Considering David Chase

Considering David Chase

Essays on *The Rockford Files*, *Northern Exposure* and *The Sopranos*

EDITED BY THOMAS FAHY

McFarland & Company, Inc., Publishers
Jefferson, North Carolina, and London

LIBRARY OF CONGRESS CATALOGUING-IN-PUBLICATION DATA

Considering David Chase : essays on *The Rockford Files, Northern Exposure* and *The Sopranos* / edited by Thomas Fahy.
     p.   cm.
    Includes bibliographical references and index.

    ISBN-13: 978-0-7864-3284-4
    softcover : 50# alkaline paper ∞

    1. Chase, David, 1945, Aug. 22 — Criticism and interpretation.
2. Rockford files (Television program)   3. Northern exposure
(Television program)   4. Sopranos (Television program)
I. Fahy, Thomas Richard.
PN1992.4.C49C65   2008
812'.54 — dc22   [B]   2007034047

British Library cataloguing data are available

Cover photograph: David Chase, creator of *The Sopranos*, January 1999,
(HBO/Photofest)

Manufactured in the United States of America

McFarland & Company, Inc., Publishers
  Box 611, Jefferson, North Carolina 28640
  www.mcfarlandpub.com

In loving memory of
Gerald Francis Fahy (1948–2006)

Contents

Introduction

Thomas Fahy

Growing up in New Jersey (first in Clifton, then in the suburbs of North Caldwell as a teenager), David Chase was drawn to what he calls "the idea of writing" at an early age. In high school, he enjoyed penning short stories as well as reading Freud — an interest that would intensify when he started going to therapy himself in the 1970s. In a recent interview, Chase recalls this early fiction with amusement: "[These stories] were sort of mindblowers, like somebody spies the Apostles sneaking Jesus' body out of the tomb, right before they go, 'Oh, my God, he's resurrected!'" (Longworth 24). Chase dismisses these juvenilia, in part, because of his lack of discipline at the time, saying, "I didn't understand about rewriting" (24).

He continued to focus on his writing as an English major in college, first attending Wake Forest University in Winston-Salem, North Carolina, and then transferring to New York University when he was a junior. During these years, his preoccupation with rock and roll suggests that music was never far from his mind either, but despite his dreams of becoming a rock musician, he decided to pursue his burgeoning passion for writing and film. After graduation, Chase moved across the country to enter the graduate film program at Stanford University, hoping to make features in Hollywood one day.

Some of his inspiration for pursing this career came from foreign films. Chase recalls his introduction to Fellini's *8½* in 1965: "I didn't totally understand it but I liked it. I saw my family in there. I saw those Italians, I saw those faces looking into the lens. I saw those gestures, I saw those 'operatic' men and women and I thought, 'I'm home, this is where we came from'" (Rucker). His fascination with *8½* was, to some extent, about belonging and

1

identity — themes that characterize Chase's work on *Northern Exposure* (CBS, 1990–1995) and *The Sopranos* (HBO, 1999–2007).

Chase's interest in these themes can be traced back to his time at Wake Forest University, which exposed him to some of the complex racial politics of the South. And these experiences informed his early work on the Civil Rights–era drama *I'll Fly Away* (NBC, 1991–1993). In an interview with James Longworth, Chase explains, "it was because of my experience in Winston-Salem in the early sixties that I was drawn to that show. Because [...] I remembered how unhappy I felt about the situation for black people then" (26). As a student in North Carolina, Chase witnessed KKK rallies, the mobilization of the National Guard after Martin Luther King's assassination, and a general acceptance of racism that unsettled him. All of these things contributed to his feelings of alienation and displacement there: "I never felt really welcome on that campus as a Yankee. [...] And it wasn't an atmosphere I liked. It's not that I'm some freedom fighter, I just found the South to be at that time stodgy, strange, and bigoted, and kind of unsophisticated. I mean, I was from New Jersey, I grew up twenty-five miles from New York City and I missed that" (Longworth 25). For Chase, growing up near Manhattan imparted a sense of urbanity and a tolerance for racial difference that was lacking in the South. Not surprisingly, on *The Sopranos*, ethnic identity and race shape how Chase's characters view and interact with others. His comments in this interview also highlight the importance that he gives to place (where one lives and comes from) and its role in defining who a person is.

Even though Chase made three films at Stanford, he was unable to find work as a director after he graduated. In 1971, he moved to Los Angeles and eventually began writing for the television show *Kolchak: The Night Stalker* (ABC, 1974-5), penning five episodes, and later for *The Rockford Files* (NBC, 1974–1980), joining the writing and production staff in the third season. Chase won his first Emmy for his work on *The Rockford Files* in 1978.[1] His second Emmy came for his television movie *Off the Minnesota Strip* (ABC, 1980), about a young girl who moves to New York, becomes a prostitute, and returns to Minnesota to try to integrate back into a "normal" Midwestern life.

After creating his own show, *Almost Grown* (CBS, 1988-1989), and spending two years writing for the series *I'll Fly Away*, Chase became executive producer for *Northern Exposure* in its last two seasons (1993–1995). He has pointed out that he didn't care much for this show prior to his arrival. In part, he was critical of its self-congratulatory tone: "It was ramming home every week the message that 'life is nothing but great,' 'Americans are great' and 'heartfelt emotion and sharing conquers everything'"

(Rucker). In later work on *The Sopranos*, Chase would openly reject the kind of closure and clean resolutions that typify *Northern Exposure* — a show about a young doctor, Joel Fleishman, who has agreed to work for the state of Alaska to pay off his medical school loans. In Chase's tenure as executive producer, he began to sap away at the kinds of expectations that *Northern Exposure* had established.

The episodes filmed under Chase's watch undermine the theme that "sharing conquers everything" in a number of ways. One example occurs with Joel's departure in the final season. The impetus for this perhaps surprising move was the actor's (Rob Morrow's) decision to leave, and his final two episodes raise questions about the effectiveness of the kind of community offered in Cicely, Alaska. After his girlfriend, Maggie O'Connell, throws him out in "Up River" (6.8), Joel decides to "go native," and he starts living in a Manonash village away from town. He returns in "Quest" (6.15) to make one last journey with Maggie. Their search for the "Jeweled City of the North" plays with the Arthurian legend of the Holy Grail, as Joel and Maggie defeat a "dragon" (a retired Japanese solider whose first name means dragon), are tempted by the siren song of a luxurious spa, and answer the gatekeeper's riddle in order to cross a bridge ("How do you keep the one you love?"). In the end, Joel discovers that his quest for self-understanding and belonging lies in Manhattan — home — the place to which he should return. When he has a vision of the New York skyline, he asks Maggie to come with him. But she refuses: "New York City. The thing you've dreamed about day and night for five years. [...] Whatever that is, it's for you. That's your place, not mine. [...] This is *my* place. This is where I belong." Like Joel, she can't leave her home, not even for love.

The struggle to understand the self — relative to geography, ethnicity, gender, sexuality, and the psyche — preoccupies most of the characters in Chase's writing. Tony Soprano and his crew, for example, feel disconnected from Italian culture when they return to Italy in "Commendatori" (2.4). And in the sixth season, when Vito Spatafore, Tony's top earner, is outed as a homosexual, he must flee the violently homophobic world of the mafia. Vito ends up in Dartford, New Hampshire, a town with a visible gay community, and he subsequently gets involved in a loving homosexual relationship with Jim, a local cook and volunteer firefighter. But Vito is quickly drawn back to New Jersey — even at the expense of his sexuality and ultimately his life. In "Moe n' Joe" (6.10), he decides to cook an Italian meal for Jim before returning to his life as a mobster, as a husband and father, and as an Italian American. While listening to Dean Martin's "That's Amore," Vito puts the finishing touches on his meal, chopping onions and garlic, pouring red wine, and lighting candles. He tells Jim: "I thought I'd make a little dinner like we do back home. We got pasta badan, macaroni and potatoes, real peasant food. We got a little salad. Then pork chops and vinegar peppers. I fuckin' miss this shit, I gotta say." Italian food and music signal the ways that Vito misses home — even a home that forces him to deny and reject (to some extent) his sexual identity. Once again, geography defines who these characters are, and in Chase's work, being true to oneself requires a certain truthfulness about where one is from.

These conflicted experiences with identity shape the narrative arcs of *Northern Exposure* and *The Sopranos*, and they resonate powerfully with our own struggles to understand the world around us and our place in it. Despite Chase's dismissal of *Northern Exposure*, it's important to note that he brought several writers from this show to *The Sopranos*, including Robin Green, Mitchell Burgess, Andrew Schneider, and Diane Frolov. Not surprisingly, there are a number of thematic and stylistic connections between these shows, as well as with his early work on *The Rockford Files*. The essays collected here focus on these television shows, arguably the most significant that David Chase has been a part of. This is not an attempt to give Chase more credit than he is due. Television is inherently a collaborative art, and Chase learned his craft from years of working in the television industry. But in mapping the trajectory of his career, we can get a better understanding of the professional and personal experiences that led up to and influenced *The Sopranos*, while also revisiting and discussing exceptional shows such as *Northern Exposure* and *The Rockford Files* in their own terms.

Victoria E. Johnson begins the collection with her analyses of the televisual innovations of *The Rockford Files*. Her essay "From Paradise Cove to the Precinct: Mapping *The Rockford Files*' Urban (Tele)Visions" challenges the ways in which television has been traditionally associated with low-brow, mainstream culture. This association, Johnson explains, has fostered a "popular and scholarly resistance to thinking critically about the aesthetics, address, function, pleasures and, indeed, *quality* of 'typical television.'" In the case of *The Rockford Files*, these biases have also contributed to the general exclusion of this show from most discussions about Chase's oeuvre. Johnson's essay counters this by offering a rich critical assessment of this hybrid drama and arguing that it "should be seen as 'typically televisual' and part of a *broader* televised field of city-set, character-driven series that actively engaged and re-imaged the urban landscape of 1970s America."

Robert F. Gross continues this discussion of *The Rockford Files* in "Driving in Circles: *The Rockford Files*," arguing that the show stands apart from other detective series in the 1970s by speaking to widely held anxieties in America following the Vietnam War and the Watergate scandal: "*The*

Rockford Files is the reflection of a period in which postwar prosperity was coming to an end and the middle class was under increased economic pressure, pressure that led to anxieties about masculinity, upward mobility, societal values—and especially suspicion about the values of those on top." In this way, Rockford's financial troubles resonated with viewers in the 1970s: "Rockford is the hero for a decade in which the dream of upward mobility was becoming increasingly remote for many Americans—at a time during which the wealth began to be increasingly concentrated in the upper brackets." Part of Rockford's appeal comes from the fact that his financial concerns are typically a result of his integrity and often occur at his own expense, literally.

In "Going Native in Cicely, Alaska: American Archetypes and Hybridized Identity on *Northern Exposure*," Heather E. Epes considers the issue of hybridity in regard to ethnic identity, examining the stereotypes associated with images of the pioneer-frontiersmen and Native Americans in the series. Despite the show's awareness of such biases, it tends both to reify and redefine stereotypes about these mythic constructions—primarily through Joel Fleishman, who represents the stereotypical "modern man," and his relationship to Cicely's community. As Epes explains, "[Fleishman's] perceptions of Indianness are influenced by exposure to its representation, never its reality. Even as he learns to accept the complexity of Native Americans around him, he reverts occasionally to his engrained worldview." Ultimately, the questions that *Northern Exposure* raises about identity are reconciled, to some extent, by Fleishman's quest for self-understanding and for redefining the self.

Thomas Fahy's "'You Don't Have to Eat Every Dish of Rigatoni': Food, Music, and Identity in the Works of David Chase" considers the role that food and music play in identity formation. Eating meals and listening to music typically bring people together. They provide communal experiences that not only help Chase's characters understand themselves, but they also point to tensions that we all share "in creating an individual identity both in relation to and distinct from the broader forces that have influenced us— such as family, ethnicity, and geography." Throughout *The Rockford Files*, *Northern Exposure*, and *The Sopranos*, the music of a certain singer or composer can function like the sonorities of eating. It provides a pulse for the scene as we listen to the sounds of wine glasses ringing during a toast and silverware grinding against a plate. When meals occur without music, other sounds—chewing, drinking, and passing around dishes—establish a distinct rhythm. "The rhythm (or time spent consuming a meal) and the harmonies (or exchanges that occur when sharing food) reflect the characters' state of mind as well as their anxieties, desires, and resentments." Ultimately, both music and food encapsulate the need in Chase's fiction for social and cultural belonging. The songs that characters listen to and the aromas of the dishes they eat speak to something visceral about identity, something that transcends words.

In "'This Art's Kind of a Girly Thing': Art, Status, and Gender on *The Sopranos* and *Northern Exposure*," Kirstin Ringelberg turns our attention to visual art and its association with masculine power and social status on these shows. In *The Sopranos*, a woman's ability to understand art, which is often associated with upper class sophistication or intellectual superiority, threatens male power. As Ringelberg explains, "Art in American culture is often linked with the feminine, particularly when it is being denigrated, and *The Sopranos* relives this idea that the 'girly' images are tricky and artificial — not to be trusted much less loved and understood, like the women on the show." In the world of the Jersey mob where men cannot be perceived as weak, it comes as no surprise that Tony and his crew would be suspicious of art and the women who understand it. Even in the more egalitarian world of *Northern Exposure*, art is still gendered. It may be presented as communal and democratic here, but as Ringelberg reminds us, the art in Cicely is created primarily by men.

Susann Cokal continues this discussion of gender in her essay "Narrative Ergonomics and the Functions of Feminine Space in *The Sopranos*." Specifically, she argues that the feminine spaces on the show function as a sort of visual code or shorthand to define and refine male characters and their narratives. Three spaces are primarily identified with women — the Soprano home (run by Carmela), Dr. Melfi's office, and the Bada Bing — and each of these establishes boundaries for women: boundaries that Tony tries to reinforce as a way of maintaining control over his own life narrative. Despite the limitations placed on women, these spaces enable the storytelling of the series. They create pauses in the larger, male-dominated gangster narrative. Cokal points out, for example, that "If there were no Melfi, there would be no *Sopranos*, for Tony would continue to bottle up his feelings with Gary Cooper–like stoicism, and the show would stop at the shiny metal surface of a gun or knife, the crimes themselves, rather than the gleaming tissue box and the penetrable reflections in the office." Tony needs Melfi's office to facilitate his own narrative, just as he needs his home and the Bada Bing to restore conservative gender hierarchies.

Ann C. Hall reads the narrative structure of *The Sopranos* in terms of violence. In "Crooked Reading: Postmodernism and *The Sopranos*" she draws parallels between the mob's use of violence in this show and the violence that Jacques Derrida links with his theories of signification and deconstruction. "Of course," as Hall points out, "the problem with either method, on the theoretical or practical level, is that nothing is ever 'erased' completely, there is always something left over: for deconstructionists it is 'play' or 'difference'; for the mob, body parts, nightmares, and maybe even twinges of guilt and fear." These remnants raise questions about power and control, and Hall applies this to Chase's deconstructive strategy in *The Sopranos*, which reminds us "that existence is insecure at best and our personal power frequently a vain delusion."

The next two essays focus on the portrayal of family in some of Chase's work. Mardia J. Bishop's "Wackos in the Wilderness vs. Getting Whacked in Newark: Dueling Family Models in *Northern Exposure* and *The Sopranos*" examines representations of the American family on these shows relative to President Clinton's and President George W. Bush's definitions of family and family values. "Both programs," Bishop argues, "portray families that are dramatically different from each other but representative of their eras' definitions of family." Using the linguistic studies of George Lakoff as a critical framework, Bishop discusses how the political subtext of these shows not only engages with contemporary moral politics but also reveals fundamental differences between the worldviews of liberals and conservatives. Specifically, she highlights two parenting models from Lakoff's work that resonate with Clinton's and Bush's definition of the nuclear family — the Nurturant Parent Model and the Strict Father model — and she discusses how *The Sopranos* and *Northern Exposure* expose the strengths and weaknesses of each.

Lorena Russell's "Defense-of-Family Acts: Queering *Famiglia* in *The Sopranos*" analyzes the ironic tension between the violence characterizing the mob and the violence threatening the security of the Soprano family — a tension that the show uses to critique conservative social politics about family values. "Family is staged throughout the series as a kind of social bulwark, a comforting retreat to traditional values, but then this conservative gesture is repeatedly undercut through the violence, cruelty and thoroughgoing criminality of the *famiglia*." As Russell goes on to explain, this critique of family values also comes from the portrayal of homophobia and masculine anxiety. Russell traces this homosexual panic throughout the series, which culminates in Vito Spatafore's coming out and murder in the final season. Prior to his death, Vito experiences a loving same-sex relationship — a relationship that starkly contrasts with "the material-driven heterosexual relationships that the other mobsters call marriage" and calls into question how "the ideology of family supersedes its real value" in American culture.

Keith B. Mitchell takes this discussion of sexuality and links it with the construction of male bodies in "Until the Fat Man Sings: Body Image,

Masculinity, and Sexuality in *The Sopranos*." Mitchell asserts that "fat male bodies, both heterosexual and homosexual, have become sites of contestation about how society views masculinity, virility, and power." Fat bodies tend to be viewed as weak and degenerate in Western society — an association that is often emasculating for men — and Mitchell's essay addresses the ways that *The Sopranos* engages with this problem. Specifically, he focuses on Tony, whose body represents the ways in which excess defines his life, and Vito, whose bodily transformation in season six signals his growing acceptance of his own homosexuality. Mitchell concludes that "their bodies engender multiple signs that manifest fluidity which on the one hand reinforce societies' imagined construction of fat bodies as innervated, weak, depraved, and out of control while simultaneously imbuing the very same body with notions of power, wealth, and unimpeded libidinal energy. These fat bodies express a kind of liberation from cultural norms and expectations."

The volume concludes with Michael Calabrese's personal and literary reflections on *The Sopranos* in "From Troy to 95 Lincoln Place, Irvington, NJ: A Virgilian Reading of *The Sopranos* Underworld." Through the lens of his own experiences as an Italian American growing up in New Jersey (where the series takes place), he examines the epic scope of *The Sopranos* and its ability to resonate across cultures, nations, and ethnicities. For Calabrese, the show's Classical and literary allusions clearly place it in a larger epic tradition —from Dante's *Inferno*, Virgil's *Aeneid*, and Homer's *Odyssey* to *The Godfather* trilogy. "Chase crafts such moments of epic 'connectedness' to shape the *Sopranos* as part of the continuing Mediterranean, Classical, and specifically Italian saga." This tradition highlights one of the show's primary thematic preoccupations— its concern with betrayal and loss. But as Calabrese explains, the world of Tony Soprano and his crew only offers a parodic vision of these epic narratives. "Chase gives us the blood, the tears, and the cascading sacrifices of the *Aeneid* but not the guarantee of a mythic destiny fulfilled." Something has been lost indeed.

The range of these essays and the scholarship that informs them suggest that there is something powerful about David Chase's fiction and the worldviews offered in *The Rockford Files*, *Northern Exposure*, and *The Sopranos*. These works continue to resonate with viewers on many levels, and they invite us to reexamine them again and again. Whether it's the gritty realism of *The Sopranos* or the more idealized vision of community offered in *Northern Exposure*, these shows ask us to think about our place in the world. They challenge us to recognize the ways in which society defines, regulates, and limits identity. In fact, Chase's work as a writer and filmmaker has continually engaged with the impact of contemporary social problems on the individual. Even his preference for open-ended narratives reflects this ongoing challenge in his writing — a challenge for us to think about our complacent acceptance of violence, racism, homophobia, gender roles, social hierarchies, and consumerism. In many ways, television has been the ideal medium for David Chase. Despite his long-held desire to make films, it is the serial nature of television that best captures this artistic vision and challenge. It is the medium that enables his work — and the questions it raises — to reverberate with us week after week.

Notes

1. *The Rockford Files* won the Emmy for Best Drama in 1978.

Works Cited

Longworth, James L. "David Chase: 'Hit' Man." *TV Creators: Conversations with America's Top Producers of Television Drama*. The Television Series. Syracuse: Syracuse University Press, 2000: 20–36.
Rucker, Allen. "An Interview with David Chase." *The Sopranos: A Family History*. New York: New American Library, 2004.

From Paradise Cove
to the Precinct:
Mapping *The Rockford Files'*
Urban (Tele)Visions

Victoria E. Johnson

In the winter of 2007, *Newsweek* published a cover-story intended to mount a defense regarding "Why TV is Better Than The Movies."[1] The feature article proposed that while, historically, television had witnessed periodic "golden age[s]," contemporary TV was notable for the breadth and volume of series that now challenged cinema's presumptively higher cultural standing both "narratively *and* visually." States author Devin Gordon, "The best shows tell their stories slowly, carefully and with exquisite detail, putting viewers inside the experience of another person with unparalleled intimacy. This is the grand achievement of *The Sopranos*, and it's why the show's final season ... is a safe bet to be the cultural happening of the year."[2] It is not coincidental that the David Chase–created HBO series, *The Sopranos*, is singled out here as the pinnacle achievement of this "new" era. The series is often understood (in interviews with Chase and in popular and trade industry press, in particular) to represent the culmination of his career as a story consultant, writer, producer, and creator of series that have often gone against the grain of mainstream commercial television and, therefore, been hailed as *exceptions* within TV's "typical" flow.

Significantly, however, *Newsweek*'s and other such features considering Chase's career do not write of "quality" TV in *televisual* terms.[3] Series singled out as being more *cinematic* than cinema are hailed, explicitly, as *literary* and *theatrical* triumphs. Television is praised as a venue in which "'the writer is king,'" and "'The people working in television right now are the Shakespeares of the medium,'" inspired by the "standard" of "'Balzac's Paris, or Dickens's London, or Tolstoy's Moscow.'"[4] Praise of literate programs extends, in such articles, to praise of those series' dedicated and discriminating audiences. Such viewers are portrayed as smart, literate, adult, and as early adopters of *alternate* platforms for TV-viewing. "Quality" TV audiences, such articles suggest, like their television to *not* be "TV." They prefer "niche," "sutured," all-enveloping experiences evocative of the presumptively more considered, individuated pleasures of reading a novel or of watching film or stage play. The post-network contemporary television era is, thus, described as a *qualitatively* revolutionary age in TV programming and viewing. "Smart" viewers no longer have to deal with "dumbed down" programming that might also appeal to those who are "12 years old." Such viewers can avoid the "crowd-pleasing" pandering presumed to characterize other kinds of TV "(because the dummies have their own channels)."[5]

It is in this context — and with such "tasteful" subscriber demographics in mind — that cultural trendsetter HBO branded itself with the slogan, "It's *not* TV. It's HBO." As the network's most successful original series ever, *The Sopranos* became iconic of TV that's "not" televisual — TV that was, instead, cinematic, literate, theatrical and, even, operatic. While certainly *The Sopranos* can and should productively be analyzed in such terms, it should also be asked what is at stake in the apparent institutional and critical investment in taking "television" out of "quality" TV. Why is HBO simultaneously iconic of the "best" of television *and* "not" television at all? Why, historically, have scholars been unwilling or unable to think more broadly about the potential richness of television aesthetics and address in its own terms?

These questions are significant because — in spite of *Newsweek*'s claim that the early 2000s represent a completely "new" quality TV context — such claims for "exceptions" to TV *as* quality TV have been cyclically crucial to television historiography. In each instantiation, "quality" genres have suggested the "promise" of TV to be allied with "official" culture and the attendant educational, social, and economic capital characteristic of "high" art and enlightened intellectual pursuits, *against* "popular" culture and its associated "mass" appeal, and "typical" or, further, "low" capital. The standards of what constitutes "quality" in television have, in this respect, remained stable throughout broadcasting history: portrayed as "not" like the "typical" TV of its era; notable for its indebtedness to "high" cultural forms of expression; acceptable for viewing by an actively engaged, discriminating viewer; exemplifying "intimacy," truth-value, literate dialogue and depth of characterization; and privileging the "socially conscious" text.

In the 1950s, the drama anthology was hailed in these terms, particularly considering its frequent use of talent from the Broadway stage (or, "legitimate" theater), and for its apparent contrast with "typical" television of its era, as exemplified by panel and quiz programs, westerns, and action-adventure series. In the 1960s, the documentary series was promoted as TV's counter-balance to a postwar culture of consumption, as a genre that might help redirect national attention toward pressing social issues from the Cold War and Civil Rights to environmental concerns and the space race. Such news programs were seen as ballast within the "vast wasteland's" broader schedule, populated by suburban sitcoms, "rural" comedies, and variety programming, in particular.[6] In the 1970s and 1980s, the "socially conscious" sitcom and the "hybrid" "dramedy" were, respectively, embraced as the next interruptions in the flow of "standard" televisual fare, character-driven and engaged with the real social world beyond the TV screen.[7]

As Laurie Ouellette's history of public television has recently outlined, such claims are problematic for a medium "awkwardly situated between the notion that the people need 'enlightenment' from above and the democratic access implied by its claim to 'publicness.'" While writing specifically about PBS, Ouellette's argument might apply also to "quality" TV more broadly, as it, rhetorically, "is situated above popular culture, billed as 'better' TV for unusually discriminate 'viewers like you.' It secures cultural distinction — and invites recurring charges of elitism — by defining the public that it exists to serve against a negative image of an indiscriminate mass audience glued to uncivilized afternoon talk shows, insipid sitcoms, cops-and-robbers dramas, sensationalistic tabloid news, and formulaic movies-of-the-week."[8]

Thus, while not challenging the idea that *The Sopranos* is "quality" TV, following that claim, it remains productive ask several related questions: Why, historically, has there been such a popular and scholarly resistance to thinking critically about the aesthetics, address, function, pleasures and, indeed, *quality* of "typical television," as opposed to TV that is *not* TV?[9] What broader, lingering power and significance has the constitutive exclusion of the *televisual*, popular genres, and "mass" audience appeal programming from such discussions had for scholars of arts and media? How have such exclusions ratified, as well as mystified, broader cultural and institutional investments in who and what *count* within postwar culture? Might such exceptions imply a "rule" that *is* TV — series that are more "televisual" than literary, more "shared" than niche? Looking at such "typical" television, in fact, calls attention to blind spots in both academic and popular TV theory regarding TV aesthetics, address, and appeal to its audience.

Several series for which David Chase was a story consultant and on which he was a writer and producer have been discussed as "quality" TV or — at the extreme, as *not* TV. These include *Kolchack: The Night Stalker* (ABC, 1974-1975), *Almost Grown* (CBS, 1988-1989), *Northern Exposure* (CBS, 1990–1995), *I'll Fly Away* (NBC, 1991–1993), and *The Sopranos* (2000–2007) but, notably not *Switch* (CBS, 1975–1978) or *The Rockford Files* (NBC, 1974–1980, with CBS's made-for-TV movies of the 1990s). The following challenges this typical exclusion of *The Rockford Files* from most discussions of Chase's oeuvre and from canonical understandings of "quality" TV as writerly, literary and theatrical rather than "televisual" in order to complicate boundaries of quality, distinction, and prized demographics in television and to illuminate key blind spots in academic and popular television criticism.[10] This essay focuses on *The Rockford Files* to revisit and challenge critical understandings of television emergent at the peak of the U.S. network-era and to posit the series' generic and narrative hybridity and place-specificity as, in fact, *quintessentially* televisual.

Through the 1970s—concurrent with *The Rockford Files'* network run — academic considerations of TV typically defined the medium negatively, theorizing it as an "apparatus," field of visual expression, and site of viewing/consumption according to what TV was *not*. Specifically, theories of TV that emerged from art, architecture, film, theater, and literary studies in this period, conceptualized TV as *not* art, *not* public, *not* "masculine" or spectatorial, *not* interactive, *not* literate, and radically commodified (i.e., *not* market-transcendent). The following proposes that *Rockford* challenges these understandings of television's "essential" properties. It argues that the series should be seen as "typically televisual" and part of a *broader* televised field of city-set, character-driven series that actively engaged and re-imagined the urban landscape of 1970s America.

It thus takes up the late Ernest Pascucci's call to challenge early and powerfully lingering interpretations of "television watching" (vs. "*not* TV") "as escapist behavior that is symptomatic of a lost public deprived of face-to-face interpersonal encounters. ... [whereby] the rise of television accompanies the decline of our metropolitan centers, effectively atomizing the public in isolated suburban homes."[11] Explicitly positing questions of local identity as *central to* television production and expression, *Rockford*'s textual properties, characterizations, and emphasis on place-specificity challenge conventional critical assumptions about "typical" television programs and viewers, TV aesthetics, address, and appeal. The following interrogates why, to a surprising degree, scholars have remained resistant to theorize television aesthetics and address in its own terms, and to include certain types of television within "quality" TV history. I am inspired, here, by those who *have* taken up the theorization of TV in these terms and who have, further, argued that television has always been at the leading edge of narrative and aesthetic experimentation within U.S. visual culture, while *simultaneously* occupying the position as the preeminent *quotidian* medium of postwar U.S. life.[12]

Theorizing "Quality": TV, Its Opposites and Analogues

Early critical, academic understandings of television published contemporaneously with *The Rockford Files* network run have remained significantly influential in the present day. Though social science and mass communication scholars in the U.S. had been writing, critically, about television since its inception, early scholarship from humanities and arts based visual theory emerged, in part, following the social upheavals of the 1960s.[13] Such tensions encouraged consideration of the potential of popular media forms for social action and of the possibilities of television for *art* practice. In a somewhat defensive position in relation to "acceptable" academic discourse, early discussions of television from art, architectural theory, and film and literature scholars, were thus often focused on justifying TV as an object of study by theorizing the medium as, alternately, an analogue for postwar cultural transformations, and, through models that defined television as, fundamentally, *opposed* to art and to film.

Gene Youngblood's "Art, Entertainment, Entropy," for example, contrasts the aesthete in the museum to "the viewer of commercial entertainment" who "does not want to work; he wants to be an object, to be acted upon."[14] Given that television is, here, *not* like museum art or like film, its "essential" properties must then be defined in opposition to those media. If film viewers and museum-goers were "sutured" into the completed work of art through the focused attention of a concerted "gaze," television viewing seemed to be always-already in process, characterized by "liveness" and simultaneity between event and address, inviting viewers to engage the medium with a distracted "glance." By extension, television viewers were "by nature distracted and inattentive."[15] As John Caldwell has argued,

> This extreme dualism between film and television — this mythology of "essential media differences" ... forms the categorical basis for many future speculations on television, including the glance theory. Once one assumes that there are innate differences between the two media, then critical theorists are merely left to explain, post-facto, the cultural and political reasons for those differences.... Even recent updates of the glance theory are based on the very

problematic notion that television viewers are not actually *viewing* television but that the television is on in the background while viewers are actually doing something else.[16]

For scholars like Youngblood, theories of the television viewer's innately distracted relation to television were extended to support arguments that TV "culture" was characterized by an apolitical lack of engagement in broader, public life. Television, here, diffuses or destroys the capacity for political awareness and for public engagement, primarily via its presumed contrast to the focused attention and labor associated with engaging high-art practices. Of course, such an argument rather problematically implies that "high" cultural objects transcend the market, ideological determinants, and limits of production and dissemination. However, in this context, television's detractors are put into a contrastingly favorable light — reaction *against* television is allied with that which culturally *matters* and speaks for a recovery of public engagement, imagination, and control. In these theoretical frames, TV becomes a metaphor for a changed affective, spatial, and political *culture* characterized by malaise, placelessness, dis-ease, and loss.

In related terms, scholars of the 1970s and 1980s theorized that television was one of several postwar analogues characteristic of "mobile privatization" — the experience of a post-modern disconnect from the public sphere that was simultaneously characterized by enhanced "travel."[17] TV's "placeless" analogues, here, include, most famously, the suburb, the freeway, and the mall as, "a nexus of interdependent two- and three-dimensional cultural forms which ... observe similar principles of construction and operation" and which are characterized by an "attenuated fiction effect" — a "partial loss of touch with the here and now."[18] According to Roger Silverstone, for example, "television is not simply the result of the suburbanization of the world, but is itself responsible for the 'suburbanization of the public sphere.' It is characterized for him by what he calls the suburban genres, par excellence, of soap opera and situation comedy, largely devoted to the representation and working through of the problems of domestic life."[19]

Such theoretical claims helped to shape the arguments of post–1980s humanistic television and media studies, as a field emergent, largely, from film studies and literary studies programs. Building arguments about TV upon its presumed "distinctiveness" from other media through the "essential" properties established in 1970s theory, early work focused, particularly, on genres that emphasized television's capability for "liveness." While critically important work — particularly for carving out a place for the study of television alongside film, within academia — focus on "liveness" as definitive of television at-large, prevented other kinds of questions about television program aesthetics and address from being pursued. According to Caldwell, "As long as high theory continues to overestimate the central-ity of liveness in television ... it will also underestimate or ignore other modes of practice and production: the performance of the visual and sty-listic exhibitionism."[20] Television studies scholars of this period also actively wrote *against* the 1970s models, however, by approaching TV from an explicitly feminist and cultural studies perspective engaged with questions of popular forms and their pleasures (e.g., early studies on soap operas and their "feminized" address) in ways that recuperated previously disdained texts and audiences. And yet, with rare exceptions, it has only been in the last decade that concerted attention has been paid to televisual *aesthetics* of prime-time, particularly as regards television of the 1970s.[21]

Rockford's *Televisual Qualities:* *Tongue in Cheek, with Your Fist on Your Hip*

Pascucci's intervention is critical, here. In surveying architectural the-ory of the early 1970s that "associate[s] television with the death of public life," he asks, "What are we to make of a book announcing the decline of urban public life in 1974 that makes no mention of civil rights, the migra-tion of rural southern blacks to large northern cities, women's liberation and gay liberation?"[22] As David Morley notes, "We must recognize the con-stitutive exclusions on which the definition of the classical public sphere was based." In so doing, we might also imagine television *otherwise*, con-sidering that, perhaps, "Communications technologies can function as dis-embedding mechanisms, powerfully enabling individuals (and sometimes whole families or communities) to escape, at least imaginatively, from their geographical locations."[23] For Pascucci, television explicitly allowed a "bet-ter view" of a life in the city that was racially mixed, "emphasized the every-day bonds of community life" and enabled "a subjectivity that" otherwise "had no recognizable place in the 'spaces of appearance' available" to him in his otherwise "nearly evacuated cul-de-sac" in suburban New Jersey. Television, Pascucci argues, allowed him to "traverse the avenues of great American cities week after week" and to map his own move to Manhat-tan — and his subsequent activist, public engagements in that city — with confidence and encouragement.[24]

What Morley and Pascucci encourage is a consideration of TV the-ory's own "constitutive exclusions" and the potential limits of imagining TV aesthetics and address through "suburban" genres and in terms of the medium's presumed "placelessness." While a comprehensive analysis of TV arguably requires attention to each element of television as a social insti-tution (with industry interests, regulatory concerns, textual analysis, and audience relations each considered), the following offers a beginning analysis of *The Rockford Files* as "typical" prime time television of the 1970s that offers a "better view" of a diversified Southern California via a thoroughly televisual, "hybrid" mode of address.

The phrase "typical" television comes from John Fiske's *Television Culture*, which argues for critical attention to the best institutionally-supported and "the most popular, mainstream, internationally distributed programs, for these are the ones of greatest significance in popular culture."[25] *Rockford* fits this designation for several reasons. The series had a comparatively long run with successful ratings and, with its success in syndication, it has not been off the air since the end of its network run. Though not stellar, *Rockford*'s ratings were always stable. The series' debut season saw it rank twelfth overall, after which it hovered between the top-twenty and top-sixty shows in prime time. Such stability was encouraged by NBC's institutional support, shown in the program's fixed location within 1970s scheduling "flow," its stable "hammock" of series on either side of it within the schedule, and its lack of direct generic competition from CBS or from ABC during its time-slot (with the exception of *Rockford*'s second season, when it had to face *Hawaii Five-O* directly, on CBS). Indeed, *Rockford* never changed its time-slot (from 9:00–10:00 P.M., Pacific time, each Friday night on NBC from 1974 to 1980). Its lead-in was always a comedy—from *Chico and the Man* (1974–1978) to *Who's Watching the Kids* and *Shirley* in the series' last two seasons. And the series was always paired with another detective or mystery series at 10:00 (ranging from 1974's *Police Woman* to the final season's lead-in to *Eischeid*). With season two as the exception, CBS and ABC counter-programmed *Rockford* with series that, ostensibly, would not compete for its same audience (featuring shows aimed at children, science-fiction/fantasy dramas, or telefilms).

Visually, aurally, and narratively, *Rockford* represents a transitional televisual text for its time. Visually, as a Universal studios production (in partnership with James Garner's Cherokee Productions), *Rockford* represents a transition between the backlot-bound telefilm series of the 1950s and 1960s (including Garner's own *Maverick* [ABC, 1957–1962 though Garner only appeared until 1960]), and 1980s dramatic series' "extreme self-consciousness of style" (as evidenced, for example, in the private investigator series, *Moonlighting*, ABC, 1985–1989).[26] *Rockford* was atypical for Universal TV productions of the period. It was not characterized by Universal's 1970s "zero-degree film-based style ... with uniform settings, lightings, looks, and cutting." [27] The series often shot on location, featuring nighttime and outdoor sequences characterized by a textured look that featured Los Angeles and its surrounds with an unusual specificity. Aurally, *Rockford* was distinguished by its theme music which is considered the first rock-based theme for a television series. Narratively, *Rockford* represents a revision of the detective series and detective persona for prime time. This narrative hybridity is theorized as "cookie jar noir" in the analysis that follows.

The opening titles sequence of *The Rockford Files*—designed by Jack Cole with musical scoring by Pete Carpenter and Mike Post—economically establishes the series' dry humor, setting, and its star's "quotidian heroism." The titles open on a black screen, with all-white lettering reading "James Garner in" as a phone rings. A hand-held tracking shot glides over a desk cluttered with an audio cassette machine, dot-matrix printout, a half-finished game of solitaire laid out on a desk featuring a governor's pardon, pencil cup, desk calendar, photo of an older man, and a quarter-full coffee cup. The title, "The Rockford Files" is superimposed on screen and the camera pauses at the answering machine and phone and the machine picks up and the greeting sounds, "This is Jim Rockford. At the tone, leave your name and message. I'll get back to you." Each week's different caller's message is then left as the title, "Also Starring Noah Beery" is superimposed and the camera closes in on an extreme close-up of the phone.

The theme song enters as the title visuals transition to a series of still photographs and step-photography that features Jim Rockford personally navigating Los Angeles' freeways (explicitly identifying the 10 freeway, the 101 Hollywood/North, and the 134 to Pasadena), and the city's surface streets in his golden Pontiac Firebird (featuring Jim traveling eastbound on Hollywood Boulevard at night, and in Chinatown). Interspersed with scenes of Rockford driving are shots of him in action on the job as a private investigator, and in quieter, domestic everyday routines: He walks toward the camera while on a downtown city street; he's shown in an exhausted pose in a phone booth at night; he's captured on the phone in his trailer's kitchen while putting on a shoe, his jacket, and exiting; he laughs with a date at a drive-in; he talks with a woman who points him to what appears to be a lead; he's in the squad room and shown being led to a jail cell by a policeman. In a montage that pictures him in the squad room, responding to a comment by a cop in an apparently "heated" way, and then standing next to a hall-of-records file cabinet with an unresponsive clerk, Rockford is clearly established as a sympathetic "everyman" hero, exasperated by bureaucracy and short-sightedness. These qualities are affirmed in the sequence's next set of images, which feature the "domestic" side of Rockford, including photographs of him shopping for groceries and fishing with his dad, Rocky, off the Malibu pier.

The titles sequence concludes by featuring more abstract, generalized shots of Los Angeles without the Firebird or Rockford present, inviting the viewer to occupy this space — from Chavez Ravine to the beach — on her/his own. In the fourth season, the series core regulars were added into the title photographs, including shots of Rockford interacting with Angel Martin (his former cellmate), Beth Davenport (his lawyer and former love-interest), and Dennis Becker (his friend and police force insider). When Beth Davenport's character left the show, the remaining seasons' titles were tailored, respectively.

Musical scoring is essential to establish the feel of the series, its locale and, chiefly, its characterization of Rockford as an everyman hero, beleaguered but, nonetheless, undaunted. According to composer Mike Post, Garner was the inspiration for the theme's instrumentation which was explicitly designed to evoke *geographic* references that viewers would consciously link to the star's persona beyond the series. The score was also designed to quickly communicate and *Rockford*'s unique generic tone and sensibilities.

> We talked about the kind of guy Rockford was.... And that he was kind of quirky — how, because he'd been in the joint, he had a "Kiss my ass" attitude toward the police ... and how he also had a wryness and sweetness about him, which you could see in his relationship with Rocky.... We tried to write music that has humor, ... that was tongue in cheek, but at the same time, with your fist on your hip — as if you're saying "Hey, kiss my ass!"[28]

Significantly, here, though the series was set in Los Angeles, the characterization of Rockford also consistently referenced Garner's own Oklahoma roots and resultant, presumed, "common sense" values and lack of patience with pretense. Post and collaborator Pete Carpenter thus wanted a theme that "'could also sound Midwestern,'" to tap into what series producer and Garner's former agent, Meta Rosenberg, calls his "'kind of country wisdom and humor.... It's a certain vulnerability he has.'"[29] Thus, the composers considered their theme to sound "'if not country, then country rock,'" evocative of "'exactly what James Garner is,'" by featuring blues-rock instrumentation (with key passages given over to harmonica and the Dobro), accompanied by a driving rock beat and "'a strange orchestra, ... half-legit, half-rock 'n' roll.'"[30] The composers emphasized the contemporary setting and "Los Angeles-ness" of the show in their scoring of the interstitial music for action sequences and "spooky scenes" that could build tension with "'more contemporary music.'"[31] In these interstitials, Post and Carpenter explicitly avoided Mickey Mousing — or, direct punctuation of action with sound — for a more sophisticated, urbane, underscore that accompanied rather than led and commented upon the action. Such underscoring, arguably, emphasizes the viewer's engagement with the *image* on-screen, over reliance on sound cues that would allow for a distracted gaze or "glance," that could still keep track of the story. *Rockford*'s theme thus cues viewers to tone, setting and characterization while simultaneously urging and requiring engagement with the visuals and narrative for full immersion in Rockford's milieu.

Cookie Jar Noir and The Rockford Files' "Better View"

Existing critical praise for *Rockford* has focused on the series' revisionist approach to hard-boiled detective narrative. The series shares key characteristics with literary and cinematic *noir*: It is "recognizably set in a specific city," Los Angeles; It is "masculine" in its focus on action, centered on the point-of-view of its anti-heroic central character, Jim Rockford; and, it shares with *noir* the underlying "suggestion that American capitalism and economic prosperity were not synonymous with the best of all possible worlds.[32] Given the theoretical traditions established, above, such characteristics are explained in literary and cinematic terms largely because of traditional associations of cinema with masculine "ways of seeing," public traversal, and the haptical fascination of urban experience and form, as opposed to typical associations of television with homogeneous "nonspace," suburbia, domesticity, and feminine engagements. That is, when praised as revisionist *noir*, *Rockford* is simultaneously praised for its literary and cinematic qualities as *counterintuitive* to typical televisual flow, offering an updated detective persona for the 1970s.

And yet, it might instead be argued that *Rockford*'s revisionist qualities and narrative hybridity are established through the series' emphasis on character and relationships over strict attention to crime and detection. As noted above, these are "feminized" narrative characteristics. Thus, the series' revisionism is its unique balance between Rockford's public, action-oriented, investigative realm and his intimate, personal, and domestic private realm, in scenes focused on quotidian routines set at Rockford's trailer home and favored taco stand in Paradise Cove, or in conversations involving the detective's close cohort of friends or family. *Rockford*'s masculine/feminine, public/private, city/beach hybridization might thus be characterized as a truly "televisual" mediation, "cookie jar *noir*" (in reference to the spot in his Malibu trailer home where Rockford hides the gun he is loathe ever to use with his beloved Oreos). Specifically, *The Rockford Files* articulates domesticity to detective work through the figure of Jim's Pontiac Firebird. The Firebird mediates Rockford's navigation of life, work, and greater Southern California. In the process, audiences are offered a "better view" of a

Californian urban life and culture, characterized by mobility and individuality, diversity and community.

Regulatory transformations and industry pressures in the early 1970s encouraged all studios and independent television producers to minimize violence in prime time — particularly gun violence. Partly as a response to these conditions, *Rockford* substituted "car action" for "gun action" and, wherever possible, emphasized chase sequences and Rockford's outsmarting of the bad-guys instead of fight sequences and resorting to violence.[33] Perhaps more significantly, however, the Firebird Esprit immediately underscored Jim Rockford's quotidian heroism as an iconic extension of the series' closely hewn fit between Garner as star and Rockford as titular character. The car's license plate, "853 OKG," is a reference to Garner's Oklahoma roots and the date when he signed his first contract-player contract in Hollywood. Garner did all of his own stunt-driving during the run of the series (and in the subsequent made-for-TV-movies). He recalls, "That was my fun — driving the cars. I was always behind the wheel." Garner chose the Firebird for the series "because it could just handle it — you could do anything with that car."[34] Further, the car's neutral color (while it appears gold on screen, its paint is technically "medium camel tan"), its unadorned body (though other models of Firebird were painted with the "screaming" bird logo on the hood, Rockford's Pontiac is notably stripped down), and General Motors bloodlines, by extension, mark the character as an unassuming but dependable figure.

The Firebird is the visual and motive link between Rockford's home in Paradise Cove, Malibu to the Precinct downtown, and to the wide-ranging geography of Los Angeles, with frequent forays up the 101, near Santa Barbara, down south to Orange County, inland to canyon country, the desert, and, periodically, out-of-state (including full-company location shoots in Las Vegas and Honolulu). While Stage 23 at Universal Studios' lot was home to *Rockford*'s interiors (the inside of Jim's trailer, the rooms of the police station, and the interior of Rocky's house), the show often went on location and depended, to an uncharacteristic degree, upon exterior locations and action that were *not* confined to the Universal Studios backlot. The Firebird was thus prominent in most episodes of the series, especially as Garner/Rockford was in almost every shot and, "they took Rockford and the camera went wherever he went."[35]

By *Rockford*'s third season, the series had more institutional clout (as a proven success) which allowed the show additional resources and supporting rationale for such location shooting and emphasis on visual and narrative mobility. When David Chase became a producer in this season, the series also began to be hailed as more "literate" and smart, featuring more well-rounded characters, deeper (and darker) explorations of its hero's personal life — including story-lines that tackled broader social questions than previously had been considered. Chase's episodes frequently underscored that Rockford was a success at his job (with characters referring to him as "the best private detective in L.A."), and, unlike in earlier seasons, the character was, now, regularly paid for his labor.

A less often discussed strength of the series, from season three on, however, is its diverse representation of a range of "California-ness" through locations, topical story-lines, and "localized" characterizations. According to writer-producer Juanita Bartlett, *Rockford* portrayed "the Southern California lifestyle without ever resorting to stereotypes":

> We tried to show that there's a lot more to Los Angeles than sun worshippers and movie stars and the like.... They're certainly part of the makeup of L.A., but there's also a richness to the populace that goes beyond that. There is a variety. We tried not to stereotype anyone because you have to look at your characters as human beings.[36]

Indeed, many of the episodes written and produced by Chase specifically play with presumed assumptions about California "types" by exposing "pretenders" to the California dream through their deflation at the hands of the "true" Californian spirit, embodied by Jim Rockford. Rockford, in each such instance, represents the triumph of the typically *unseen*, ordinary, everyday Californian (even — or, especially — as this ordinariness, for Jim, is significantly inflected by his Oklahoma roots). This narrative restoration of ordinariness-as-a-way-of-life in California of the 1970s is a notably atypical characterization of the "left coast" in popular arts and media of the period. In Pascucci's terms, it implies a "better view" of L.A.'s urban life and culture in the era, in ways that viewers from elsewhere might find familiar rather than off-putting, "human" rather than stereotypical, and, thus, enabling of "another" kind of subjectivity and geographic imagination.

In "The Oracle Wore a Cashmere Shirt" (3.2), for example, psychic Roman Clementi embodies pop celebrity at its worst, using Rockford to figure out a murder case while he pretends to divine each development along the way. As Rockford travels from Malibu to the precinct, to Topanga, then Hollywood, he encounters a range of Angelenos—from drug dealers to record producers— none of whom is the "kind of lowlife" Clementi represents, making money from others' sorrow and conning the public with his "gift." Rockford's "everyday" cohort — Beth, Rocky, and Becker — never buy in to Clementi's rhetoric, thus underscoring Rockford's expert position and eventual exposure of Clementi's ruse. "Three Day Affair with a Thirty Day Escrow" (5.7) takes on several California obsessions and "types," with Jim restoring "common sense" to those who have over-invested in skewed ideas regarding class standing, real-estate, the lifestyle of the idle rich, while simultaneously critiquing those who have invested in traditional codes of family and gender "propriety" that appear outmoded in the "here, *now*." Focusing particularly on real estate and romance in Pacific Palisades, Jim takes on a missing persons case for Sean Innes, who turns out to be a professional gigolo. After Rockford tutors Sean in how to be honest about his feelings and to value relationships over lifestyle, Sean is able to help him find Khedra Azziz and to untangle a real estate and murder conspiracy constructed by Beverly Hills realtor, Cy Margulies.

Chase's "Quickie Nirvana" (4.7) and his 1994 Rockford made-for-TV movie, "Godfather Knows Best," both invoke "typical" California character types as a route to interrogate and complicate Rockford's character and the potential limits of quotidian heroism. "Quickie Nirvana" features Rockford's acquaintance with Sky Aquarian, a forty-year-old woman who keeps searching for enlightenment in all the wrong places, in the form of the most current California "fads" for self-realization. Sky's general disposition lacks any of Rockford's common sense. She seeks "nirvana" through meditation, sweat-lodges, communal living, gurus, consciousness collectives, sensory depravation, and, eventually, through charismatic Christianity.

Characteristic of the series, this episode moves around Southern California, featuring location work at Venice Beach, as well as story points that take Jim and Sky from Malibu to Laurel Canyon, Hollywood, Placerita, Century City, and "La Questa" spa. While much of the episode plays Sky's search for laughs ("You here for 'pre-death'?" one commune member asks Jim), the episode is also very dark (Sky says, of Jim, "you know, you're sweet, hang-loosey, but also kind of a fascist," an assessment with which he does not disagree). In the end, the episode reinforces *both* characters' inability to change and emphasizes that Sky's and Jim's friendship is thus doomed. Jim's quotidian heroism is not up to the exceptional task that would be required to "save" Sky and recuperate her for "everyday" functioning in Jim's realm. Similarly, the 1994 "reunion" movie, "Godfather Knows Best" (7.4), places Jim at the center of an attempt to "save" his godson, Scotty Becker (Dennis Becker's son) from a life on the streets as a homeless grafter in Santa Monica. To escape a homicide charge, Scotty takes refuge in a Zen Doha tucked away in the Hollywood Hills. Jim's skepticism is palpable ("it was my material wealth you were divesting yourself of," he tells the retreat's new pupil). Unlike Sky, however, after Scotty's predicament is proven to be a frame, the film concludes with his successful restoration to "ordinary" life in the city, picturing his graduation from the Los Angeles Police Department academy, apparently restoring Jim's faith and good judgment.

"Like a Home Movie, Taken Before I Was Born"

While the era of a multi-generational, cross-continental, shared national TV audience simultaneously tuned in to the same program is lost in a niche-network era, this same niche moment — with its promotion of alternate exhibition and delivery platforms — might, conversely, encourage viewers to "time travel" through the streets of America's urban centers with series' new life on DVD. Rather than argue (or refute) that quality TV is "not TV" or that "typical" TV is unremarkable, there is a need to interrogate the broader institutional, textual, and social stakes behind these powerfully entrenched claims, both to consider how such tropes have functioned historically and in the contemporary context. "Quality" TV historically ratifies a particular kind of TV viewer and consumer for her/his economic, educational, and social capital. As noted above, this is a viewer who is flattered as allied with "high" culture, distinctive taste, "masculine" rationality, and active engagement in culture against those imagined to take pleasure in "low" culture's accessibility, "mass" appeal, "feminized" disposition, and distracted engagement. Such discursive appeals simultaneously mystify "quality" programming's real market imperatives *and* presume that "typical" series lack critically significant aesthetics and address.

The above subheading was taken from an Opinion piece written for *The Los Angeles Times* in 2005, on the occasion of the DVD release of its author's favorite TV series, *Remington Steele*.[37] In the essay, Robin Rauzi indicates the potential power of television's portrayals of place to literally and figuratively move viewers to engage community and interrogate assumptions regarding public mobility, and civic identity, in both heroic and heroically quotidian terms. According to writer Frankie Montiforte, *Rockford* is, likewise, "a particular treat because it captures the look of a Los Angeles that no longer exists. 'Rockford was one of the last shows to really depict L.A. as it was before the era of skyscrapers and multiplexes.'"[38] What new ways of theorizing television, its "quality" and its use within the rhythms of everyday life might open up if, following Pascucci and others, we consider the ways in which television is not *necessarily* synonymous with either suburban experience, "nonspace," or the "death" of public life in postwar America? What, Pascucci asks, of the "better" view of the city offered on television? A view that does not inhibit interpersonal relations but, in fact, might encourage or enable subjective relations otherwise unavailable to the viewer?

Notes

1. Gordon Devin, "Why TV Is Better Than the Movies," *Newsweek* (26 February 2007): 52–57.

2. Ibid., 54.

3. Throughout the chapter I will use the term "televisual" to refer to TV's unique formal (aesthetic/aural/textual) and industrial characteristics. John Caldwell has theorized the term "*televisuality*" as historically specific, referring to the early 1990s "collision of cineastic taste and streetwise sexuality, auteurism and rap" that, "for at least a decade," enabled American TV to exploit "the programming potential of visual style." That is, for Caldwell, the shift to a "post-network" or neo-network era in the 1990s represented a distinct transition in television aesthetics and address, from "primarily ... a form of word-based rhetoric and transmission, ... to a visually based mythology, framework, and aesthetic based on extreme self-consciousness of style." See, John Caldwell, *Televisuality: Style, Crisis, and Authority in American Television* (New Brunswick: Rutgers University Press, 1995), viii, 4.

4. Gordon, quoting, respectively, Carlton Cuse, Executive Producer of *Lost* (ABC, 2001–present); radio host, Ira Glass; and David Simon, co-creator of *The Wire* (HBO, 2001–present), 54, 52.

5. Ibid., 53.

6. The term "vast wasteland" appeared in FCC Chair Newton Minow's inaugural address to the National Association of Broadcasters in which he called for more public service oriented programming in prime time, as a ballast to "the old complacent, unbalanced fare of action-adventure and situation comedies." See, Newton Minow, "The Vast Wasteland," *Equal Time: The Private Broadcaster and the Public Interest*, Ed. Lawrence Laurent (New York: Atheneum, 1964), 51.

7. For excellent close analyses of each of these genres of "quality" TV, historically, see, for example: William Boddy, *Fifties Television: The Industry and Its Critics* (Urbana: University of Illinois Press, 1993); Michael Curtin, *Redeeming the Wasteland: Television Documentary and Cold War Politics* (New Brunswick: Rutgers University Press, 1995); Jane Feuer, Paul Kerr and Tise Vahimagi, Eds. *MTM "Quality Television"* (London: BFI Publishing, 1984).

8. Laurie Ouellette, *Viewers Like You? How Public TV Failed the People* (New York: Columbia University Press, 2002), 12, 4.

9. While, arguably, television studies within the academic humanities has been largely dedicated to rectifying such exclusions, much work remains to be done on broadly popular prime-time series from, particularly, the 1970s, which are only just now becoming available to many scholars thanks to greater DVD releases.

10. As regards *The Rockford Files* quality, it should be noted that, with the third season's addition of Chase to the writing and producing staff, it has been argued that "the stories got better ... and the shows started winning awards." Indeed, the series was recognized with the Outstanding Dramatic Series Emmy in its fourth season (1977-1978) when lead actor, James Garner, was also nominated for the Best Actor Award. Additionally, the popular *TV Guide* recently named the series the "Best Detective Show Ever." See: Ed Robertson, *Thirty Years of The Rockford Files: An Inside Look at America's Greatest Detective Series* (New York: ASJA Press, 2005), xxv.

11. Ernest Pascucci, "Intimate (Tele)Visions," *Architecture of the Everyday*, Eds. Steven Harris and Deborah Berke (Princeton: Princeton Architectural Press, 1997), 40. See also, Victoria E. Johnson, "'You're Gonna Make It After All!' The Urbane Midwest in MTM Productions' 'Quality' Comedies," *Heartland TV: Prime Time Television and the Struggle for U.S. Identity* (New York: New York University Press, 2007).

12. See, for example, Caldwell, above, and Lynn Spigel, *Welcome to the Dreamhouse: Popular Media and Postwar Suburbs* (Durham: Duke University Press, 2001).

13. It should be noted here that while humanistic scholarship regarding popular television, arguably, does not begin to flourish in the U.S. until the early 1980s, scholars in other national contexts had been engaging these questions from the immediate post-

war era, as is evidenced, for instance, in early work by scholars such as Richard Hoggart and Raymond Williams, in Great Britain.

14. Gene Youngblood, "Art, Entertainment, Entropy," *Video Culture*, Ed. John Hanhardt (Rochester: Visual Studies Workshop Press, 1987), 226. Originally published in 1974. Youngblood's gender-specific terminology is significant here, because it compromises his essay's early proclamations that his generation is responsible for questioning "all that has been held essential" in society.

15. Caldwell, 25.

16. Ibid.

17. Raymond Williams, *Television: Technology and Cultural Form* (Hanover: Wesleyan University Press, 1992), 20.

18. Margaret Morse, "An Ontology of Everyday Distraction: The Freeway, the Mall, and Television," *Logics of Television: Essays in Cultural Criticism* Ed. Patricia Mellencamp (Bloomington: Indiana University Press, 1990), 193. See, also: Roger Silverstone, Ed. *Visions of Suburbia* (London: Routledge, 1997); Roger Silverstone, *Television and Everyday Life* (London: Routledge, 1994); Mary Ann Doane, "Information, Crisis, Catastrophe," *Logics of Television: Essays in Cultural Criticism*, 222–239; and, E. Ann Kaplan, Ed. *Regarding Television: Critical Approaches* (Frederick, MD: University Publications of America, 1983).

19. David Morley, *Home Territories: Media, Mobility, and Identity* (London: Routledge, 2000), 128.

20. Caldwell, 30.

21. Early examples include: John Fiske and John Hartley, *Reading Television* (London: Methuen, 1978); and David Morley, *The Nationwide Audience: Structure and Decoding* (London: BFI, 1980).

22. Pascucci, 40, 44. Pascucci is referring, particularly, to Richard Sennett's *The Fall of Public Man* (New York: Knopf, 1976).

23. Morley, *Home Territories*, 114, 149.

24. Pascucci, 44, 45, 47, 46.

25. John Fiske, *Television Culture* (New York: Routledge, 1987), 13.

26. The mid-to-late 1950s is the period in which Hollywood film studios "became the predominant suppliers of the networks' primetime programming." See: Christopher Anderson, *Hollywood TV: The Studio System in the Fifties* (Austin: University of Texas Press, 1994), 4; and, Caldwell, 4.

27. Caldwell argues that the majority of Universal programs of this period were characterized by this "zero-degree" style, including "shows like *Columbo, Quincy, Delvecchio, The Incredible Hulk, The Six Million Dollar Man, The Bionic Woman*, and, later, *Knight Rider*." 57.

28. Mike Post, quoted in Robertson, 129.

29. Quoted in Tom Shales, "The Garner Files: Marshmallow Macho," *The Washington Post* (13 May 1979), N1.

30. Mark Post, quoted in Robertson, 129.

31. Ibid.

32. Edward Dimendberg, *Film Noir and the Spaces of Modernity* (Cambridge: Harvard University Press, 2004), 26, 17.

33. James Garner speaks to the series' emphasis on "car action" versus "gun action" in his interview on *The Rockford Files* season one DVD (Universal, 2005). Producer and writer Stephen J. Cannell has also spoken to this issue in interviews emphasizing Rockford's distaste for physical violence.

34. Ibid. And, according to Ed Robertson's history of the series, "Rockford had a brand new car each year (a 1974 model for the first season, a '75 for the second, and so

on) except for the last two seasons, when Garner elected to continue using the '78 model for the balance of the show," Robertson, 182.

    35. James Garner Interview (*The Rockford Files* Season One DVD, Universal, 2005).

    36. Quoted in Robertson, 307.

    37. Robin Rauzi, "Here and Now: Following Her Fedora, a Laura Holt Fan Goes on Location, Sort of, with Her Hero." *The Los Angeles Times* (8 September 2005): E2.

    38. Robertson, quoting Montiforte, 307.

Driving in Circles:
The Rockford Files

Robert F. Gross

In the 1970s, evening viewing on American television was awash in detective series. The cowboys had ridden off into the sunset; the spies had gone back into the cold. The sleuths, however, had a stronger hold on the ratings than ever. It seems that the viewing public could not get enough of engaging personalities who could solve riddles, defend the innocent, and put the world to rights in ninety minutes or less.

A few detective series carried over from the previous decade, most notably CBS's *Hawaii 5-O*, featuring colorful Hawaiian locations and a somewhat colorless Jack Lord in the lead. It would run until 1980, establishing a record for longevity broken only decades later by *Law and Order*. More indicative of later developments, however, was NBC's *Ironside* (1967–75), which individualized its detective by giving him a disability that confined him to a wheelchair. For, throughout the 70s, the detective needed to be strongly yet tersely characterized. The plots, after all, were largely familiar, even mechanical — who could hope to dazzle an audience well-versed in detective plots with fresh variations in under ninety minutes? And the formulaic plotlines brought with them a gallery of type characters fated to play out their all-too-familiar roles. It was the personality of the detective, distinctive, likeable, and immediately identifiable, that became the focus of the series.

The 70s spate of new detective series began in 1971, with NBC introducing no fewer than three successful detective dramas on its *NBC Mystery Movie*, which was introduced on Wednesday nights, but was moved to Sunday for the rest of its seven-year run (leaving Wednesday night free for yet another set of detective shows). The *Mystery Movie* rotated ninety-minute episodes of *Columbo*, starring Peter Falk; *McCloud,* with Dennis Weaver, and *McMillan and Wife*, with Rock Hudson and Susan St. James. In 1973, CBS entered the competition with Telly Savalas as *Kojak*, which would run until 1978. Each detective had his eccentricity: Kojak had his shaved head and lollipops; Columbo, his rumpled trench coat; McCloud, his cowboy hat, and McMillan, his wife. There were others as well: CBS offered *Cannon* (1971–76) with William Conrad as a middle-aged, overweight detective and *Barnaby Jones* (1973–1980) with Buddy Ebsen portraying the senior citizen as sleuth. Less long-lived attempts included: NBC's Polish-American *Banacek* (1972–1974); its Western-frontier detective *Hec Ramsey* (1972–1974); ABC's world-weary cop on disability, *Harry O* (1974–1976), its homoerotic "buddy" coupling of *Starsky and Hutch* (1975–78), and its pairing of an undercover cop and his pet cockatoo in *Baretta* (1975–1978). And the list goes on....

For all their trademark distinctions, however, the successful detectives of the 70s are, in retrospect, distressingly similar — all white (the African American *Tenafly* only lasted four episodes), male (short lives for both *Amy Prentiss* and *The Snoop Sisters*), gentile (few viewers for *Lanigan's Rabbi*), and heterosexual (no way). In retrospect, the distinctive markers of the protagonists only serve to underscore the basic homogeneity of the genre and its presuppositions throughout the decade.

David Chase entered the world of television detection in 1976 and stayed on for four seasons on NBC's *The Rockford Files*. The series had begun in 1974 as a ninety-minute *Movie of the Week*, and became a one-hour weekly series soon after. One of the most consistently popular of the 70s spate of detective dramas, its reputation has fared better than most with the passing of time. Mark Alvey has summed up the critical consensus of *The Rockford Files* as "one of the finest private eye series of the 1970s, and indeed of all time" (1942). It is worth viewing, not only for its entertainment value, but also for the insights its particular blend of realism and fantasy offers into American culture in the anxious years following the Vietnam War and Watergate scandal. *The Rockford Files* is the reflection of a period in which postwar prosperity was coming to an end and the middle class was under increased economic pressure, pressure that led to anxieties about masculinity, upward mobility, societal values — and especially suspicion about the values of those on top. These concerns are articulated largely through private detective Jim Rockford, a figure who exists simultaneously inside the system and without, is both macho and sensitive, hardworking and hedonistic, stressed and successful.

The Rockford Files was the creation of Roy Huggins and Stephen J. Cannell at Universal Studios.[1] Huggins had scored a success in 1957 by starring James Garner as a suave gambler in a decidedly unheroic variation on the Western —*Maverick*. The success of the series, an innovative amalgam of adventure and comedy, relied to a great extent on Garner's ability not only to play both action-hero masculinity as well as relaxed, self-deprecating roguishness, but to fuse them into a single character. From the beginning, *The Rockford Files* set out to do for detectives what *Maverick* had done for the West, using Garner's laid-back screen persona and understated acting style to bring a distinctive touch to the series. Rockford had a cool, amused sense of humor that communicated confidence and self-control, even in disconcerting circumstances; the sort of man who could ask a bullying thug, "Does your mother know what you do for a living?" ("The Kirkoff Case," 1.2).[2]

As Cannell has observed, the major strategy in writing *The Rockford Files* was to add realistic touches that would de-mythicize its protagonist. Unlike Auguste Dupin, Sherlock Holmes, and their erudite successors, Jim Rockford never comes up with recondite references or obscure knowledge; what he knows is simply what a man in his line of work *should* know. He is eager not to alienate the police (though often winds up doing so), reticent about taking open cases, and will often urge prospective clients to go through official channels first. He is averse to violence, does not carry a gun, and, although he is capable of landing a well-aimed punch on an assailant, he only resorts to fisticuffs when there is absolutely no alternative. He is as tough as the situation requires, but would far prefer being out fishing or home watching the football game. He is, quite simply, the Ordinary Guy as detective.

In his *Critique of Cynical Reason*, Peter Sloterdijk identifies three figures who embody three attitudes toward the heroic ideal in society: (1) the hero, the rare individual who unreservedly embraces the ideal; (2) the coward, the much more common anti-hero who resists even the slightest internalization of the ideal, and (3) the hesitater, or "relative hero" who occupies a middle ground between the two extremes (221). Hesitaters, Sloterdijk explains, "constitute the main mass of a 'reasonable middle position; they fight when they have to, and then they fight energetically, but they also curb the danger that can come from the bravado of heroes" (220). Rockford is clearly a hesitater. He regularly weighs the heroic code against his own safety, and tries to reach an accommodation between the two whenever possible. Although he is often skeptical in his analysis of human motives, he is never cynical in his overall comprehension of the system. Rather, he is an idealist. His idealism can verge on sentimentality, as when he tells a wealthy Los Angeles socialite trying to hide her past as a prostitute, "You're just a girl from southern Illinois. If I can, I'll help you" ("The Countess," 1.4), but it is precisely this occasional openness to sentimentality that proves Rockford's ability to remain humane in the most hardboiling of occupations—the L.A. private eye. When a one-time fiancée of Rockford's reacts to some unusually acid remarks with the observation, "You changed. You used to be a hopeless romantic" ("Claire," 1.18), the regular viewer of the series knows that she is mistaken. Rockford's harshness is merely self-protection; beneath the thinnest of veneers, we know he is *still* a hopeless romantic.

Because of this strain of idealism and deep compassion, attempts to put Rockford in the tradition of hardboiled L.A. private investigators such as Raymond Chandler's Philip Marlowe and Ross Macdonald's Lew Archer miss the mark (Alvey 1942). While the series does portray a Los Angeles rife with greed and deception, one close to the "metropolis of lies" that Liahna Babener identifies in Chandler's fiction (128), it also creates a core of regulars around Rockford who share his values and are honest, loyal and compassionate, most notably his father Joseph "Rocky" Rockford, his lawyer, Beth Davenport, and Police Detective Dennis Becker. Many of Rockford's clients are similarly decent. Unlike Philip Marlowe, Rockford rarely turns up an increasingly lurid tangle of crime and corruption that cannot be set to rights. Although some episodes end on a note of sadness or regret, others are lighthearted, and the overall tone throughout is hopeful. While the series abounds in *noir*-ish motifs (gangsters, thugs, corrupt tycoons, femme fatales, and the city of Los Angeles itself), their presence is repeatedly tempered by an affectionate and even comic tone, rooted in the pleasures of family and companionship, fishing, driving, and walks along the beach. Although *The Rockford Files* adopts many of the motifs of hardboiled detection, it distinctly softens its tone, often producing a "noir lite."

Although Huggins said that he fashioned Rockford as an outsider (Marc and Thompson 150), it would be more accurate to say that this detective occupies the threshold, both an insider and an outsider. Rockford's romantic idealism is by no means iconoclastic; he supports the status quo, albeit from a marginal and therefore problematic position. Not a member of the Los Angeles Police Department, he works on the fringes of the law enforcement system in an occupation that often raises the hackles of those at the center. He has enemies on the police force, but continues to have an inside track through his good friend Detective Dennis Becker, though even that relationship is subject to frequent renegotiation and testing of boundaries. The original concept for the series might have made Rockford's relationship to the police less fraught with tension; he was supposed to work only on cases that had been closed.[3] But that idea was soon abandoned, and Rockford often finds himself working on cases that have not only attracted the attention of the local police, but of state and federal agents as well.

Rockford's profession carries a degree of social stigma. His father, Rocky, wishes his son had followed his footsteps in the safer, more dependable and respectable profession of driving a truck: "You never gave trucking a chance" ("The Dark and Bloody Ground," 1.3), he complains. Embarrassed by his son's profession, Rocky does not tell his friends how his son makes his living — unless they suddenly need his help ("The Four Pound Brick," 1.21). The job may be on this side of the law, but not safely and unambiguously so.

Rockford's situation with the law is rendered even more vexed by the fact that he is an ex-convict. The series' handling of this piece of exposition is revealing. Although Rockford spent five years in the state penitentiary, he was released with a full pardon ("Exit Prentiss Carr," 1.5). This invention puts the series' protagonist as much as possible into the world of felonious crime while still preserving his innocence. The series, in those gentler, pre–*Oz* years of television drama, leaves that miscarriage of justice intentionally vague, and his entire experience with the penal system seems neither to have embittered him nor rendered him an embittered critic of society. Garner's clean-cut good looks and affable manner bear no trace of his unfortunate experience. For the most part, Rockford's penal experience seems little more than time spent in a somewhat louche prep school that encourages intense male bonding. Beyond its walls, a string of colorful and sometimes dangerous ex-cons come to enlist Rockford's services, while others have skills or information that he can draw upon during his cases. Professionally, the state prison works for Rockford much as the Jaycees or Elks might work for a more conventional businessman.

"The Daily Grind"

The Rockford Files repeatedly makes a point of underlining Rockford's situation as a self-employed businessman in a service economy. Although Cannell's description of his character as "the Jack Benny of private eyes" (qtd. in Alvery 1943) is clearly overstated, it is true that his finances put pressure on him to an extent unprecedented in television detection. Rarely does an episode go by without a reminder that Rockford's fee is "200 dollars a day — plus expenses." Although the fee seems to promise a comfortable lifestyle, especially by 70s standards, it is clear that Rockford is not making anywhere near the $52,000 annual income that a five-day workweek at that rate would suggest. As a freelancer, he is often worried about where his next paycheck will come from. The series underscores the point each week during the opening credits. Panning across the desk, the camera reveals a game of solitaire that Rockford had obviously been playing between jobs, waiting for the phone to ring. His answering machine sometimes gave further evidence of his financial woes. The phone message beginning the first episode conveyed it with amusing terseness: "Jim, it's Norma from the market. It bounced. Do you want us to tear it up, send it back, or put it with the others?" ("The Kirkoff Case," 1.2).

There is no reason to suspect Rockford or accuse him of Benny-like miserliness when he describes his bank statement as "a nightmare in red" ("The Kirkoff Case," 1.2).

Rockford's financial worries no doubt resonated with many of his viewers. The 1970s were a decade marked with economic difficulties. In June 1970 the unemployment rate reached five percent, and would hit six percent in 1978. The worldwide economy underwent the worst recession since the Great Depression of the 1930s. And while unemployment grew, so did inflation. Wage and price controls were briefly instituted in 1971 to deal with the problem, but prices rose throughout the decade, reaching sharp price increases of 13.3 in 1979 and 12.4 in 1980. Over these same two years, personal bankruptcies rose from 209,500 to 367,000 (Trager 1025–1078). 1973 has become the commonly agreed upon year for the flattening of household incomes, the starting-point for the "middle class decline" that affected more and more American household over the coming decades (Philips 24).

Against this background, Rockford's professional adventures reveal a more troubled aspect. Each episode is another job, another *paycheck,* and yet none of this perilous work seems to leave him any more secure by the end of the episode. Instead, Rockford all too often finds himself incapable of collecting his "200 dollars a day — plus expenses" from clients who are no better off than he is, and sees the promise of substantial finder fees vanish before his eyes. As the series unfolds, you get the feeling that he will never be able to improve upon the dark, cramped, and modestly furnished mobile home that serves as both his residence and office. Rockford is the hero for a decade in which the dream of upward mobility was becoming increasingly remote for many Americans — at a time during which the wealth began to be increasingly concentrated in the upper brackets (Philips 25).

Yet Rockford, a man unembittered by a bum prison wrap, seems largely unaffected by economic pressures. Although he repeats that he only does detective work for the money — "I don't take charity cases" ("The Dark and Bloody Ground," 1.3) — he finds himself again and again working for clients who are incapable of paying him, and displays a generosity that remains untainted by circumstances.

Although Rockford seems unblighted by the effects of the economic situation, the series is not. It is greed — not lust, jealousy, envy, or rage — that motivates the majority of the crimes committed on *The Rockford Files*. The desire for wealth divides friends, spouses, lovers and business partners. Rockford's boyhood friend and sometime foster brother does not hesitate to set him up as a patsy when a dangerous pyramid scheme goes sour ("The Aaron Ironwood School of Success," 2.1). One of Rockford's ex-girlfriends tries to revive his romantic feelings towards her, only to trick him into carrying counterfeit bills for her, and turns him over to be killed without turning a hair ("A Bad Deal in the Valley," 2.22). The most pervasive conflict of values throughout *The Rockford Files* is between loyalty and greed. It is the desire for wealth, the series implies, that is destroying the social fabric of America.

The paradigmatic villain in the series is the Man in the Suit, a sinister figure tied to some vaguely defined corporation with a paneled office in the upper reaches of some generic high-rise office building. His Suit is — along with its inevitable accessory, the necktie — the most frequent sartorial indication of moral turpitude. Businessmen gone wrong (an all-too-frequent occurrence) wear them, as do shady lawyers, sleazy PIs, and, surprisingly, the thugs who work for the higher-ups. Federal agents dress in suits and drive the four-door sedans similar to those of the Man in the Suit, a similarity that leads to no end of plot complications and lends a vaguely sinister connotation to law enforcement agents from Washington, D.C. (The Watergate Affair had, after all, been a matter of Men in Suits....)

The necktie sometimes helps to differentiate between two ethically opposed characters. In "Profit and Loss" (1.13 and 1.14) there are two investment advisors: one corrupt (with necktie) and one honest (without). In "A Bad Deal in the Valley" (2.22), the tie-less, suit-less Rockford confronts the shadow side of his profession in the person of a cigar-chomping sleazebag in a three-piece suit — and red necktie. Rockford only wears a tie if he is attending a funeral, romancing a glamorous but suspicious dame who moves in the world of Suits, or is impersonating a Suit himself. Otherwise his wardrobe is at once professional and casual — a sports coat, slacks, and a pastel or print shirt, open at the neck. One must momentarily suppress the suspicion that Garner's casual wear probably cost more than many of the suits worn by the supporting nasties and read the dress code as an indication that, although Rockford is a professional, he is by no means the stooge of a corrupt and often criminal system motivated by greed.

On the whole, women are more likely to be guiltless than men, and when guilty, less blood-bespattered. They are less involved in the greedy workings of corporations, and hence are less implicated in their machinations.

The lament of one improbably naïve gangster's moll, "I thought I knew him" ("The Kirkoff Case," 1.2), recurs with variations throughout the series as women are confronted with the misdeeds of their sons, husbands, brothers, or lovers who turn out to be felons. At the same time, women, as the objects of sexual desire, are more difficult to decipher than men, and Rockford is far more likely to be taken in by them. The ubiquitous pantsuit is not the equivalent to the business suit worn by men. It predominates as the female outfit of choice, and is worn by women both crooked and straight. As a general rule, however, the more revealing the outfit, the more dangerous the dame. Low-cut gowns often suggest duplicity, and bikinis are outright giveaways. Performances of hyperfemininity are generally suspect, the touchstone for female behavior is Rockford's lawyer, Beth Davenport, a highly competent, ethical, and loyal professional, whose values seem close to her client's.

The Men in Suits establish the criminal norm for *The Rockford Files*. Rather than breaking into banks, museums, or jewelry stores, they are masters of confidence games, blackmail, and white-collar crime. Even when a major heist does take place, in "The Italian Bird Fiasco" (2.19), it is over before the episode begins; the plot deals exclusively with the elaborate schemes concocted to convey the loot from London to L.A. The Men in Suits prefer to do their work invisibly; murders are often the result of unfortunate complications. Opponents or unlucky eyewitnesses are much more inclined to be dispatched efficiently than sadistically, and are staged to look like suicides ("The Real Easy Red Dog," 2.7) or mishaps ("Just by Accident," 1.22). Yet this is not to minimize the threat that they pose to the average citizen. Those unlucky enough to simply blunder in on their transactions can suddenly find themselves under sentence of death ("Sleight of Hand," 1.16 and "Gearjammers," 2.3 and 2.4). Invisibility is everything; crimes operate most effectively under the lush cover of ever-increasing corporate and bureaucratic obfuscation.

But Rockford has learned how to thrive in these thickets as well. He masterfully impersonates the officious non-entities of the bureaucratic world: insurance adjusters, assessors, accountants, and salesmen. Armed with an array of phony business cards in his wallet, and a portable printing press in his glove compartment (to produce more if the situation demands it), he is able to bluff his way into many well-patrolled homes and offices, and get otherwise privileged information. "The whole secret of a good confidence game is having the right props," he explains ("Tall Woman in Red Wagon," 1.6). For Rockford, the right business card, a confident manner, and a convincing line of bureaucratic patter proves more effective than "Open Sesame" in the "Arabian Nights." The very circumstances that allow crime to thrive also create opportunities for a private inspector with a gift for improvisation. Part of the pleasure of seeing Rockford at work is in his ability to get the better of the system, as Garner momentarily masks his star-conferring charm and dives beneath the radar screen of corporate culture to mimic the officious nerd. Even his leading man good looks seem to momentarily fade behind the unglamorous façade of minor officialdom. Rockford's gift for impersonation adds an element of comic playfulness to his serious undertakings.

Although he profits from his ingenious, protean nature, it also runs the risk of branding him a weasel. A rival gumshoe characterizes Rockford to his face as a "con bull artist. You never run a straight line in your life" ("A Bad Deal in the Valley," 2.22)—a brutal assessment, but not his alone. Rockford's gift for impersonation sometimes makes him appear more the confidence man than the private eye, working to defeat con with con. A few episodes give this impulse full rein; "The Farnsworth Stratagem" (2.2) develops an elaborate con done in the cause of justice, protecting the preyed-upon citizen from the legal but outrageously unethical deceits of entrepreneurs. But the series also places limits on Rockford's improvisatory skills. He fails miserably when he tries to unenthusiastically bluff his way through the world of art dealers in "The Italian Bird Fiasco" (2.19), and uncharacteristically puts out almost no effort to succeed. From his first interaction with an effete art dealer, it is clear that for Rockford to pass in this world, he would endanger his status as Ordinary Guy, both in class affiliation and heteronormative masculinity. Impersonation dare only go so far, after all.

"The Endless Pursuit"

Jim Rockford's most important tool, however, is not his skill at impersonation, but his car. Rockford's Pontiac Firebird, updated to the latest model each season, is at once a practical necessity and a fantasy inspiring fetish that continues to be admired by Ordinary Guys. This sporty compact car had undergone extensive redesign in 1970, and was available in both a base model and a more powerful and highly styled Trans Am. In the interests of verisimilitude, it was decided that Rockford should drive the base model, the Trans Am being too clearly beyond his means. General Motors' Pontiac Division supplied a "veritable fleet" of Firebirds not only to Garner, but to the production company as well, keenly aware of the advertising value of the car's weekly screen appearances.[4]

The automobile had long been a standard part of the detective's equipment, and the injunction; "Follow that car!" had passed into cliché decades before *The Rockford Files* arrived on the scene. But movies had recently proven the audience appeal of high-powered displays of automotive choreography with *Bullitt* (1968), *The Italian Job* (1969), and *The French Connection* (1971), and *The Rockford Files* exploited that appeal for the small screen. The car chase became a frequent set piece and a distinguishing mark of the series. Indeed, it is surprising how much screen time that could have been spent on more character development or the smoother and more digestible exposition is given over to footage of the Firebird. The amount of time and ingenuity lavished on cars and car chases, renders *The Rockford Files* far more of an action series than the usual 70s detection drama, augmenting fistfights with glossier, less gruesome, and more varied action sequences. The vehicles involved run the gamut from a Rolls Royce to a Volkswagen Beetle, from a semi-trailer to a beat-up pizza delivery car. They usually are confined to the streets, but can easily veer off into a construction site, junkyard, or the swimming pool of an apartment complex. Any approach to *The Rockford Files* that ignores its cars misses a substantial part of its appeal.

Simply as a *car*, the Firebird is needed for each episode to unfold. The crime is no longer committed within the confines of a country estate, as in the classic British detective tradition, or even within a neighborhood. Unlike, say, Agatha Christie's Hercule Poirot, Rockford does not summon all the mystery's characters into a single room to announce his findings. Whereas Siegfried Kracauer identified the hotel lobby as the central locale of the 1920s detective novel (128–137), a public meeting place to which strangers could gravitate, there are no similar shared spaces in Rockford's L.A. It is a city of dispersal and distance in which fraud and impersonation are accomplished easily among strangers, and even violent crimes rarely affect the neighbors. One repeated motif of *The Rockford Files* is the character who has come to Los Angeles with a new identity, leaving an old scandal behind ("The Countess," 1.4 and "The Reincarnation of Angie," 2.12), but the city is sufficiently vast that it is even possible to reinvent oneself without leaving town ("The Hammer of C Block," 2.14). Even intimates, we find, exist at a distance from one another. When Rocky is threatened in "Gearjammers" (2.3 and 2.4), his son quickly realizes that he knows next to nothing about his father's social life, professional activities, and daily routines. The distances between people are both the precondition and result of personal independence, with results that are often dangerous.

The Men in Suits often profit from these distances. They rarely live alongside their victims, and they prefer indirect methods. The investigation establishes a complex web of relationships between strangers, linking rich and poor, criminals and cops, victims, bystanders, and perpetrators across physical distance. The truth can only be uncovered through repeated traversals of the city, not through the common spaces of mass transit, but through the private operations of a car. The process of detection becomes inextricably linked with driving.

As the car speeds along to the next clue, the city is revealed. *The Rockford Files* depends to a great degree on its extensive location shooting of the streets of Los Angeles and its environs for its sense of realistic verisimilitude, grounding the complex and often improbable plot lines in a recognizable milieu. Repeatedly, the dialogue makes a point of telling us street addresses, giving us the sense we could drive to these places ourselves. If we were so inclined and familiar with the area, we could map out entire episodes. We see the Safeways, Taco Bells, and Holiday Inns, as well as the innumerable gas stations and car dealers. The street, rather than any building, is the one common place shared by all the characters — the democratic *topos*, open to all — and the one place that links all the others.

In this democratic space, the Firebird functions as a metonym of its owner. Like Garner's Rockford, it is at once grounded in realism and bathed in unostentatious glamour. It is smart but unpretentious, nimble and responsive. It emerges with its good looks miraculously unscathed from countless murderous onslaughts. Indeed, it strains credulity that a car that undergoes so much rough handling should spend so little time in the shop. Even when it is totaled (a surprisingly rare occurrence), the screenwriters contrive to replace it instantly and effortlessly — the Firebird is dead. Long live the Firebird ("Just by Accident," 1.22).

Throughout *The Rockford Files*, car culture is tied to masculine identity. Although the series never descends to obnoxious gibes about women drivers, it very rarely lets women behind the wheel during a chase. Motor vehicles (along with fishing) constitute a major shared topic of interest between Rockford and his father, and their differences in this regard illuminate the class differences between them. Rocky, a retired truck driver, owns a (General Motors) truck, in line with his working class background. His son, who has, however uncertainly, moved out of that class, owns a (General Motors) sports coupe. In both cases, however, the very importance of their vehicles is a major indicator of their masculinity.

Although the car chases can often seem over-extended or even gratuitous in their relationship to the overall plot, they reveal the fundamental dynamics of the series. If we step back for a moment from the common assumption that the most basic dramatic formula of the series is solving mysteries, a second, less obvious pattern emerges: the mystery simply exists as a pretense for putting its protagonist in danger and mistreating him. Indeed, the extent to which the series regularly foregrounds the persecution of its detective is amazing. Deceived, exploited, humiliated, tailed, arrested, threatened, beaten, and framed, Jim Rockford undergoes a weekly ritual of abuse unimaginable in the pages of Conan Doyle and Agatha Christie — and unusual even by the standards of 70s television detection. The car chase is repeatedly the most extended, energetic, complexly shot and edited presentation of a threat posed to Rockford. And yet it also shows him at his best. Behind the wheel of his car, he seems emancipated. Driving allows him to transcend the limitations imposed on him by circumstances: his marginalized status, financial woes, romantic misadventures, and prison time. Here, the hesitater becomes the hero. In the car chase, we see an Ordinary Guy with guts, ingenuity, and split-second judgment outmaneuver the malevolent intentions of the Men in Suits at high speed. It is at once a nightmare of persecution and a compensatory fantasy of mastery.

These sequences become even more significant when considered in the light of contemporary considerations of the dynamics of melodrama. Detective drama, with its conflicts between the highly polarized forces of good and evil, usually ending in the triumph of good, is fundamentally melodramatic, and most episodes of *The Rockford Files*, despite their moments of lightness and outright comedy, are no exception. Geoffrey Nowell-Smith's highly influential analysis of stylistic excess in the film melodramas of Vincente Minnelli reveals that excess in the mise-en-scene can function as an outbreak of hysteria, manifesting the energies that the work otherwise is laboring to repress:

> The tendency of melodramas to culminate in a happy end is not unopposed. The happy end is often impossible, and what is more, the audience knows it is impossible. Furthermore, a "happy end" which takes the form of an acceptance of a form of castration is achieved only at the cost of repression. The laying out of the problems "realistically" always allows for the generating of an excess that cannot be accommodated [117].

Hysterical outbreaks of heightened mise-en-scene and musical underscoring in film melodrama are the manifestation of a tension that cannot be expressed otherwise.

Sequences of stylistic excess are often grounded in the gender dynamics of film melodrama, in which the character who is allowed to suffer openly and become a figure of hysteria is usually female (think Joan Crawford, Lana Turner, Dorothy Malone), while the suffering male is marked by the very fact of his suffering to be insufficiently masculine (think John Kerr, Montgomery Clift, Tony Perkins). Psychoanalyst Juliet Mitchell has shown how male hysteria has largely been disavowed in our culture because of its linkage with femininity: "Where hysteria in women shades easily into femininity, hysteria in men appears as the very opposite of masculinity" (159).

In *The Rockford Files,* Rockford is sufficiently compassionate and enlightened to accept the therapeutic value of masculine tears, and can even admit to his own tears without embarrassment ("Where's Houston?" 2.20), but he is usually seen to accept his daily humiliations with stoicism or anger rather than suffering. In many a car chase, there is a persecuted female in the car with Rockford, but the sequence focuses on Rockford as the persecuted figure. But he cannot be seen to be suffering, let alone hysterical. Rather, he must be masculine, that is, totally in control. The character's fear is displaced onto the mise-en-scene: rapid camera movement and cross-cutting, sounds of racing engines, squealing tires, and musical underscoring.

What is the source of the hysteria that crops up in these action sequences? Juliet Mitchell's analysis of hysteria is illuminating in this regard. She sees the origins of hysteria in the child's recognition that a rival, usually a sibling, can replace him in his parents' affections. For Mitchell, the hysteric "starts as a displaced person" (205). His identity usurped by his rival, he suffers both from "the desperate need to *be* someone" (47), as well as a desperate mixture of both love and hatred toward the imagined usurper. In *The Rockford Files,* this dynamic appears most clearly in "The Aaron Ironwood School of Success." In that episode we learn that Rockford grew up with a foster child named Aaron Ironwood, who has grown up to be a millionaire as the leader of a human potential movement. He has the charm, and we learn later, the confidence skills of Rockford, but has been able to parlay them into a fortune. From the opening of the episode, Rocky (dressed uncharacteristically but revealingly in a suit and tie for Aaron's visit) belittles Rockford for his failure to match Aaron's success, leaving Rockford to experience once again the loss of love and identity that accompanies his father's preference for his rival. Ambivalence reigns as Rockford feels both rage and affection for Aaron, an affection that leads him to play the patsy in Aaron's shady dealings, and almost leads to his death. When the Aaron Ironwood School of Success turns out to be a pyramid scheme, Rockford is able to regain his place in his father's affections. The episode begins with Rockford, the innocent ex-convict lost in the shadow of his successful sibling, and ends, in a triumph of wish-fulfillment, with Rockford vindicated, while his felonious rival is revealed as such, and is sent off to prison.

The specter of Aaron Ironwood, Rockford's wildly successful but criminal alter ego, haunts the series. Rockford is unfairly punished, in episode after episode, by the figures who embody success on both sides of the law; he is scorned by both criminal and crime fighter as inadequate. In vain, Rockford tries to establish his credentials by hard work, and win affection with his charm. The basic structure of the series shows this unfortunate sibling always being judged inferior to an imagined figure of success, subjected to suffering, and achieving a momentary triumph by the end of the hour. Yet by the next episode, he is back where he began, struggling to justify himself against the standards set by an imaginary successful sibling.

America in the 70's found itself caught between increasingly polarized visions of masculinity.[5] Still reeling from a disastrous war abroad and the resignation of a president who had chosen the hypermasculinity of Teddy Roosevelt as a model (Dubbert 279), struggling with the challenges of feminism, gay liberation, and the countercultural critique of the previous decades, masculinity became an increasing topic of debate. Should traditional masculinity be reasserted or jettisoned? Was the 1974 sight of football quarterback Joe Namath modeling Hanes Beautymist pantyhose on a television commercial a cause for celebration or alarm? The same year that saw Joe Namath's shaved legs saw the publication of both Warren Farrell's *The Liberated Man* and Marc Fasteau's *The Male Machine*, just two of the many masculinity critiques to appear during the decade. More than ever before in American society, masculinity was postulated as a problem.

One solution was put forth in the 1970s action films of Clint Eastwood. In his essay, "Eastward Bound," Paul Smith finds in those movies a pattern of physical suffering and abuse similar to that in *The Rockford Files*: the heroic body is objectified and subjected to pain, creating a temporarily masochistic moment whose homoeroticism is disavowed by the film's conclusion. By the end, he writes, the male body and its limitations seem to have "vanished into air" (86), leaving behind reinforced norms of masculinity, as well as a "hysterical residue" (80) similar to that identified by Nowell-Smith in Minnelli's melodramas. But although *The Rockford Files* can be seen to share a similarity with Eastwood's movies in their common testing of masculinity through suffering, the differences may ultimately be more significant than the similarities. While Eastwood embodies the hero, Garner embodies the hesitater. His annoyance with the system never leads to a break with it, only to complex tactics of accommodation and subversion. For Rockford, masculine maturity requires the abandonment of the heroic stance whenever possible. It is not unusual for Rockford to be saved at the last moment by the police who he has called to surround the building in which he is being held captive ("A Bad Deal in the Valley," 2.22), or to cannily summon the police to close in on his car chase and put an end to it ("In Hazard," 2.18). The series rejects the ethics of Solitary Heroism for one of Collective Hesitation. The basic movement of an episode is to bring a world of Ordinary Guys and Gals back into equilibrium.

Despite all the beatings Rockford endures, *The Rockford Files* does not communicate the intense paranoia of traditional white masculinity under attack, as seen the Eastwood films that Smith has analyzed, or the later action vehicles of Sylvester Stallone that David Savran has seen as paradigmatic of the 80's conservative backlash (187–206). Instead, the series plays with a fantasy that the best of old and new masculine values can be painlessly integrated.

In a 1978 article, sociologist Paul Starr described a new kind of hero that was making its appearance in the recent motion pictures, *Coming Home, An Unmarried Woman* and *Alice Doesn't Live Here Anymore.* In all three, Starr identified "the emotionally competent hero," distinct from the anti-heroes played by Dustin Hoffman and Jack Nicholson, the troubled and emotionally immature heroes of Marlon Brando and James Dean, and, he might have added, from the emotional Neanderthals of Clint Eastwood and Charles Bronson. The new figure shows the influence of 70s feminism and an emerging critique of traditional American masculinity on the popular imagination. As a man who can be "masculine without being dominating," Starr observes "He is the man to whom women turn as they try to change their own lives: someone who is strong and affectionate, capable of intimacy." (26) Jim Rockford anticipates these cinematic figures by five years. He can help women negotiate the emotionally painful terrain of mourning for a dead father ("2 Into 5:56 Won't Go," 2.10 and "Where's Houston?" 2.20), cope with overidealized crushes on other women ("Tall Woman in Red Wagon," 1.6), and begin to realize the emotionally crippling effects of being overly dependent on an older brother ("The Reincarnation of Angie," 2.12). Rockford is a fantasy figure that can reconcile both old and new values for men: good with cars and his fists, yet competent in his relationships and in touch with his feelings. He can hold the men who threaten his father at gunpoint, and yet also hear his father's cry of emotional frustration, "I want you to *understand!*" and put a comforting arm around him ("Gearjammers," 2.3 and 2.4). The new values, the series implies, can simply be added onto the earlier ones without any tension or contradiction; Rockford can be counted on to punch out the thugs, not his girlfriends. In this liberal gender fantasy, sensitivity and skill at impersonal relations are imagined as graceful add-ons to the masculinity of the hard-boiled detective.

While Smith has pointed to the scapegoating of women and queers as a necessary strategy to ensure the triumph of normative masculinity in Eastwood's films (92), and Savran has uncovered similar dynamics in vigilante films of the 80s and 90s revealing sexism, homophobia, and racism at work (200–210), *The Rockford Files* is surprisingly free of racial, ethnic, gender, and queer scapegoating in working out its solutions. The villains exist, first and foremost, as wealthy white males, ostensibly straight (though their greed seems to have often rendered them strangely asexual), who stand as threats to the world of Rockford and his friends. Rarely graced with individual histories or distinguishing touches, they are largely anonymous personifications of an avaricious impulse.

Although Robert J. Thompson and David Marc have claimed that "Rockford is arguably the first detective to arrive on prime time schlepping something resembling existentialist baggage" (208), a closer examination of the luggage reveals it to be less purely philosophical than social. As this paper has shown, from some angles the series appears bitter, even grim. But with only a slight shift in perspective, amusement and affection suddenly rise to the top. The system may be desperately flawed, but not so severely that it needs to be repudiated, or alternatives explored. The series turns a blind eye to the fact that Men in Suits market cars and even produce television shows, and intimates that the invasions of greed into middleclass life can be successfully patrolled by efforts of the middle class. Compared to the world of *The Sopranos. The Rockford Files* appears innocent. The Ordinary Guy may be having a tough time, but ultimately, we are assured, he does o.k. He may only be driving in circles, yet you can enjoy being taken for a ride.

Notes

1. For the origins of the series, see the entries on Roy Huggins and Stephen J. Cannell in *Encyclopedia of Broadcasting,* Alvey 1942-43, and Marc and Thompson, 144–150.
2. For examples, I have drawn on representative episodes from the recently released DVD versions of the first two seasons, for accessibility.
3. See interview with Cannell, *The Rockford Files: Season Two,* disc 6.
4. For the history of the Pontiac Firebird and *The Rockford Files,* see Parker.
5. For a thoughtful and contemporary view of 70s masculinities, see Dubbert 278–283.

Works Cited

Alvey, Mark. "*The Rockford Files.*" *Encyclopedia of Television.* Ed. Horace Newcomb. New York: Fitzroy Dearborn, 2004: 1942–1944.

Babener, Liahna. "Raymond Chandler's City of Lies." *Los Angeles in Fiction: A Collection of Essays.* Ed. David Fine. Revised edition. Albuquerque: University of New Mexico Press, 1984: 127–149.

"Cannell, Stephen J." The Museum of Broadcast Communications. http://www.museum. tv/archives/etv/C/htmlC/cannelstep/cannelstep.html.

Dubbert, Joe L. *A Man's Place: Masculinity in Transition.* Englewood Cliffs: Prentice-Hall, 1979.

"Huggins, Roy." The Museum of Broadcast Communications. http://www.museum.tv/ archives/etv/H/htmlH/hugginsroy/hugginsroy.html.

Kracauer, Siegfried. *Der Detektiv-Roman. Schriften I.* Frankfurt am Main: Suhrkamp, 1978: 103–204.

Marc, David, and Robert J. Thompson. *Prime Time, Prime Movers: From* I Love Lucy *to* L.A. Law — *America's Greatest TV Shows and the People Who Created Them.* Boston: Little, Brown, 1992.

Mitchell, Juliet. *Mad Men and Medusas: Reclaiming Hysteria.* New York: Basic Books, 2000.

Nowell-Smith, Geoffrey. "Minnelli and Melodrama." *Screen* 18.2 (Summer 1972): 113–118.

Parker, Steve. "Car Nut TV. Cars as Stars: High Performance Films and the Cars that Make Them." http://www.carnuttv.com/articles/articles_cars_as_stars.html. Accessed 11 July 2006.

Phillips, Kevin. *Boiling Point: Republicans, Democrats, and the Decline of Middle-Class Prosperity.* New York: Random House, 1993.

The Rockford Files. Season One. 3 videodiscs. Universal. 2006.

_____. *Season Two.* 6 videodiscs. Universal. 2006.

Savran, David. *Taking It Like a Man: White Masculinity, Masochism, and Contemporary American Culture.* Princeton: Princeton University Press, 1998.

Smith, Paul. "Eastward Bound." *Constructing Masculinity.* Ed. Maurice Berger, Brian Wallis, Simon Watson. New York: Routledge, 1995: 77–97.

Sloterdijk, Peter. *Critique of Cynical Reason.* Trans. Michael Eldred. Minneapolis: University of Minnesota Press, 1987.

Starr, Paul. "Hollywood's New Image of Masculinity." *The New York Times,* July 16 1978, II: 1, 26.

Trager, James. *The People's Chronology: A Year-by-Year Record of Human Events from Prehistory to the Present.* Revised edition. New York: Henry Holt, 1994.

Going Native in Cicely, Alaska: American Archetypes and Hybridized Identity on *Northern Exposure*

Heather E. Epes

> ED: How's the mooseburger?
>
> FLEISCHMAN: Li'l gamey.
>
> ED: Oh. You'll get used to it.

For a significant part of its run, the television show *Northern Exposure* develops both plot and characters through tension created by the identity clash between Cicely natives and their newly imported resident, Dr. Joel Fleischman. A close look at *Northern Exposure's* characters reveals a narrative foundation of socially constructed Native American images and mythic American national characters. Although American national identity historically has been built upon Native American identity as constructed in the Euroamerican imagination, Cicely's natives offer us a twist. In relation to Fleischman, the stereotypical modern man, both Native American and American frontiersman stereotypes seem to inhabit the same space, metaphorically as well as physically. Additionally, *Northern Exposure* consistently undermines its archetypally constructed base, establishing a dialectic that ricochets between reifying stereotypes and redefining them. Through his interaction with and ultimate hybridization of these stereotypes, Fleischman embodies their complex dynamics as he develops into the unlikely hero of an unexpected quest of his own.

Welcome to Cicely

As we meet the cast of *Northern Exposure,* we find that most of them have arrived in Cicely from somewhere else. The characters we get to know in early episodes seem to have wended their way "North to Alaska" as part of personal journeys and searches. While their intentions may not have been to make a home in Cicely, each journey was driven by decisions intended either to satisfy a calling in the self for change or discovery, or to travel paths already decided upon. In a sense, each followed his or her own North Star home, and in so doing, found themselves.

Fleischman's journey west and north, however, begins rather unlike other quests for self, its hero kicking and screaming all the way. Hardly the archetypical hero, Fleischman already presents us with the dynamic that will offer humor and depth to the characters and myth arch of *Northern Exposure.* He is a man headed west to the wild, but hardly due to some romanticized vision of finding himself or conquering frontiers. Joel Fleischman arrives unwillingly in Cicely under what amounts to a contract of indentured servitude. The State of Alaska paid for Fleischman's newly bestowed M.D. degree, and he owes them four years of service. Rather than experiencing Cicely as a settling place, Fleischman feels only disorientation, displacement and culture shock. At the end of the first season, he sarcastically describes his new location as "somewhere between the end of the line and the middle of nowhere" ("Aurora," 1.8).

Fleischman has a clear, highly localized identity as a New York City denizen, and a doctor with a Jewish background. He apparently suffers no postmodern or nationalistic identity anxiety, only personal neuroses and perhaps post-traumatic nerd syndrome. Neither Alaska nor Native Americans represent a romantic discovery or resolution of his identity, some transcendent experience of nature or spirit. Alaska represents nothing but a barrier of wilderness between him and the rest of his life. Fleischman's only self-professed romantic vision is to be married to his girlfriend and to raise a Jewish family; his closest vision to wilderness, to be wildly successful as a doctor in New York City.

True to his experience, Fleischman operates under a unified system of interdependent specialization, capitalism, and social status. Serving as a doctor within an economy of monetary exchange, he expects in turn to be served by taxi-drivers, plumbers, utilities, and a variety of goods-providing stores. Cicely's paradigm, on the other hand, functions on equal parts self-sufficiency and close community. Cicely doesn't need a plumbing specialist for hire because, as Chris Stevens explains to Fleischman in the second episode, "Brains, Know-How and Native Intelligence," everyone knows Maggie O'Connell is the best plumber around. Cicelians understand that far more important than the services bartered or favors given, is the relationship formed around those exchanges, a nuance of small-town community and honoring individuality lost upon Fleischman.

As a dedicated inhabitant of New York City, Fleischman's experience of America has been rather specific. Native Americans have only rarely been on his imaginative chart. *Alaska* has barely made it onto his chart, made immanently clear when he explains testily to Maggie that "*this* is hardly America!" ("Kodiak," 1.7). As far as Fleischman can see on his reluctant arrival, Native Americans and Cicelians are all natives of an alien, incomprehensible land. Fleischman's identity is established in opposition to these natives. His interactions with both Native Americans and Cicelians define him as one of the stereotypes of "modern man": citified, overeducated, and neurotic. The interactions also point out Native American stereotypes as well as simultaneously subverting them.

"What the hell do Indians do?"

Despite the fact that Fleischman has had neither American Indians nor Alaska on his mind or in his dreams, even he has some vague ideas about Native Americanness. Fleischman is occasionally bemused and offended by Maurice Minnifield's racism towards both Jews and Native Americans, but seems largely unaware of his own underlying assumptions. His perceptions of Indianness are influenced by exposure to its representation, never its reality. Even as he learns to accept the complexity of Native Americans around him, he reverts occasionally to his engrained worldview.

For instance, in "Aurora Borealis," Ed Chigliak caddies for Fleischman as he attempts to practice golfing in a mountain meadow (1.8). They stumble upon a huge footprint, and Ed tells Fleischman the local folktale about Adam, a wild man. In real terror, Fleischman later tries to convince Maggie that Adam is something to fear, referring to: "Footprints that Ed, an Indian, swears don't belong to any known species!" Fleischman overstates Ed's position, which was a more casual admission that the footprint belonged to no animal he knew of and that he had never seen Adam himself. He casts Ed in the position of Indian as tied inherently to the earth, omniscient concerning nature. Ed may indeed be revealed as a wildcrafter, but at this point in the series, Fleischman can't have spent enough time exploring local flora and fauna with Ed to judge his ultimate word on the natural surroundings.

And although Fleischman may trust and even respect what he considers Ed's expertise, he relies on a stereotype to express those feelings, rather than simply referring to Ed as Ed.

Occasionally Fleischman's comments seem as if they may be a bit tongue in cheek, as with his comment to Bernard on his arrival in Cicely. When Bernard asks Fleischman where he is, Fleischman comments, "Talk to Ed. He's a Native. He's got a great sense of direction" ("Aurora," 1.8). The statement may be true, and it may intend humor since Ed is both a native of Cicely and a Native, but the humor works around an irony reliant on Indian stereotypes. [1] And occasionally, Fleischman's comments are difficult to interpret. When Ed's uncle, Anku, resists participating in doctor's appointments his family arranges, Fleischman comments to Minnifield, "I've been stood up by an Indian" ("Brains," 1.2). It's possible the reference is an ironic one, but the comment may be an oblique reference to the stereotype of the lazy or unreliable Indian. Even if it is not, the import is offensive simply by his facile association of race and what he judges as negative behavior. Elsewhere, an instance of perspective for viewers on the "unreliable Indian" stereotype occurs when Ed abandons Fleischman in the middle of an Alaska style golf game. He has discovered that the town's beloved tree, Old Vicki, is diseased ("Old," 4.25). The grief and urgency of the situation is far more important to Ed than what Fleischman perceives as an important golfing engagement.

There are a number of instances when *Northern Exposure* presents challenges to stereotypes that may serve to prop up the very stereotypes they apparently refute. Generally, the images offer several potential interpretations to a viewer. Often enough, the show's humor depends on the interplay between the stereotype and its challenge. Since humor is a complex social event, it can be difficult to tell whether the humor is meant to criticize a stereotype or merely takes advantage of it.

After Soapy Sanderson dies and inexplicably bequeaths his legacy of 100 acres to Maggie and Fleischman, Fleischman quickly recognizes its money making potential ("Soapy," 1.3). To his delight and Maggie's outrage, Chief Ronkonkoma offers to buy the land. The episode may nod to a more recent perception, sometimes scornful due to the success of a number of casinos, of American Indians as enterprising; Ronkonkoma not only will own the land to sell if he wishes, but he also likes the idea of a tax write-off. However, in the context of Maggie's anger, the episode could appeal to a sense that Ronkonkoma is abdicating a responsibility to care about the land. His motivations run counter to a common image of American Indians as indigenous people linked to the land through spirituality and primitiveness, its guardians and defenders.

In a related example, a disgruntled Minnifield discovers that one of the five wealthiest men in Alaska is Native Alaskan ("River," 5.5). The connection to the previous example hinges on the association of Native Americans with wealth and, tacitly, with both ownership and the success that wealth implies. On the one hand, Minnifield's discomfort references a stereotype of American Indians as a low income group due to their failure to make "progress" in a modern American culture. Their perceived failure has been contributed variously to an innate inability to develop socially, as well as laziness or unreliability. On the other hand, Minnifield is a clearly racist figure, perhaps indicating that his reaction is based on prejudice, and that we should be critical of his feelings.

Marilyn Whirlwind functions as the foil for the conflated stereotype of the silent Indian, either wise or unemotional. Marilyn speaks little, and when she does, she does so succinctly, delivering straightforward sentences that nonetheless seem to use wisdom as a subtext of the mundane. She is also regularly the knowledgeable source of Native Alaskan, ostensibly Tlingit, myth or legend. At all times, she maintains a steady look straight in the eye of those with whom she converses, and perhaps gives a slight smile or lift of the brow. Not only her use of language, but even her body movements seem to be minimal and deliberate.

Marilyn's stoicism may echo a stereotype of Native American silent wisdom, but it is also certainly a way to tease Fleischman, a mode of humor. Her sense of humor stands against a negative stereotypical image of the silent Indian as lacking in emotion. For example, Marilyn answers the phone and informs Fleischman that someone is on line one. Fleischman responds, exasperated, that they only have one ("Brains," 1.2). She simply looks at him with her small smile and hands over the phone, fully aware that he has completely missed her ironic reference to the small town accommodations he must endure. It is an exchange that occurs more than once at his expense. Her offer of a concoction of "hair of the dog" to Fleischman after a drinking binge with Holling completely takes advantage of his naiveté ("Things," 3.13). As he spits it out in disgust, she confirms that it is, in fact, hair of the dog.

In another example of ironic humor that plays off the silent Indian, Marilyn eloquently interprets Chris's sign language when he has lost his voice to a beautiful woman ("Big," 2.2). She watches for a few moments as Chris tries desperately to communicate to Fleischman that he can't speak. Fleischman, at a complete loss, guesses that Chris is telling him he's going to throw up. At this point, Marilyn steps in. As Chris continues to make incomprehensible gestures, Marilyn poetically and accurately renders his explanation about a beautiful woman causing his voice to fly away while

Fleischman listens incredulously. Chris's slapstick motions, Fleischman's amazement and Marilyn's translation of a silent language by verbosely breaking her characteristic silence make the moment an ironically funny one. However, it could be said that it draws its humor from an incongruence recalling an Indian stereotype, as well as evokes images of the primitive Indian employing sign language instead of verbal language, used as yet another indication of Native American inferiority compared to Euroamericans. In this case, the White man signs and the silent Indian woman speaks, heightening the irony. This situation is repeated, though in a serious context, when Marilyn translates for the mute Flying Man, Enrico Bellati, who becomes her love interest ("Get," 3.9).

Though it is evident from these examples that *Northern Exposure's* stereotype breakers are problematic in a variety of ways, the refusal to accept them as nothing but a reification of established stereotypes could sometimes amount to the denial of their possibility in Native American life and identity of the present moment. And if there's one stereotype the series successfully counters, it's the idea that Indians have vanished into the past as a result of the inability to maintain tribal identity while at the same time participating in contemporary American culture. Indeed, we see that Fleischman has considerable trouble reconciling his personal experience with modern Indians, exposing his assumptions of what it means to be a modern American.

A city dweller and medical school graduate, he has well-defined ideas of privacy, rational action, and social behavior. But Fleischman's rigid sense of boundary and lack of imagination are challenged by Cicely's inhabitants. Ed and Marilyn, however, the Native Alaskans viewers come to know the best, particularly seem to embody the forces of boundary breaking and pushing his imagination. Ed constantly breaks Fleischman's rules of spatial etiquette, and Marilyn presses his ability to imagine others as individuals even when their attributes fall outside of his experience. In the episode, "Our Tribe," Marilyn even succeeds in pressing him to imagine himself differently (3.12).

Ed Chigliak literally embodies broken boundaries, a mobile knot of stereotypical Indianness, modern Indian, and just idiosyncratic Ed. To begin with, he is the son of a full-blooded Native Alaskan father and a White mother. In *Playing Indian,* Philip Deloria asserts that the highest socially constructed authenticity for Indianness is found in a "traditional reservation-based full-blood" (143). Perceived as least authentic is the "progressive, urban, low quantum mixed-blood." (This urban mixed-blood Indian is not represented on *Northern Exposure* for reasons we will consider later.) Ed runs squarely down the middle of not only this boundary, but several others. He doesn't live on a reservation, but he's in close contact with the tribe that raised him. He has strong associations with both spirituality and the land; Ed's uncle is a medicine man, and in later episodes, Ed begins to train for the same role. In apparent contrast, Ed is a pop culture maven, especially impressive in his knowledge of cinema. He sometimes comes off as delightfully innocent, but has an IQ of 180. Even his coat is half and half: the traditional animal skin as a cool leather jacket.

Ed continually challenges Fleischman's sense of space and privacy. He begins his first morning in Cicely by awakening to find Ed standing in his bedroom doorway looking at him (Pilot, 1.1). Ed's response to Fleischman's chagrinned questioning is an elucidating one:

ED: Indians don't knock. It's rude.

FLEISCHMAN: No? What the hell do Indians do?

ED: Use the key.

Ed's explanation of his behavior highlights his perception of community and shared space compared to Fleischman's sense of privacy and ownership. Fleischman finds that Ed's communal sense of space extends to the professional workspace. He is astonished to see Ed saunter into the examining room and strike up conversation with a patient, which includes questioning him about his gunshot wound. He is perhaps just as astonished to see the patient, Walter, easily responding to Ed as if it were a completely normal state of affairs rather than a serious breach of etiquette or nosiness. Walt's response indicates that Ed's behavior is not exclusively Native Alaskan, but Cecilian as well.

Ed sometimes challenges Fleischman's imagination as well, which is limited by an exceedingly rational approach to life. For instance, in "The Big Kiss," Ed searches for information about his parents in the form of a vision quest, guided by the 256-year-old spirit, One Who Waits (2.2). Fleischman fears that Ed's conversations with One Who Waits indicate a psychotic break, but is drawn up short by Marilyn's calm assertion that "White people can't see." Clearly, in Marilyn and Ed's world, "seeing" means something other than it does for Fleischman. In Fleischman's world, Ed's experience can only be described in terms of clinical psychology, and he is unable to see other possibilities.

Fleischman's first interaction with Marilyn Whirlwind offends his sense of space and taxes his concepts of normal communication. Marilyn plants herself in Fleischman's office for the "job" that he insists doesn't exist. Offering not one word of explanation, she installs herself implacably as receptionist and assistant regardless of his complaints. Her complete disregard for the parameters of conversation to which Fleischman is accustomed makes her an uncomfortably unreadable character for him. At one point, unnerved, Fleischman weakly begs her to stop smiling at him all the time ("Brains," 1.2). Not his intelligence, impressive schooling, nor city savvy offer him any insight into her personality or her subtle communicative cues.

Late in the first season, Fleischman experiences what appears to be a moment of enlightenment that hinges on exposure to traditional Native American culture. The enigmatic Marilyn takes him by surprise in Cicely's "talent show." Deloria's use of "unexpected" in opposition to "anomalous" in *Indians in Unexpected Places* describes an "unexpected" moment as one in which stereotypes are actively questioned or redefined and an "anomalous" moment as one in which they are reinforced, or when redefinition does not succeed. It is debatable, of course, whether we can call Fleischman's moment wholly "unexpected," but perhaps it is possible for a moment to be simultaneously "unexpected" and stereotype laden.

It is undeniable that this moment caters to audience expectation, or an early lack of commitment to accuracy on the part of the creators of the show, potentially making Marilyn a representational cipher. She, as noted by Annette Taylor in "Cultural Heritage in Northern Exposure," wears a Cayuse–Nez Percé costume and performs a dance linked to the Washington-Idaho region (239). Elaine Miles, who plays Marilyn, is in fact from the Seattle area. She is a member of the Umatilla tribe, brought up in the Cayuse and Nez Percé traditions of her parents. In addition, Miles is a prize-winning traditional dancer. She explains in an interview with Catherine Taylor that the producers saw a picture of her in costume and wanted to incorporate the image. Miles admits that not only did she feel uncomfortable with the representation, but also that she did in fact receive some negative feedback from Native Alaskans. She explains that the producers eventually became more invested in research and accuracy. After the second season, they were listening to feedback both from Miles and Native Alaskans. The scene in question is one strangely and ironically fraught with the very same identity issues under discussion. Nonetheless, while the moment may not be unexpected for some audience members and is problematic regardless, it almost certainly is unexpected for Fleischman.

Fleischman attends what is variously called a "talent show" and a "pow wow" by Cicelians ("Sex," 1.6). Put off by a bad comedian, Fleischman begins to exit the talent show, explaining to Maggie that it's not his sort of thing. Maggie pointedly asks him, "What did you expect?" As he makes his way out, he hears Marilyn Whirlwind announced and is arrested by the sight of her in tribal regalia, dancing. He sits down, delight and amazement on his face. Even if Fleischman had expectations, though it's not clear that he had any definite images, it seems he isn't prepared for the sight of Marilyn in this aspect. It's not Marilyn as the evening's entertainment that affects Fleischman here, or simply a performance of Indianness; it's Marilyn. This is a Marilyn he's never seen, couldn't have imagined. It's not so much that Marilyn is a real Indian, but a real person who is an Indian. Fleischman's expression seems to indicate a realization on his part that, as complicated as he may have thought Marilyn, she is in fact more complex. Fleischman's perception of Marilyn as inaccessible has perhaps been revealed to him as resulting from his own limitation and ignorance, a trend that continues throughout the series as he comes to rely on her for information and counsel.

The scene, does, admittedly, hinge on a performance for an audience. Maggie is even eating popcorn. But for a Cicelian audience, Marilyn's dance is neither anomalous nor unexpected. It's part of the yearly talent show and a part of Marilyn's life they've participated in before. The questionable moment really lies with the television viewers. Identifying with Fleischman and as fans of Marilyn's character, they could exclaim, "Look at Marilyn!" Or, they could remark to themselves with satisfaction, "Ah! There she finally is," as if "she" could only be her Indianness.

North to the Alaskan Frontier

Cicely's non–Indian natives express another set of stereotypes, those representing some of America's favorite mythic national identities. They are all variations on the pioneer-frontiersman image of Americans as consummately self-reliant border seekers free to live the way they wish. As far from the American mainland as a state can get and home to significant tracts of wilderness, Alaska — and better yet, a small town in the middle of Nowhere, Alaska — stands in for the American west as the symbolic frontier.

Holling Vincoeur and Maggie are known to viewers as hardcore outdoor enthusiasts, frontier explorers pushing their self-reliance to the limit in adverse circumstances. Only the few can keep pace with them, as evidenced by the death of one of Maggie's boyfriends, who, to her irritation, took a nap on a glacier and froze while she was taking a walk, presumably to enjoy the glacier experience. And after Fleischman complains that he can't live without his toilet, an abiding symbol of civilization, an unaffected Maggie comments that Holling "spent the best years of his life without a toilet." To Fleischman's horror, Holling amiably verifies, "In the bush. Didn't bring no port-a-john" ("Brains," 1.2).

Maggie's vocation as a female pilot is in itself a stereotype breaker, but one that works because of the assumption that pilots are men. Fleischman echoes this assumption in the pilot episode by thinking she means she is a stewardess when she tells him she "flies," despite her use of the active verb. But Maggie's real stereotype breakers are far more interesting. We learn from her father that Maggie hated summer camp and was afraid of the dark as a child. She spent two years in law school in Michigan and one year at the Sorbonne. Her education reveals a far more intellectual outdoorswoman and mechanic than one might have imagined. It turns out that while Maggie may not have been a city girl, she was quite the child of suburbia. The details of her past indicate that at some point she made a conscious choice to abandon her wealthy and possibly overeducated roots and "head west," or in this case, very northwest, and flying.

Maggie's self-perception creates another attribute that runs counter to her image. Maggie displays high anxiety and vulnerability concerning relationships, seeing herself as a negative force in the world, due to the deaths of all her boyfriends. She also displays an unlooked for openness to the metaphysical, explaining on one occasion that color is light, and light is energy, so different colors are light traveling at different frequencies, which affects people's moods ("Democracy," 3.15). When Fleischman can't understand her need to listen to trees, or to involve him in it, she quotes a version of Hamlet at him, "There's more between heaven and earth that your philosophy ever dreamed of!" ("Dateline," 3.11). The woman quoting Shakespeare in the forest while she listens to trees in the night seems a far cry from the sometimes stringent, super independent Maggie. Her emotional complexities belie a strident feminist stereotype.

In his past, Holling was a dedicated hunter and outdoorsman, and still exhibits the supervirility of an American tall tale. He is the picture of strapping masculinity and has the animal heads on the walls to prove it. We quickly learn, however, that one of his defining features is his sensitive side. These days Holling breaks his own stereotype as the mild mannered owner of local restaurant, The Brick, a man dedicated to his eventual wife, Shelly Tambo. Explaining to Shelly why he quit hunting, he describes a dream in which every animal he'd ever killed pursued him with firearms. When he woke, he knew that, "until a wolverine could blow out my brains as easily as I could his, my gun would forever remain silent" ("Kodiak," 1.7). In "Seoul Mates," Holling discovers that Shelly misses experiencing the Catholic Christmas of her childhood, especially evening mass (3.10). He first appeals to Chris, who shies away from the codification and Latin of the Catholic services. Instead, Holling learns "Ave, Maria" in Latin, surprising Shelly by singing for her when she enters the church alone and approaches the altar. We see here the depth of Holling's characteristic sensitivity, a trait not usually associated with the hypermasculine image of an outdoorsman and hunter of his caliber.

Viewers at first may wonder what Shelly, a wide-eyed, barely twenty beauty queen, is doing in Alaska. But Shelly's from Canada, no stranger to harsh conditions, and her crown was for Miss Northwest Passage. I think it's not out of place to assert that Holling and Shelly are in one sense each other's frontier. They adore each other, which places her in an highly unconventional relationship with a man 40-odd years her senior. However, perhaps the hyperfeminine Shelly also stereotypically complements the image of Holling's hypermasculine virility. She is more than just a pretty face, however. Shelly reveals a depth and sensitivity matching Holling's own when she recasts his life in a puppet show, using the toys from his childhood ("Things," 3.13). Holling, gripped by angst over having let his life pass him by without doing anything of note, goes on a self-loathing drinking spree. Shelly re-presents his life to him, healing him through her use of narrative, by casting him as the hero. We should note the recognizable narrative of the outdoorsman, epic hunter, and, Shelly's addition, the guy who gets the girl.

Cicely's pioneer, Maurice Minnifield, comes from a conservative military family obsessed with flight. After his career as an astronaut with NASA, he decides to move to Alaska, giving up one frontier and embracing another. Minnifield's vision for Alaska's future is that of a modern American capitalist pioneer, an entrepreneur. He imagines strip malls, amusement parks, subdivisions, "progress." Minnifield also represents the racist mentality of many pioneers encountering cultures and behavior unlike their own. More insulting than dangerous, he complains about and comments on Native Alaskans negatively. He is also shown relying on positive stereotypes, like his comment in the pilot episode that he was pleased Cicely was getting "a crackerjack Jew doctor from New York." Minnifield is both well-educated and well-traveled. His house resembles a museum of precious and historical items, he has a notable wine collection, and he reveres Walt Whitman, whose poetry celebrates the wealth of difference in America. Of the worldly Minnifield and the small town Cicelians, Minnifield displays the least tolerance and seems to have the least excuse for it.

But even Minnifield has his redeeming moments, indicating his capacity to, as Chris puts it, "unlearn" ("Seoul," 3.10). His first response to the discovery of his Korean son, Duk Won, is overwhelmingly negative, and he has no memory of Duk Won's mother. By the end of the episode, he has taken to calling Duk Won, Duke, and remembers his mother. Allowing himself to remember fully what it was like to be with her in Korea at that time in his life, even that she likes cherries, he asks her warmly, finally, "How *are* you?" In another instance, although he despises homosexuality, Maurice is driven to tell Ron and Erick that he has to give them credit for following their dreams and making their business a successful one ("Final," 3.20). In an intense moment from the next season, Minnifield actually takes abuse from the couple, one of whom is an ex–Marine, when they find out he has given Duk Won permission to marry the daughter of a Korean officer responsible for horrible torture of American POWs ("Sleeping," 4.24). Duke's unhappiness was too much for him to take. We see him encourage Chris with a piano-flinging performance art piece, albeit with hypermasculine speech to make up for the fact that he's talking about artistic endeavor (as opposed to owning art) ("Burning," 3.14). He takes his turn caring for and cuddling the baby in "My Mother, My Sister," and admits that his decision to cut down the town's favorite tree, Old Vicki, has left him feeling "empty" (3.18; "Old," 4.2). He even plants a sapling at her stump.

Chris's character may not so obviously follow the stereotypes the others do, but a second look reveals a connection. Chris is a borderlander in the tradition of the American rebel and a pioneer on the frontier of the mind. An autodidact, artist, and criminal on the lam, Chris inhabits the nonconformist borders of society's imagination. As an ordained priest, Chris also represents experience that relatively few members of society embrace fully. As Ruth-Anne explains to Fleischman, "Chris goes further afield than most of us, but he usually comes up with something interesting" ("Burning," 3.14). Chris's literary, artistic, and spiritual interests fuel his tendency towards the romanticization of just about everything, including, occasionally, Native American rituals and sensibilities, the idea of returning to an earlier state of commune with nature. Though intellectual and enlightening, Chris plays into stereotypes by romanticizing.[2] He romanticizes nature, American stereotypes, his own life's path, and archetypal human experience in general. As startled viewers witness the intelligent, compassionate Chris eager to continue the family tradition of brawling with the Millers when they come to town looking for him, we find that he romanticizes even fighting ("Kaddish," 4.22). For Chris, engaging in hand to hand combat provides contact with an inner primitive self, a fundamental human experience, specifically presented as masculine.

Though Fleischman initially experiences Native Alaskans and Cicelians as a united front of incomprehensibility, the American stereotypes animated by Cicely's non–Indian natives are historically dependent on American Indian stereotypes. By socially constructing a Native American Other, Euroamericans and other immigrants have been able to define themselves nationally against it. On the one hand, a rhetoric of superiority was needed to justify rousting indigenous peoples from their land. We are familiar at this point with at least some of the negative stereotypes that resulted from this ideological move. On the other hand, a positive identification with Native

Americans has engineered a kind of proxy indigenous relationship with the land itself, a right to ownership through metaphorical kinship.[3]

At the same time that Euroamericans developed images of Indians underlining what was "civilized" about themselves, they also drew on what they saw as appealing from Native cultures in response to restrictions they felt from traditional European culture. Not only that, but Euroamericans felt a need to be more American than European. They therefore created identities that built upon features they perceived to be part of a positive Native American identity, especially self-reliance and closeness to the land, which were equated with freedom and self-definition.

Several examples from *Northern Exposure* are self-reflexive concerning these complex cultural dynamics. Leonard Quinhagak, the medicine man who apprentices Ed, studies White myths of healing ("Rosebud," 5.7). After research, he decides that non–Indian Americans have no unifying myths other than the "tall tale" genre. Ironically, as we have seen, tall tale types are well-represented amongst Cicely's inhabitants. And bitterly ironic, Native Americans have served as a unifying myth for America; the "tall tales" are in fact supercharged stories of frontiersmen, pioneers, and cowboys, identities intrinsically tied up with perceptions of Indianness. Stepping back for a moment, it would also be appropriate to consider television itself as a source of unifying narratives through the serial dramas it provides its audiences.

The rhetoric Cicely herself uses to describe the small town reflects the same legacy: "In this tiny corner of Alaska, the human spirit has triumphed" ("Cicely," 3.23). She goes on to say that Cicelians are free to be who they want. Her statements equate triumph with self-reliance and self-definition. But, given the cultural precedent, that very equation evokes a colonial mentality of manifest destiny that triumphs at the expense of Native Americans, sacrificing as needed their right to self-define so that non–Indian Americans might develop or maintain their own identities. Chris, in the middle of extolling our democratic nation and the right to vote, ironically enough, sums up both the history and the rhetoric used to avoid it: "We were outcasts, scum.... But we came here, we paved roads, we built industries, powerful institutions. Of course, along the way, we exterminated untold indigenous cultures and enslaved generations of African Americans.... But today, we're here to celebrate the glorious aspects of our past! A tribute to a nation of free people" ("Democracy," 3.15).

Following this flexible construction of Native American identities, for Cicelians and Fleischman to be defined against each other, Native American and American identities must merge with some smoothness. Several elements of *Northern Exposure* ensure that Native Americans and non–Indian

Cicelians seem to inhabit the same space in relation to Fleischman. The first and simplest is that Cicelians remain consistently unfazed by Indianness. No apparent Othering takes place, with the exception of Minnifield. In addition, contact zones are plentiful, including The Brick and town meetings. The next two are a direct reference to Native American identity: closeness to the land and a tribal community mentality. The Cicelians we know are fiercely self-reliant, undeterred by Alaska's extreme weather and comfortable in the wilderness. Even Chris, the artist-intellectual, lives in only a small trailer by the lake in which he bathes, freezing or no. Exhibiting another aspect of closeness to the land, the town reveres an ancient tree named Ootockalockatuvik, Old Vicki for short ("Old," 4.25). And as we have seen, Cicely's community seems to operate under a tribal mentality, all news shared, all dinner parties rotated, services and favors exchanged.

Northern Exposure also makes frequent use of dream sequences, psychic connections, spiritual visions, and related phenomenon. This could be a response to a perceived Native American experience related to spirituality and a mystical connection to nature. In this case, the experiences of non–Indians are brought into line with an alternative Native American perception of experience in the world. The strategy could also be intended to create what is essentially an Alaskan fantasyland that attempts to constitute its own identity, after a fashion, to establish some otherwhere that somehow supercedes or encompasses race and national identities. Either way, or both, inexplicable experiences and intuitive knowledge are accepted, in direct conflict with Fleischman's worldview and mode of experience. Eventually, however, even Fleischman is visited by his rabbi in dreams and experiences visions.

"I Already Belong to a Tribe"

Occasionally Fleischman's Jewishness provides a point of connection through race between him and Cicely's Native Alaskans. Both historical and current events sometimes unify him with Native American experience as a non–White people, throwing a bit of a wrench into *Northern Exposure's* dynamics and foundational relationships of the previously discussed stereotypes. The connection constituted by race challenges a wholly oppositional definition of Fleischman as the modern Other and serves as a reminder of the often sublimated issue of race lurking behind American archetypes.

Fleischman himself exhibits a tendency to essentialize Jews and Jewishness. Planning to take a short vacation, he becomes convinced that his substitute doctor, Dave Ginsberg, is a "Jewish imposter" who changed his name to capitalize on Jewish success ("What," 2.4). His only evidence is Dave's classically Caucasian blonde hair and blue eyes. Of course, Fleischman also despises him for fitting in, loving Alaska, fixing the radiator, and learning Tlingit words from Marilyn within twenty-four hours of having arrived. Significantly, when Fleischman kicks Dave out, he declares and justifies his position there by triumphantly flinging Tlingit her way as he reclaims his office. Fleischman also explains to Ed in "Kaddish for Uncle Manny" that the lumberjack he has picked up on the road can't be a Jew either because "Jews don't hitch ... [they] don't wear suspenders, they don't slobber tobacco in their beard, they don't hitch, and they definitely don't have names like Buck" (4.22). He returns to this idea when he tells Marilyn that all names ending with "-ner" indicate a Jew. Later in the conversation, Fleischman laughs when Marilyn asks if Kevin Costner is Jewish.[4] She looks at him squarely and points out with false innocence, "It ends in '-ner,'" putting him at a complete loss ("Things," 3.13).

Related to his essentializing perception of his cultural and racial group, Fleischman identifies himself as a Jew absolutely, indicating that to be Jewish is to be exclusionary of any other experience. He tries out a Christmas tree one year, but ends up giving it to Maggie because he can't quite get comfortable with it being in his house. Protesting Marilyn's offense when he won't join her tribe, he shouts that he is a Jew from Flushing ("Our," 3.12). In Cicely, Fleischman's Jewish identity takes on a more metaphysical meaning as well. One of Fleischman's earlier experiences of dreaming in Cicely is followed by sharing with Maggie that his name is not merely Joel Fleischman, but Joel ben Jacob, Joel the son of Jacob ("Body," 3.6).[5] However, joining Marilyn's tribe marks a point in Fleischman's journey when his stereotypes of Jewishness are challenged in a lasting way. By opening himself to a new tribal identity, he opens himself to possibility. He will discover in time that his experiences outstrip the singular identity of "the Jew from Flushing."

Mrs. Noanuk, an Elder, offers Fleischman a place in her tribe when he declines to accept her payment for treatment. When he refuses the honor, Elder Noanuk becomes indignant. Unanticipated by Fleischman, Marilyn is also offended, and it is due to her assiduous silent treatment that he acquiesces. He explains in a last ditch effort, "I already belong to a tribe. I'm Jewish. We're a very tribal people." Neither of the Native Alaskans are disturbed by the idea that he might belong to two tribes. Noanuk even refers to their shaman as "our Rabbi Ragins," drawing what seems to be a comfortable parallel. Fleischman expects a show of ritual just as he expected Anku's medicinal practice to be an "act," a largely superficial experience. He is wrong on two counts. Firstly, he must in fact undergo a ritual initiation of three steps. Secondly, becoming Mrs. Noanuk's grandson means that he and

Marilyn may consider one another as siblings, as same-age members of a moiety may.[6] A metaphorical kinship between them also appears when she tells him she has a Jewish cousin who can say kaddish with him.

After joining a local Tlingit tribe and sitting shiva with his Cicely community rather than the traditional Jewish minyan in the fourth season, Fleischman begins to redefine both Jewishness and himself as a Jew. At this point, he begins to recognize connections between himself and Native Alaskans. He decides to walk with the Native Alaskans in their Day of the Dead parade, self-identifying as a person of color by virtue of his Semitic roots, recalling cultural histories of genocide and displacement ("Thanksgiving," 4.8). He recognizes a similarity between Yiddish as a dying language and Ed's experience of his native language, Tlingit, which he can't read and which is usually used only by the oldest generation ("Sleeping," 4.24). Fleischman later discovers the impossible: a Yiddish element in Tlingit through an eighteenth century explorer from Russia ("Mystery," 5.2). Fleischman's Russian Jewish roots make this a double connection.

Sometimes these connections extend meaningfully to the realm of spirit and ritual. In a remarkable blend of identities, Ed creatively adopts an ancient Jewish ritual. He runs for Holling and the fox in Minnifield's fox hunt ("Shofar," 6.3). Ruth-Anne has squirreled away the fox, and Holling is blaming himself for his older daughter's troubles. Ed, acting on a shaman's prerogative, heals all wounds. Fleischman explains the Jewish Day of Atonement ritual. A high priest would ritually infuse a goat with the tribe's sins and release it into the desert. Mirroring the place of the goat, Ed takes the burden of Holling's "sins" upon himself as he simultaneously runs for the fox.

"Child of Asphalt" in the Wild

On Fleischman's arrival, both groups of natives are inscrutable to him. In his imaginings, everyone in Cicely is Other; they are all what he is not. Our Cicelians, as generalized mythic American characters, seem to be defined positively against Fleischman, who serves as a stereotype of modern American man. Cicelians are depicted as closer to nature, self-sufficient, and independent. There seems to be an underlying conviction that they somehow lead more authentic lives due to a supposedly unfettered transcendent experience of "the freedom to be who we want to be." Such a conviction is dependent on the idea that there exists some kind of "natural self" to be found, and that it is somehow available in their specific circumstances, as opposed to, say, New York City. Just as Fleischman is convinced Cicely is hardly America, Cicely is quite sure that city boys don't know what it means to be a real American.

In turn, their apparently unified front more clearly establishes a perception of Fleischman as egocentric and neurotic due to an effete, undeveloped personality. In contrast to self-reliance, Fleischman specializes as a doctor and therefore, though potentially useful, has been dandified due to his city lifestyle and intellect. His sense of rationality and order appears an imposed mechanistic one that breeds neuroses and dependency in comparison to the more organic lifestyle of Cicelians. It is this image of the modern man that explains why the "urban progressive mixed-blood" Indian Deloria discusses is not represented on the series. The emphasis in this case falls not on "mixed-blood," but on "urban." An Indian who fit this description could disturb the identity dynamic maintaining Fleischman's modern urban stereotype.

Fleischman's initial interactions with Maggie lead us to believe that it's not the Indians or frontiersman who are in a lower state of social Darwinian development, but instead individuals living in modern urban conditions. It's Fleischman who seems to be the child who can't take care of his heat or plumbing, who doesn't have the emotional maturity to appreciate the Alaskan splendor around him. Her derision is based on conversations like this one from the pilot episode, as she sets up Fleischman in his cabin:

FLEISCHMAN: What do you do for heat?

MAGGIE: [building a fire] This is the heat.

FLEISCHMAN: What do you do for wood?

MAGGIE: [looks at him] Chop it.

As far as Fleischman's concerned, heat and plumbing are somebody else's business, and he purchases it from them. When Maggie asks what's wrong with his plumbing, he responds irritably, "How am I supposed to know what's wrong with it?" ("Brains," 1.2). What is self-evident to Maggie is completely opaque to Fleischman: either you do it yourself or find out for yourself. Just as he was unable to imagine himself chopping wood, it did not occur to him to take a look at the plumbing himself.

Exchanges like this one abound for Fleischman, continually out of his element. His lack of imagination short circuits his ability to think rationally within his new environment's variables. The ultrarational doctor manages to miss consistently the most obvious of answers; understanding minutely and scientifically the functions of the body, he is unable to understand the functionality of things in his new life, to imagine the different ways that he himself might function. He asks Marilyn after receiving a goat as payment from Mrs. Noanuk, "What do I want with a goat?" Marilyn responds practically, "Milk." He doublechecks with Ed about the ramifications of refusing the offer to join Mrs. Noanuk's tribe. Ed offers a simple explanation: "Well, you insulted her tribe and all of her ancestors" ("Our," 3.12). In "My Mother, My Sister," he asks Marilyn desperately as she heads out the door to get talcum, leaving him with the town's new and apparently orphaned baby, "What am I supposed to do with a baby?!" Marilyn says as she leaves, "Feed her" (3.18).

Even Fleischman's medical training and methods are brought into question, significantly, by two Native Alaskan healers: Ed's uncle, Anku, and Marilyn's cousin, Leonard. After firmly explaining in agitation to Ed that "doctors do not chase patients" and the rules still apply even in Alaska, Fleischman then goes out of his way to visit Anku, Ed's uncle, at his home ("Brains," 1.2). The more Anku resists his assistance with his health, the more determined Fleischman becomes to persuade him to responsibly address his prostate cancer. In the end, somewhat surprisingly, Fleischman appeals to Anku as a doctor who "knows better" than to let the cancer go untreated. Acknowledging Anku as a peer amends his previous perception of Anku's medicinal practice as an "act" he'd like to "catch." During conversation, Fleischman recognizes two familiar tenets from Anku's description of his practices: that the physician should do no harm to the patient, and that the patient's body is the real healer. It is Anku who counsels Fleischman on his inability to connect with Maggie over the plumbing issue and as an individual in general, to cross the divide between their mindsets, a skill he and Leonard both consider necessary in creating relationships with patients. He says, in reference to a story he told earlier in the episode, "If you want to catch a fish, think like a fish." Fleischman, who previously thought the story was a joke, has a small epiphany and makes a house call to Maggie as well, who offers in exchange to fix his shower.

Indicating that Marilyn had welcomed him, Leonard explains that he wishes to observe Fleischman due to an interest in opening up to "alternative" forms of practicing medicine after all his years using the "orthodox" holistic methods ("Wake-Up," 3.19). He reverses completely the rhetoric Western doctors frequently use when referring to Native American, herbal, folk, or Eastern systems and practices of healing, setting up current Western forms of medicine as the center of healing. Leonard recenters the locus of established and effective medicine onto Native Alaskan traditions. During his time with Fleischman, he points out through demonstration one of Western medicine's major deficiencies, forcing Fleischman to reconsider not only concepts of healing, but of himself as a doctor as well.

Fleischman becomes irritated with Leonard when he engages in conversation with Shelly, attempting to find common ground on which they can build a relationship before moving to diagnosis. To Fleischman, it simply seems like off the subject chatter. When Leonard asks how she is with animals, Fleischman somewhat contemptuously says he has no idea. Leonard responds, his tone indicating a lack, "You don't ask?" Fleischman becomes furious with Leonard for later diverging from his allergy diagnosis, insisting that telling her she was sloughing her skin in order to be reborn for spring was irresponsible and ridiculous. The next time Fleischman sees Shelly, she is glowing at him with her newly sloughed skin. Quietly, he calls it "radiant." She explains that Leonard knew what was happening because they "had a heart to heart," and he listened to her story about why she doesn't like eggs. Fleischman visits Leonard before he leaves and shares with him the reason he didn't become a pathologist. Although he has difficulty relating to people, a patient influenced his decision. No one could determine the man's illness, and it was only after Fleischman spent time talking to him person to person, rather than doctor to patient, that he realized what was wrong. When Fleischman tells Leonard that he hadn't thought about that event for a while, he indicates his recognition of the role of relationship in healing, and the awareness required for it. Fleischman, "the man of flesh," must move into the mind and heart as well in order to be a healer.

Though Fleischman makes a good neurotic product of the city, there are indications from the beginning of the series that his stereotype does not tell his whole story. Immediately after his arrival, although he desperately tries to escape Cicely and repeatedly refuses his role as town doctor, Fleischman finds himself unable to leave patients untended. Twice he storms out of his makeshift office, and each time drags himself back in. While he may experience difficulty relating to people on a personal level and operating outside of his accustomed orderliness, it's clear that he does care about individuals and will go against his habit for them, though he often thinks he won't. Fleischman is also curious, despite his disgust with his surroundings. He constantly asks questions, is interested in Cicely's news and lore, and shifts into student mode when encountering new material, as when Anku teaches him to dance, Adam teaches him to cook noodles, and he tries to learn juggling when a traveling carnival passes through. According to Cicely standards, this perhaps indicates that his instincts aren't as fouled up as they appear to be.

From Modern Man to Mushroom

As Fleischman's narrative of self progresses, we can see the very concept of self being questioned. Rather than picturing the self as an immutable or "true" aspect of an individual, which indicates a classic American path of discovery of fixed identity west to the wild, Fleischman's journey looks much more like a project of identity hybridization. The archetypal journey taken by a new kind of hero involves finally consciously redefining self without simply assimilating wholesale or taking advantage of the identity of a group. These differences seem to speak to Joseph Campbell's concept of "creative mythology."[7] It seems to me that Fleischman's variation on the hero quest, which traditionally occurs within local mythologies in order to confirm them, constitutes a generative, creative response to the need for a global sense of identity and unity. For what and who are we if not a narrative about ourselves we tell ourselves and others, a myth of self in fact? Instead of being incorporated into the systemic definitions of a particular group, Fleischman incorporates aspects of various cultures and worldviews into an individual identity inclusive of several apparently conflicting ones. He integrates aspects of the American identities he encounters in Cicely, without losing his Jewishness or the desire to return to New York.

There are five main steps in Fleischman's journey: resistance, adjustment, membership, crisis, and hybridization, easily recognizable as a sort of reluctant hero's quest. We initially see Fleischman resisting every aspect of his forced move to Cicely. The length of time he's required to serve there, the conditions in which he's required to work, and the interaction with the local characters all fall outside of his imagination, creating a sense of desperateness and fear. Fleischman's adjustment to his predicament involves establishing some understanding of those around him, but continuing his resistance to imagining himself meaningfully engaged with the community and environment. A significant shift in this resistance occurs in the third season, when Fleischman refuses the offer of tribal initiation.

We've considered Fleischman's acceptance into Marilyn's tribe as a metaphorical meeting of race, the acknowledgment of two identities standing counter to the non–Indian American archetypal identities represented in Cicely ("Our," 3.12). In the present context, however, he is nevertheless forced to question his ideas about "tribal" identity in general and his own identity. The demands of the initiation trials in reality overwhelm him. The actual forfeiture of personal property as part of the ritual surprises him, leading him to plead with Marilyn, "I feel like an invisible man! Every time I turn around, another piece of me is gone! Please, just tell me when it's going to stop." Marilyn, witness to the shift in perception of self that step of the ritual was meant to evoke, confirms its completion. Fleischman, somewhat pleased with himself, admits feeling "chastened" as a participant in consumer culture.

However, as he begins his fast and realizes that he will receive replacement items from the tribe in exchange for his actual possessions, Fleischman is truly chastened, following a wracking junkie-like outburst about his things with ruminations about tribal identity. "I belong to the Jewish tribe, so to speak, but I'm mostly American. But what does that mean? I mean, is there an American tribe? ... Maybe we've outgrown tribes. It's the global village.... [W]e all belong to the same tribe." Fleischman's speech accomplishes two things: firstly, he questions his own identity as Jewish and/or American; and secondly, he moves to a comprehension that human experience can be archetypally understood on a global level. Ed checks his intellectualizing, however, saying, "That's true. But you can't hang out with five billion people." Fleischman concedes that this is a good point. Paradoxically, Fleischman's concept of a global tribe provides the rationale by which he can eventually form a composite identity. If Jews, Americans, and Native Americans, New Yorkers and Cicelians, are all in the same global tribe, a local tribal identity should not preclude kinship with any other. Taking the name "Heals with Tools" doesn't replace "Joel ben Jacob," but joins them together.

Northern Exposure's seasons reflect the stages of Fleischman's journey. The first and second seasons, and part of the third season, are clearly a stage of resistance for Fleischman. But in the third season, the landscape changes a bit. Although death reappears thematically throughout *Northern Exposure,* it figures significantly in this season. Holling loses an uncle, which sends him on a drinking spree until Shelly puts him right; and he and Minnifield also lose a mutual friend, which sends them into the wild to bury him. Holling's longtime foe, Jesse the Bear, dies, and Holling must renew a feeling of connection to the life affirming danger of the hunt. Chris discovers a frozen eighteenth century man, Pierre le Moulin, whose journal rewrites history as they knew it. Maggie's latest boyfriend dies, but she also has a healing relationship with a man who is also a bear, an ancient symbol of death and rebirth. She loses her house and possessions in a fire, providing a piano for Chris to fling as part of his performance art piece. Ed buys Ruth-Anne a grave plot, and they both dance on it. We even witness the death of Cicely herself, who leaves behind a town of promise. This is also the season in which Shelly sloughs all her skin. In each event, the spectre of death or loss gives way to redefinition, rebirth or rediscovery. The theme is appropriate for a hero adjusting to his new world, experiencing the death of previous social constructs and identities in preparation for redefinition.

In "Lost and Found," Fleischman clearly reconsiders his concepts of community and redefines his relationship with Cicely citizens (3.17). After hearing a voice in the night, Fleischman learns that a previous inhabitant of his cabin committed suicide, a literal death of the self. Maggie matter of factly tells Fleischman that if he were to commit suicide, no one in Cicely would mourn him. When Holling seems surprised at the idea of being friends, Fleischman realizes that he cannot assume interacting with people regularly constitutes friendship. Friends must be brought into his life, which he must open to them. He reaches out by inviting them all to a barbecue in the tradition of Cicely's reciprocal dinners.

At the end of the fourth season, a season of unions and reconciliations, Fleischman makes the monumental decision to sit shiva with Cicelians instead of the nine Jews they set out to find for him ("Kaddish," 4.22). He receives news of his Uncle Manny's death, but to sit shiva for him, ten Jews are traditionally required. However, after Cicelians display their support for him by searching for nine other Alaskan Jews, he decides that the experience would be more meaningful if he shares it with his day to day community rather than a community based solely on ethnicity and religion. He explains to them, "...it seems to me that the purpose of saying kaddish is to be with your community. And what I realized this week is that you're my community." Fleischman has redefined his sense of authentic experience and community, and his Jewish identity as well.

Not long after Fleischman's religion, which is inextricably bound to race in his case as a descendant from Russian Jews, provides a bonding point with Cicely's community, he discovers an unlikely infusion of Yiddish in the Native Alaskan Tlingit language ("Mystery," 5.2). Rather than resisting or discrediting this link as he might have previously, Fleischman researches the linguistic source and unearths evidence of an eighteenth century Jewish explorer stranded in the area. In what smacks of a search for connection, Fleischman subsequently imagines himself as the modern manifestation of this figure, infusing medical knowledge rather than language. His efforts seem centralized around layering local identity onto both his Jewishness and his modernity.

By the end of Season 5, Fleischman is making absolute statements of a Cicelian identity, affirming his membership in Cicely's community. In "Lovers and Madmen," he states unequivocally that he is a Cicelian (5.24). Fleischman's experience of losing his discovery of "a gold mine of prehistoric history" to Walt Kupfer, who informs him that mammoths are especially tasty, offers a bizarre point of entry into the understanding that "Life is a mystery. One man's life-altering experience is another man's tenderloin." It's as if the decidedly Cicely-flavored event serves as initiatory ritual, startling Fleischman into a greater recognition of possibility and variation in what Campbell might call "an actual shock of experience," an event that results in the awareness of self as spirit, self "in the consciousness of being" (92–3). Fleischman's comment on the mystery of life may indicate that his awareness of self and identity has begun to include a spiritual aspect. In another instance, Fleischman accidentally drinks one of Ed's medicines. He hallucinates his Cicely friends transplanted in Manhattan, leading essentially bleak lives with unpleasant personalities ("Dinner," 6.1). The hallucination ends with his revelatory shout, "I'd rather practice in some hick rural outback than stay here another minute!" His identification with Cicelians allows him to finally experience a negative critique of modern city life.

The next step in Fleischman's journey towards identity hybridization occurs when Maggie breaks off their relationship in the sixth season. As a result of this crisis, a turning point in the hero's quest, Fleischman chooses to remain in the Indian village of Manonash after traveling there for a house call ("Up River," 6.8). It is in Manonash that Fleischman alters his identity yet again and undergoes the project of incorporating both Native American and national American archetypes while retaining his Jewishness and his wish to return to New York. His choice to stay in Manonash echoes the classic tradition of identity definition as a project for White males by journeying into a native space to gain a transcendent experience of self. Typically, the native space is also depicted as a primitive one. Robert Baird notes the idea that "only by going backward into history, back into tribalism, could the American hero hope to go forward" (196). However, Manonash and *Northern Exposure's* Native Alaskans aren't depicted as primitives of the past, and Fleischman has self-identified as Semitic rather than White. And though Fleischman may be on a journey towards redefining self, his final step of hybridization is atypical.

Maggie finds Fleischman carving a totem, and they have a conversation in which Fleischman employs what sounds like the rhetoric of Native American spirituality while looking more like a Grizzly Adams frontiersman ("The Big Mushroom," 6.11). He tells her that he has never left her because they are all connected, like the fungal mushrooms in a field, which are connected by organic threads underground. Perhaps Ed was correct when he said during Fleischman's vision quest initiation, "Maybe you have to believe in visions to have one" ("Our," 3.12). Apparently, Fleischman has reconciled his rational and irrational sides. In this same visit, we also find that the list of ingredients in Fleischman's meal reads somewhat like a list for Ed's cures, including bear root, fiddlehead fern, and crowberries. The humor here is elicited from not only a Native American image, but the image of a frontiersman or trapper using the land to sustain himself.

Fleischman could also be read as acting in the role of shaman when he tests Philip Capra's suitability as his replacement in Cicely ("Realpolitik," 6.10). However, the test location is on his mountainside regulation golf course. At the same time that he counsels Capra to access mind-body connection in order to play golf better in the moonlight, he discusses medical matters expertly. At this point, he hardly looks the part of a Western medical doctor, a traditional Jew, or a child of asphalt. And as he argues with Marilyn in "Our Tribe," "nobody's ever going to mistake me for an Indian." Shortly after their game, Fleischman burns most of his possessions, including his medical school degree and golf clubs, in a final commitment to his quest for hybridizing identity, which at this stage seems to embrace a spiritual identity in addition to local and national ones ("Horns" 6.13). His actions recall Chris's pithy observation from "All is Vanity" that everyone dies alone: "But it's that solitude in death that's our common bond in life.... Only when we understand all is vanity, only then it isn't" (2.3). As Fleischman strips himself of that which previously defined him completely, invoking a ritual death of ego, he moves closer to his earlier perception of humans as part of a global tribe, and thus, paradoxically, closer to a return to an integrated self that may experience the kinship and identities of multiple tribes.

North(east) to the Future

The end of Fleischman's course of hybridization is indeed steeped in Native American identity. We know that he has achieved a new identity not only from his actions, but because Marilyn verifies it ("Mi Casa, Su Casa," 6.12). When she attends a potlatch at Manonash, she perceives that Fleischman has changed through her perception of a bowl he crafted. She sees with mystical vision the culmination of his quest. In response, she makes him goose feather babiches[8] and tells him to "go lightly through life." Marilyn's authority as the measure of Fleischman's change is her spiritual vision, a trait closely linked with Native Alaskan experience throughout the series, and Native Americans in general. She understands Chris's sign language when Fleischman cannot, sees One Who Waits when he cannot, and perceives that his mother has an eagle spirit. When Holling learns to dance as her Cajun two-step partner, he tells Shelly that Marilyn has a special ability to recognize hidden talents in others ("Sleeping," 4.24). It's not necessarily Marilyn's spirituality that should be questioned, but her role as an authenticated authenticator. Native Alaskan culture may foster certain spiritual sensibilities that Marilyn in reality exhibits, but one could also interpret her role as a use of her Indianness to affirm the success of a White man's developing identity.

Marilyn also serves as a kind of spiritual guide for Fleischman. She often generally educates and enlightens by relating the stories of legendary characters, like Eagle and Raven, or providing counsel. But "Our Tribe" illustrates more specifically the depth of Marilyn's contributions to Fleischman's journey. Ultimately, Marilyn is the reason Fleischman agrees to join her tribe, which essentially establishes a kinship between them. At her insistence, he undergoes an experience that challenges his definitions of self, community, and tribe. It seems that she also bears the responsibility of determining the duration of his first step, living without possessions. The step is crucial in that it must prepare him for the trials to come, must render its participant disoriented and vulnerable to transformation. As is her wont, Marilyn can see when Fleischman is ready to move to the next step. I find it significant that despite his initial anger, Fleischman thanks Marilyn publicly, saying he would not have made it through the ordeal without her. It is indeed as if one previously disgruntled sibling makes up with another, and it recasts their typical bantering relationship. Marilyn annoys Fleischman, who actually appreciates her, and she often takes advantage of his limitations while simultaneously seeing his potential.

Though the hero's quest is not a ritual unique to Native Americans, given the context of *Northern Exposure,* it is difficult not to interpret Fleischman's final engagement with his quest for identity as part of a Native American tradition of the vision quest. He and Maggie search for "The Jeweled City of the North," undergoing a series of mythic trials before reaching a vision of the Manhattan skyline, north and east this time rather than northwest ("Quest," 6.15). However, his companion is Maggie, not an Indian guide, recalling the ubiquity of meaningful dreams and psychic connections among Native Americans and non–Indian Cicelians alike. The ordeals themselves include various ethnicities and locations. Fleischman leaves Cicely by walking straight out of his clearly heroic adventures into his life in New York City. Unsurprisingly, Marilyn senses him as he goes, as sibling, as seer, saying "Good-bye" from her chair at home, witnessing Fleischman's steps out of Cicely and into New York, as she has been watching his steps all along.

With all the conflations of stereotypes and identities, one might argue that Fleischman's quest is the latest best attempt to employ Native American identity in the development of a national American one, in this case the modern American city dweller. However, this White man's identity is the product of a hybridizing effort rather than an attempt to replicate or deny the identity of another group. We don't see Fleischman trying to convert to Indianness or become a frontiersman in his quest, or trying to urbanize or convert those around him. He does not change his name to Heals With Tools or don his bearskin vest for the return home. And though home is in fact still New York City, the culmination of his quest is not a vision of the wild or an exotic Other against which to define himself in a fixed manner. He is still Joel Fleischman, who has become Joel Fleischman, a hybrid of Native American and American identities, Jewishness, and the child of asphalt who in the end chooses to return to his original urban home, albeit with longer hair and a somewhat enigmatic expression. He has moved beyond local myth, what he refers to earlier as "special interest groups," to a more inclusive identity that reflects an "acceptance of difference within oneself" (Romeyn and Kugelmass 260).

Northern Exposure does not always succeed in questioning stereotypes or providing its audience with "unexpected" moments. Indeed, it is impossible to deny the historical roots of American national identity and its construction and exploitation of Native American identity. But neither does it completely fail. Instead it presents a dynamic of stereotypes which inform modern day identity and the journey of an individual attempting to create an identity that encompasses the range of his experiences. It is possible that Fleischman subverts older stereotypes by choosing to belong to more than one "tribe."

Perhaps whether use of race as a foundational center redefines or reifies depends on the use and function of ethnicity at any given moment. Perhaps it can never be more or less than both. And perhaps whether it's one or the other depends on the viewer's perception. To bring it home, Fleischman's lot is our lot: to accept our conditions and break with previous dearly held identities, to reconnect, to redefine, and in redefining ourselves, see the world differently as well. While Fleischman has been enacting and encountering stereotypes, working with archetypes, undergoing rituals, interpreting dreams, and finally leading his own course of self-exploration in order to creatively accomplish his transformation, the audience has been exposed to, and perhaps living, all these things as well. Taylor points out that we, as viewers, can "choose our myth to suit our problems" or our particular point in the quests of not only Fleischman, but in the identity developments of any of *Northern Exposure*'s characters (*Northern* 84). The final element in the dynamics of relationships between American and Native American identities rests with the experience of the viewer. In the end, the presence of unexpected moments lies with the audience's experience, both of their lives and of the series.

Notes

1. I would feel remiss if I did not mention at this point that the series itself participated in a double irony by hiring Armenia Miles, Elaine Miles's mother, to play both Mrs. Anku and Mrs. Whirlwind. The parts were very small ones, but it does seem to play out in an odd way the stereotype that all Native Americans look alike.

2. Chris's enlightening influence on Cicelians through literary and philosophical ruminations on his radio show, as well as some of his art pieces, has prompted Iain Crawford to argued that Chris is in fact *Northern Exposure*'s pivotal character.

3. Alaska wasn't purchased from Russia until 1867 and didn't become a state until 1959. The Alaska Statehood Act included a provision against taking Native Alaskan tribal lands, as well agreements over land use. The unique history is nodded to on *Northern Exposure* in several instances. For example, Holling voted against statehood, and Marilyn receives a biannual check for $5000 from Proudhoe Bay Corporation. It should not be forgotten, however, that certain tribes endured exploitation by both Russians and Americans. And though Alaskan Natives have a significantly different set of historical circumstances from other Native Americans, many of the same socially constructed stereotypes apply precisely because they are stereotypes.

4. This is also probably a veiled reference to *Dances with Wolves*. *Northern Exposure* is rife with allusions to the history and present of Native American identity in Hollywood.

5. Thanks to Rhonda Wilcox, whose article reminded me to review this important episode. As she notes, it's also in this episode that Fleischman says somewhat with dismay, "I feel like I'm changing.... My faculties, my sense of self, I'm losing it." Maggie replies, "It's life growth."

6. Although we usually only hear "tribe" on *Northern Exposure*, Tlingit are socially structured into two moieties, Raven and Eagle, within which are various clans, including Raven and Eagle, respectively. Membership is traced through the mother (not unlike Judaism), and historically, members must marry outside their moiety, ensuring kinship crosses those boundaries as well. As far as I can glean, Ed belongs to the Raven moiety and Marilyn to the Eagle, and they possibly belong to the Raven and Eagle clans, respectively. "Tribe" could be substituting for clan or moiety. The idea of pairs and halves, moieties, figures largely in Tlingit concepts and structures. If a person is part Haida and part Tlingit, for instance, one can describe her tribal membership as either the Tlingit or Haida moiety. Perhaps Mrs. Noanuk and Marilyn saw Judaism as a moiety in conjunction with theirs.

7. Campbell says the fourth most important function of mythology "is to foster the centering and unfolding of the individual in integrity, in accord with" himself, his culture, the universe, and "that awesome mystery which is both beyond and within himself and all things" (6). Creative mythology builds meaningful relationships between self, others, and the cosmos "from the insights, sentiments, thought, and vision of an adequate individual, loyal to his own experience of value" (7).

8. Snowshoe webbing.

Works Cited

Baird, Robert. "Going Indian: Discovery, Adoption, and Renaming Toward a 'True American,' from Deerslayer to Dances with Wolves." *Dressing in Feathers: The Construction of the American Popular Culture*. Ed. Elizabeth Bird. Boulder: Westview, 1996. 195–209.

Bird, Elizabeth S. "Introduction: Constructing the Indian, 1830s–1990s." *Dressing in Feathers: The Construction of the American Popular Culture*. Ed. Elizabeth Bird. Boulder: Westview, 1996. 1–12.

Campbell, Joseph. *The Masks of God: Creative Mythology*. New York: Arkana, 1968.

_____. *Myths to Live By*. New York: Bantam, 1972.

Carafiol, Peter. "The Nationalist Model for American Ethnic Narrative." *"Writing" Nation and "Writing" Region in America*. Ed. Theo D'haen. Amsterdam: VU UP, 1996. 166–85.

Crawford, Iain. "Reading TV: Intertextuality in Northern Exposure." *Mid-Atlantic Almanack* 3 (1994): 14–22.

Deloria, Philip. *Playing Indian.* Yale Historical Publications. New Haven: Yale University Press, 1998.

_____. *Indians in Unexpected Places.* Culture America. Lawrence: University Press of Kansas, 2004.

Erdoes, Richard, and Alfonso Ortiz, Eds. *American Indian Myths and Legends.* New York: Pantheon, 1984.

Johnston, Jessica, and Josef Raab. "The Utopian Community of Northern Exposure." *Popular Culture Review* 5.2 (1994): 73–85.

Miller, Jay. "Alaskan Tlingit and Tsimshian." U of Washington Library Digital Collections. 2005. 15 Feb. 2007 <http://content.lib.washington.edu/aipnw/ miller1.html>.

Romeyn, Esther, and Jack Kugelmass. "Writing Alaska, Writing the Nation: 'Northern Exposure' and the Quest for a New America." *"Writing" Nation and "Writing" Region in America.* Ed. Theo D'haen. Amsterdam: VU University Press, 1996. 252–67.

Swann, Brian, ed. *Coming to Light: Contemporary Translations of the Native Literatures of North America.* New York: Vintage, 1994.

Taylor, Annette. "Cultural Heritage in Northern Exposure." *Dressing in Feathers: The Construction of the American Popular Culture.* Ed. Elizabeth Bird. Boulder: Westview, 1996. 229–44.

_____. "Landscape of the West in Northern Exposure." *Mid-Atlantic Almanack* 3 (1994): 23–33.

_____, and David Upchurch. *"Northern Exposure* and Mythology of the Global Community." *Journal of Popular Culture* 30.2 (1996): 75–85.

Taylor, Catherine. "Marilyn Speaks! A Conversation with Elaine Miles." *Radiance* Fall 1993. *Radiance Online.* 2007. 13 Jan. 2007 <www.radiancemagazine.com/issues/ 1993/ elaine.html>.

Wilcox, Rhonda. "'In Your Dreams, Fleischman': Dr. Flesh and the Dream of the Spirit in *Northern Exposure." Studies in Popular Culture* 15.2 (1993): 1–13.

"You Don't Have to Eat Every Dish of Rigatoni": Food, Music, and Identity in the Works of David Chase

Thomas Fahy

In the sixth season of *The Sopranos,* Dr. Melfi tells Tony: "You don't have to eat every dish of rigatoni. You don't have to fuck every female you meet" ("Kaisha," 6.12). Her declaration highlights the ways in which consumption has come to define Tony Soprano. As boss of the New Jersey mob, he has the power to take what he wants with impunity. Tony consumes money, material goods, political favors, women, and even the feigned affection of his crew as he does food: with a seemingly insatiable appetite. As this appetite suggests, eating embodies one of the primary activities and rhythms that regulate life on the show. Most characters in *The Sopranos* eat quickly and voraciously, and this excessive consumption reflects a pervasive need — both here and in David Chase's writing more broadly — for belonging. Chase's characters tend to share food as a way of asserting their familial, cultural, and professional allegiances. In some cases (at restaurants, at the Melfi home, and at the Bada Bing), meals are accompanied by music — music that, as Chase himself has explained, tends to "[comment] on events in the story" and "[foster] a feeling or mood" ("Introduction," x). During these moments, the music of a certain singer or composer functions like the sonorities of eating. It provides a pulse for the scene as we listen to the sounds of wine glasses ringing during a toast and silverware grinding against a plate.

Most meals at the Soprano house, however, occur without music. Instead, chewing, drinking, and passing around dishes establish a distinct rhythm. These aspects of eating punctuate conversation and often draw attention to what the characters aren't saying — what they are holding back from each other. The rhythm (or time spent consuming a meal) and the harmonies (or exchanges that occur when sharing food) reflect the characters' state of mind as well as their anxieties, desires, and resentments.

Of course, *The Sopranos* has not been David Chase's only show, and this use of music and food can be found in his earlier work as well. For Chase, these elements typically comment on the struggles that we all share in attempting to understand ourselves relative to place and community. Food and music bring people together. They fill in the silence between characters— when they either don't know what to say to each other or prefer not to speak. And they give characters time to think about who they are relative to what they are eating and hearing. All of these elements are crucial for establishing a sense of belonging to a social and cultural group. Throughout *The Rockford Files, Northern Exposure,* and *The Sopranos,* moments of personal crisis, including feelings of alienation, betrayal, and guilt, are mitigated by the shared activity of eating and/or music. For Chase, music and food not only establish essential rhythms for pacing drama, but they also operate as artistic tools. They highlight the tensions that we all experience in creating an individual identity both in relation to and distinct from the broader forces that have influenced us— such as family, ethnicity, and geography. Ultimately, Chase suggests that these forces are both liberating and restrictive and that a true understanding of self is found in these tensions, in this ongoing negotiation between the self and others.

"One Big Pulsating Symphony":
The Role of Music in Chase's Work

As a young man, Chase dreamed of being a rock-and-roll musician. He played the drums and the bass. He listened to records while smoking pot with high school friends. And in college, he claims, "what I was really studying, this is no joke, was the Rolling Stones" (Rucker). In the same interview, Chase even recalls some of his early observations about music and television:

> When I was like 17 or 18 back in Jersey, my friend Donny and I, we used to get high in his basement and we'd put a single on the stereo, like "Peppermint Twist," and play that single against *whatever* was playing on the TV, and turn the TV sound off. You would notice strange synchronicities like the rhythm of

the cutting of the TV show would miraculously fall in with the rhythm of the song. [...] It blew out the idea of "score."

In many ways, Chase's work in television has continually challenged the idea of "score." Chase explains that his short-lived show *Almost Grown* (1988-1989) shifted between past and present, "using rock and roll and pop music as a memory device" (Rucker). As the executive producer for *Northern Exposure*, Chase became part of a show that used music as a powerful voice for the community. Music permeates every aspect of Cicely, Alaska — in Holling Vincoeur's bar, The Brick, on Chris Stevens's radio show, and through the stereos that play in Ruth-Anne's general store, Maggie O'Connell's home, and at the various dinner parties hosted by millionaire and former astronaut Maurice Minnifield. Music not only ties these characters together, but it also captures the emotional pitch of their lives on the show — from Joel Fleishman's indignation and Maurice's explosive temperament to Ed's unflappable calm. Cicely might seem like a quiet, slow paced town, but music helps reveal the dynamic emotional lives of its inhabitants.

In Chase's first season as executive producer, the episode "Mite Makes Right" (5.13) articulates the importance of music for the show and arguably for Chase as well. After an allergic reaction to dust mites, Maggie becomes obsessed with the unseen bugs and creatures that live in her home. She tries a variety of methods to kill them but to no avail. Through the help of Chris Stevens's sculpture of a dust mite, her own dream of meeting a human-sized mite at Holling's bar, and Joel's advice and affection, she comes to terms with her shared place in the earth's ecosystem:

MAGGIE: Listen. Do you hear it?

JOEL: What?

MAGGIE: *Life*. Life is everywhere. The earth is throbbing with it.... It's like music ... one big pulsating symphony. [...] We're all in this together.

At this moment, the camera pulls away, and we see Maggie and Joel kissing in an open field at daybreak (where they have been having this discussion). Their bodies are small amidst the towering trees, thick snow, and rocky mountains of the Alaskan wilderness; in effect, they have become just another part of the landscape and its pulsating symphony.

With this tableau of Joel and Maggie's kiss, we start to hear the second movement of Bach's G minor Violin Sonata (BWV 1001). The steady, interweaving voices of this fugue — a contrapuntal composition that layers one theme on top of another — parallels the episode's theme about the harmonious connection between humanity and nature, about the ways in which we all overlap and intermingle on this planet through love, friendship, work, and creative endeavors. This piece is being played by Cal, a violinist obsessed with Maurice's new investment, a 1728 Guarneri del Gesù violin. Cal is horrified by Maurice's plan to keep the violin in a safe until its value appreciates. As Cal explains, "You don't understand. You can't do that. [...] You have to play it, or it loses its tone. It dies. [...] You can't keep it locked in that box." Maurice isn't convinced. He sees the instrument — and most of the world — in terms of economic exchange, and though he enjoys upper-class refinements, such as fine foods and wine, expensive furniture, and classical music, he lacks any real understanding of the passions that create art — although he ultimately gives the violin to Cal and helps him escape a nearby asylum ("Lovers and Madmen," 5.24). The message here, in part, is about community, about the things that tie people together regardless of class and socioeconomic background. Cicely is a town where the inhabitants are just as conversant with the philosophy of Hegel, the music of Bach, and the films of Fellini as they are with baseball statistics, community gossip, and hunting. It is not unusual for the same piece of classical music to be playing in Ruth-Anne's general store and Maurice's extravagant living room. In this way, *Northern Exposure* uses music as one of the many tools that forge the community of Cicely. Likewise, the diversity of music in the show (which includes jazz, blues, classical, country, Native American folk songs, rock and roll, pop songs, heavy metal, and more) suggests a universal appreciation of so-called "high" and "low" culture; it implies that understanding and accepting a variety of artistic expressions can bring people together.[1]

Source music (drawn from preexisting recordings, as opposed to a score written specifically for the show) is an integral part of *The Sopranos* as well. In an interview with HBO, Chase explains the role of music in his creative process: "I listen to music while I'm trying to think of ideas and I just like it. So even from the beginning I said [that] we really need to have a good music budget."[2] After the pilot was rejected by every major network, HBO expressed interest in developing the series, and this venue enabled Chase a great deal of flexibility to capture the contemporary sights and sounds of New Jersey mob life. As David Lavery and Robert J. Thompson explain, "having the series on HBO permitted Chase to use nudity, violence, and profane language in ways that would have been impossible on network television, greatly facilitating its verisimilitude, but perhaps more importantly it enabled the uninterrupted-by-commercial construction of hour-long narratives" (*This Thing of Ours* 21). We can certainly add music to this list. The flexibility and funding provided by HBO enabled Chase to use source music in most of the spaces on the show — the Bada Bing, Tony's car and boat, the stereo in Anthony Junior's room, Chris and Adriana's apartment, Artie Bucco's restaurant, Dr. Melfi's home ... just to name a few.

Chase elaborates on the thematic significance of this music in his introduction to *The Sopranos: Selected Scripts from Three Seasons*: "I sometimes
see the music as another character, the lyrics of songs functioning as a Greek
chorus, sometimes—but not always—summing up or commenting on
events in the story. Or not. Mostly the music fosters a feeling or mood.
There's no question that the music and this particular cast of actors are my
favorite parts of *The Sopranos*" (x). On one hand, the lyrics (as Greek chorus) often provide a language to guide our interpretation of what is happening in a particular episode. They highlight themes and reflect inner
truths about the characters. As scholar Kevin Fellezs argues, "dialogue and
imagery convey information that the soundtrack either supports or emphasizes" (165). For example, songs can fill in the silences between dialogue,
foster tension by pacing the action, and reinforce the psychological and
emotional states of the characters.

On the other hand, the mood or feeling evoked by some of this music
also develops apart from the lyrics. In a world of secrets and lies, filled with
characters who often lack the ability to articulate feelings, songs without
words seem particularly fitting for the characters of *The Sopranos*. The closing scene of "Pax Soprana" (1.6) offers an interesting example. The dinner
celebrating Junior's new title as "Boss" of the New Jersey mob is accompanied by Xzibit's rap "Paparazzi" (an instrumental version). As the title suggests, this rap is about unwanted photographs, one of the costs of celebrity
and notoriety, and the photographs in this scene are being taken covertly
by the FBI. These images are part of the government's mounting case against
the Soprano family, and subsequently they appear on a corkboard in an FBI
field office, revealing how closely the mob is being scrutinized.

Removing the lyrics of this song, however, draws attention to the fact
that the melody was written not by Xzibit but by nineteenth-century French
composer Gabriel Fauré. To the original composition, *Pavane* (Op. 50),
Fauré eventually added a choral part, setting a poem by Robert de Montesquiou. Some of Montesquiou's stanzas, which focus on the anguish of
love, resonate with the angst that Tony and many of the other characters
feel about family and loyalty—including the infidelities that threaten to
break apart marriages, the betrayals of one's oath to the mob, the feelings
of being trapped in a certain life (as a mobster, a spouse, a Soprano, etc.),
the power struggles within the mob, and the potential costs of breaking the
law (losing one's freedom and being separated from family). As Montesquiou's poem laments, "And it's always the same. We love each other,
hate each other, curse our loved ones!"[3] This tension drives much of the
action in the series—including Livia's, Tony's mother's, sanctioning of a hit
on her son in the first season ("Nobody Knows Anything," 1.11 and "Isabella,"

1.12), Christopher's agonized life-or-death decision to reveal Adriana's role as an informant for the FBI ("Long Term Parking," 5.12), and Tony's ambivalence about having Vito Spatafore killed because of his homosexuality ("Live Free or Die," 6.6).

The use of a pavane in "Pax Soprana" captures another critical tension in the show — the nostalgia for looking back to a romanticized vision of the past. The pavane was a courtly dance that first originated in sixteenth-century Italy, and as such, it conjures the finery, rituals, and elegant lifestyle of the aristocracy.[4] In a similar way, Tony Soprano and the more senior members of his crew cling to idealized visions of the old days of the mob. They desperately want to see themselves as part of a venerated tradition (as they do when the travel back to Italy in "Commendatori," 2.4), but these visions are corrupted by greed, violence, infidelity, Hollywood films, widely held stereotypes, and the ways in which silence (*omerta*) has given way to self-interest. Likewise, Fauré's original composition has been corrupted by this synthesized, pop-rap version. This modern incarnation is not the real thing — just as this dinner celebrating Uncle Junior is a farce: He is de facto boss only. Tony is really running the mob, while Junior is just a "lighting rod" for federal scrutiny.

The use of classical music in *The Sopranos* doesn't raise the typical questions about class and high culture that one might expect. Tony and Carmela are *nouveau riche.* They have the money for a nice house and expensive things, but their taste is often garish — from the roman pillar that supports the television in their bedroom and the "bar with the goombah Murano glass"[5] to the constant need for new things (furniture, cars, boats, and clothes). Not surprisingly, classical music is largely absent from the show. We wouldn't expect Tony or Carmela to have a deep appreciation for Bach or Brahms. Unlike the characters on *Northern Exposure,* the world of organized crime in New Jersey is not conversant with high art and culture. Here, education is something that parents provide for their children by sending them to college — even though this education typically creates barriers between generations. Meadow often uses academic learning to distance herself from her family, for example.[6]

Nevertheless, as the Xzibit/Fauré example suggests, the high class and elitist associations with classical music tend to be leveled in *The Sopranos.* Instead, its sporadic use reinforces questions of ethnic identity and belonging. The Italian aria heard during Tony's panic attack in the pilot episode is part and parcel of his quest to understand himself as an Italian American and as a mobster at a time when the cultural traditions of the Mafia (honor, loyalty, respect, family, and silence) are eroding. Likewise in "The Legend of Tennessee Moltisanti" (1.8), the Melfi family debates Italian-

American identity and Italian stereotypes in American culture while eating pasta and listening to music by the Italian keyboard composer Domenico Scarlatti. Classical music — like other forms of music on the show — is associated with a range of characters. It is not reserved for the social, intellectual, and cultural elite.

In the third season, for example, Antonio Vivaldi's song "Sposa Son Disprezzata" ("The Scorned Wife") accompanies Carmela's emotional response to Jusepe de Ribera's painting of *The Mystical Marriage of Saint Catherine* ("Amour Fou," 3.12). This musical selection links classical music with the high art of the Metropolitan Museum of Art — which is not surprising on the surface. Yet the artwork in the Soprano house is not accompanied by such music. In fact, the Sopranos never seem to look at the paintings in their own home. Art merely fills up space in the way couches, lamps, and flat-screen televisions do. In the museum, where Carmela and Meadow have gone specifically to look at paintings, "Sposa Son Disprezzata" serves as the Greek chorus for Carmela's viewing of Saint Catherine and the baby Jesus. As the title, lyrics, and the repeated chords that drive sections of the song suggest, Carmela is both angry with Tony and frequently tormented by guilt — about her marriage and her life, which has been financed by crime, Tony's infidelities, her growing fear that God intends to punish her with ovarian cancer, and her conflicted desires to have another child with Tony. "Look at her," she tells Meadow as they stand in front of the painting, "The little baby's hand against her cheek. She's so at peace. The beautiful, innocent, gorgeous little baby." Carmela has lost her own sense of peace, and she has watched her children lose their innocence. The moral and ethical justifications she has used to maintain her comfortable life of wealth and privilege have been called into question (most notably by the psychiatrist in "Second Opinion," 3.7). Even though Carmela will ultimately stay with Tony (despite their separation in season four and her attempts to get divorced in season five), the pathos of Vivaldi's music, the repetitive accompaniment, and the text of the song encapsulate her ongoing angst for the viewer:

> I am a scorned wife,
> faithful, yet insulted.
> Heavens, what did I do?
> Yet he is my love,
> my husband, my beloved,
> my hope.[7]

While still standing in front of the Ribera painting, Carmela quickly collects herself and tells Meadow that they should eat. Vivaldi's music —

and subsequently food — will substitute for the words that Carmela is unwilling to utter — the truth about her own complicity in Tony's misdeeds.

Interestingly, Vivaldi's "Sposa Son Disprezzata" is first heard at the end of the previous episode, "Pine Barrens" (3.11). After a botched collection and killing leaves Paulie and Christopher stranded in the icy woods, this music accompanies their drive back to civilization with Tony and Bobby. The four men — all part of a family in the context of the Mafia — are mostly silent as we hear Vivaldi's music as part of the soundtrack. This silence is broken only when Tony chastises Paulie for having mayonnaise on his chin. Here Paulie is wearing a mark of his sloppiness — representing his sloppy failure to get the money from Valery in this episode, which is part of his growing shortcomings as a captain in the mob — and Tony treats him like a disobedient child. By the end of this season and throughout the fourth, Paulie's relationship with Tony will be further strained. Paulie will contemplate switching allegiances from Tony Soprano to Carmine of New York ("Army of One," 3.13, "Watching Too Much Television," 4.7, and "Eloise," 4.12, for example). The closing lament of Vivaldi's song, like the mayonnaise, reflects Tony's strained relationship with Paulie and the rest of his crew — a relationship that is increasingly defined by incompetence, drug abuse, and unchecked rage. There is no fidelity in this family, and these words parallel Carmela's feelings for Tony when it comes to his affairs.

Finally, this music provides a segue to the image of a nude statue of a woman in Dr. Melfi's office and one of Tony's therapy sessions, where he is complaining about the mental stability of Gloria, the woman with whom he is having an affair: "And by that I'm supposed to know she's going to throw a fucking roast beef at my head. Why does everything have to be so hard?" ("Pine Barrens," 3.11). Tony's obsession with women and food come together here. He samples women as he does various meats from Satriale's, but he fails to understand the significance of the sustenance they offer him. Gloria throws the London Broil because he has shattered her fantasies about domestic harmony and love. He is a cheating husband with no intention of leaving his wife. The lyrics of this song not only speak to Carmela's feelings but also to Gloria's (which lead, in part, to her suicide ["Everybody Hurts," 4.6]) and Irina's before that.[8]

"No More Weight Remarks, Tony": Food and Belonging

Food in David Chase's most significant shows, *The Rockford Files, Northern Exposure,* and *The Sopranos,* tends to reflect a set of cultural and personal values. It is associated with social status, class, ethnic identity, body image, and feelings of belonging and alienation. As E. N. Anderson argues in *Everybody Eats: Understanding Food and Culture*, "food is used in every society to communicate messages. Preeminent among these are messages of group solidarity; food sharing is literally sacred in almost all religions and takes on a near-sacred quality in many (most?) families around the world" (7). He goes on to explain that "one main message of food [...] is *solidarity*. Eating together means sharing and participating. [...] The other main message is *separation*. Food marks social class, ethnicity, and so on. Food transactions define families, networks, friendship groups, religions, and virtually every other socially institutionalized group. Naturally, one group can try to use food to separate itself, while another is trying to use food to eliminate that separation" (125). This tension between solidarity and separation is certainly evident in Chase's fiction through the use of food. Just as certain types of meals help define characters in cultural and socioeconomic terms, they also get in the way of relationships. Not everyone enjoys the same foods. People eat too much or too little, too quickly or too slowly. They eat instead of communicating with those around them. And just as eating can be about community, it can also be about selfishness. Eating someone else's food without returning the offer, snacking on candy while you're on a diet, or letting someone else pick up the bill — all of these can be moments that violate trust and strain relationships. These types of complicated and conflicted exchanges occur throughout *The Rockford Files, Northern Exposure,* and *The Sopranos.*

In the opening montage of *The Rockford Files,* for example, food helps establish Jim Rockford's financial troubles. In addition to still photographs of his car, of his contentious relationship with the police, and of him behind bars, we see him at a grocery store trying to decide what to put in his shopping cart, as if he's not sure what he can afford or what he really wants. Another image features Rockford and his father, Rocky, fishing off the Santa Monica pier. Throughout the series, Rockford fishes not for recreation but for food. He struggles to pay the bills, so catching his own food and eating inexpensively are ways for him to save every last penny. When Rockford does dine out, money defines both his choices and the eating experience. At the end of "The Dark and Bloody Ground" (1.3), for example, Rockford and Beth, his attorney and part-time girlfriend, meet at a cheap taco stand at the end of the pier. As soon as he realizes that Beth isn't going to pay him for the work he's just done, he walks away without eating. Once again, Jim is reduced to cheap food or no food at all — an indication of his financial struggles. And in "Aura Lee, Farewell" (1.15), Jim's friend Sara takes him to lunch at Sara's Place, a casual sandwich shop that she owns. He protests, joking that she made her invitation sound more formal. She replies: "Well, I did sort of make it sound like that. I confess. But this is less expensive, and it gets us even for the time you asked me to go out to dinner and then stuck a fishing pole in my hand."

This is certainly a playful moment, but it is also part of the ongoing way that inexpensive food characterizes Rockford's socioeconomic status. He doesn't hesitate to take women on cheap dates. Despite the fact that he charges "two hundred dollars a day plus expenses," his clients, more often than not, fail to pay the bill. His soft spot for helping people (regardless of payment) thus gives him little hope for improving his financial situation.

Rockford's consumption of fast food is a fitting choice for both his nomadic personality and Los Angeles itself, where the show takes place. Fast food and Rockford's fast life may explain the absence of source music on the show as well. The roar of car engines and screeching tires provide most of the soundtrack here. In fact, car chases and movement define Rockford's life. They set the tempo for his actions and the pace at which events unfold. He is a man always on the go—tailing people in his signature Pontiac Firebird, living in a trailer (which presumably can be moved), and having romantic liaisons with a variety of women. He is not one to settle down, and fast food provides a fitting metaphor for the fast rhythms of his life. It is something to be consumed quickly and, in many cases, without enjoyment. Rockford simply doesn't have time to savor what he eats, and by extension, there isn't much time to listen to music either.

The use of food in *Northern Exposure* and *The Sopranos* also reinforces themes, reflects truths about the characters, and speaks to a need for community. But unlike *The Rockford Files,* the meals on these shows often work in conjunction with the music being heard. Perhaps this link isn't surprising. As historian Donna R. Gabaccia explains in *We Are What We Eat: Ethnic Food and the Making of Americans:*

> Key to identity and culture in both American music and eating is the tension between people's love of the familiar and the pleasure they find in desiring, creating, and experiencing something new. [...] To the degree that American culture is a consumer culture, Americans will probably always hunger for the tastes and long for the sounds we believe we have lost to commercial producers. And our efforts to find "authentic foods" and "authentic sounds" will generate demand for small food stores and live jazz clubs, and for face-to-face relations between the shopkeeper and the consumer or the musician and the audience [229–230].

As Gabaccia suggests, food and music have the power to express a shared ethnic identity. Singing and eating together are acts that can reinforce a sense of belonging to a particular group. Once these things become part of consumer culture and mass production, however, they tend to become somewhat diluted. The New Jersey mob in *The Sopranos* certainly finds this transformation difficult to accept. Paulie, for example, resents the way that Starbucks-like cafés have appropriated and capitalized on Italian culture: "We invented this shit. [...] It's not just a money thing. It's a pride thing. All our food — pizza, calzone, buffalo mozzarella, olive oil. [...] But this is the worst. This espresso shit" ("46 Long," 1.2). Paulie laments the distillation of Italian culture in the commercial marketplace,[9] in part, because it highlights the ways that distinct cultural practices can be subsumed in American culture by mass production.

In the first episodes of *Northern Exposure,* food is one of the barriers between the community of Cicely and Joel Fleishman. He reluctantly tries a moose burger in the pilot episode and quickly gives up. Joel does eventually find himself fitting into the town of Cicely (despite his best efforts to resist), and this growing participation in communal life includes eating. In the opening moments of "Thanksgiving" (4.8), he muses on the meaning of this holiday, saying it doesn't matter what is served but the celebration. "Thanksgiving [...] it's the only holiday that's for everyone. Christians. Jews. Muslims [...] No one's left out in the cold." This egalitarian philosophy is called into question when Ed Chigliak, an amateur filmmaker, shaman in training, store clerk, and general errand boy, throws a tomato at him. Even when Joel learns that one of the holiday rituals in Cicely includes Indians throwing tomatoes at white people, he remains outraged. As his assistant, the laconic Marilyn, explains, "we [Indians] have a lot of anger." She goes on to tell him that the red of tomatoes represents blood: "Tomatoes look like blood, but they don't hurt." Food here signifies the wrongs of the past. It stains the clothes of white people to make public the brutal history that has largely been hidden in the United States. Food — the kind that will be shared at the Thanksgiving feast at the end of the episode — starts out as a marker of difference. It symbolizes a latent cultural hostility that still requires some kind of outlet, and it reminds us that the community of Cicely has its limits.

To Joel, the act of throwing tomatoes violates his sense of civility and propriety, and more importantly, it challenges his sense of self. He claims that he isn't white but Jewish, a fellow "victim of oppression." As a result, he doesn't feel that he deserves to pay reparations for the wrongs committed against Native Americans. Joel tries to explain this to Dave, the Native-American cook who works at the Brick:

JOEL: I can understand that you would harbor a certain amount of hostility toward white people — small pox, the Trail of Tears ... I saw *Dances with*

> *Wolves.* But do you really think hurling tomatoes is an acceptable way to express that hostility?
>
> DAVE: It could be worse [...] baseball bats, bicycle chains, tire irons.

Joel's reference to *Dances with Wolves,* though amusing, is part of the problem. Mainstream America tends to become aware of historical tragedies and wrongs through Hollywood films and quickly forgotten news cycles. For Joel, the problem with the tomato throwing is that it actively disrupts his complacent acceptance of the near-annihilation of Native Americans as justified by American imperialism and Manifest Destiny. His indignation gets sidetracked, however, when he discovers that he must spend one more year as a physician in Alaska. The prospect of additional servitude to the state — a place that has made him feel trapped and disempowered from the outset of the series — sends him into a depressive funk. He even dreams of meeting Sisyphus and being forced to take his place underneath the boulder. At the nadir of his desolation, Marilyn invites him to join the Indians in their Day of the Dead Parade on Thanksgiving. "You have no hope left," Marilyn observes of Joel. "You can march with us. [...] You're not white anymore."

The message is a sober one for *Northern Exposure:* Being white in western culture means occupying a place of privilege and power, and to really understand the Native American experience, whites would have to lose everything, even hope itself. However, this message is quickly mitigated by the images of the parade (which is accompanied by the communal message of Louis Armstrong's "Life Is a Cabaret"[10]) and, at the end of the episode, the Thanksgiving meal.

In many respects, all of the plots in this episode are resolved through the act of eating. Chris realizes that his best Thanksgiving was celebrated in prison — sharing a meal among the community of his fellow inmates. Maggie and Mike discuss cooking together, and it becomes an image for their burgeoning romance. The episode even culminates in a potluck Thanksgiving feast at the most social place in town, The Brick. In the closing moments, Joel sits next to Ed, who threw a tomato at him at the opening of the show, and he joins the rest of the town in this feast. Though he is still angry and frustrated about the job, Joel is eagerly partaking in and enjoying the food being passed around.[11] He is part of this town, yet as always, Joel tends to eat quickly — as if he can't let himself be too comfortable here.

Just as music can be heard in most of the spaces in *The Sopranos,* hardly a scene goes by without food — family meals, catered parties, mobsters eating lunches or dinners, people grabbing a slice of pizza or picking up meat at Satriale's Pork Store, men consuming alcohol at the Bada Bing, groups ordering food at Artie's restaurant, and Tony hovering in front of the refrigerator or eating ice cream on the couch. Business, love, infidelity, arguments, family events—they all happen around food and drink in this show. Food is not only an act of sharing and community—one distinctly associated with Italian-American identity here—but it is also associated with excess and self-indulgence. The cast of *The Sopranos* may, in fact, be the heaviest on mainstream television—apart from reality shows like *The Biggest Loser* that are intentionally exploiting obesity. David Chase even made some of them gain weight; Edie Falco, for example, struggles to lose it after every filming. Jamie-Lynn Siegler lost weight after the pilot and was told to put it back on. Her own struggles with an eating disorder also inspired her to become a spokesperson for the National Eating Disorders Association.

An early episode, "The Legend of Tennessee Moltisani" (1.8), juxtaposes two family dinners in which Italian-American culture and community are the focal point of discussion. The Melfi family—Dr. Jennifer Melfi, her ex-husband, Richard, her son, Jason, and her parents—are gathered around a nice wooden dining room table, eating a home-cooked meal of spaghetti and meatballs (with Grandmom's "Ginzo gravy"), drinking red wine, and listening to a Scarlatti keyboard sonata in C Minor. At one point, Richard complains that people like Tony are responsible for perpetuating stereotypes about Italian Americans: "Italians against Discrimination did a study, and at its height the mafia had less than 5000 members. And yet that tiny, insignificant fraction casts such a dark shadow over twenty million hard-working Americans."

Richard's resentment stems from his own anxieties about ethnic identity. He is both proud of being Italian and hyperconscious of the ways that mainstream culture views ethnic groups. Throughout the series, Richard fervently supports anti-defamation organizations (similar to the American Italian Defense Association, which filed a lawsuit against HBO for the portrayal of Italian Americans in *The Sopranos*).[12] Richard fears that someone like Tony, who perpetuates a negative image of this culture, reflects poorly on hard-working Italian Americans like himself, so he rails incessantly against his ex-wife's choice to work with Tony as a patient. In part, Richard and the rest of the family are faced with a challenge when it comes to the food at the table. Spaghetti, meatballs, and red wine are staples in American cuisine, but for an Italian-American family, they are downright clichés. In many ways, the discussion here is about the struggle to define oneself in relationship and in opposition to stereotypes, to find ways to consume and savor this meal for its cultural distinctiveness. When the grandfather concludes this conversation with a toast ("To we ... the twenty million"), this is a moment of reclaiming and celebrating this food as part of a proud heritage. It can reaffirm meaningful traditions just as easily as it can be used by others to perpetuate prejudices.

The Melfi dinner is set up in contrast with a Soprano meal later in the episode. After the FBI searches the Soprano house for evidence linking Tony to organized crime, the family also discusses the place of Italian Americans in the United States over dinner. They are not eating one of Carmela's home-cooked meals, however, because they have been displaced from the house for the day. Instead, they are eating Chinese fast food and drinking Coke. Tony begins by heatedly announcing that Italians are discriminated against in mainstream society.

> MEADOW: Who invented the mafia? *La Cosa Nostra,* who invented it? [...]
>
> TONY: Is there something you want to say to me?
>
> MEADOW: I just like history like you, Dad. [...]
>
> TONY: The Bank of America [...] one of the biggest banks in the world, started by an Italian. [...] And here's something else I bet you didn't know. More Italians fought for this country in World War II than any other ethnic group. [...] And, of course, Francis Albert [Sinatra].

Tony tries to impart a greater degree of cultural appreciation here through an aggressive presentation of statements, not a calm discussion accompanied by soothing classical music, and he repeatedly raises his voice in frustration with his children's ignorance about Italian-American accomplishments.[13] His message is undercut, however, in several ways. First, he silences any discussion of *La Cosa Nostra.* Meadow's "interest" in history, which is both an act of youthful rebellion and an attempt to get her father to acknowledge the truth about her own family's connection to the Mafia, is antithetical to Tony's shadowy life of crime. While the Melfi family is willing to discuss the mob, Tony denies it. In large part, he does this to protect his children — though Meadow already knows the truth. The problem is that Tony is the stereotype. He is one of the five thousand that Richard criticizes — a mobster who deals in the lawless world of organized crime, violence, and actions without consequence. Nevertheless, Tony recognizes the stigma that this association can bring to his family. He even dreams of his children becoming professionals, and he explicitly tells Dr. Melfi that he does not want them involved in his business. Thus, in order to have a discussion that validates mainstream Italian-American accomplishments, Tony must, in effect, deny his own role in society.

This tension between what Tony wants for his children and the life he has inherited from his own father resonates with Marlisa Santos's analysis of food in the first two *Godfather* films. In "'Leave the Gun; Take the Cannoli': Food and Family in the Modern American Mafia Film," she argues that "food highlights the power structure of the 'family' as a military hierarchy, but also highlights the family as the foundation of home and tradition. The depiction of food in these films is the glue that binds together the often contradictory elements of the American Mafia way of life — the seeming incongruities of family, tradition, and religion joined with murder, bloodshed, and brutality. Food becomes the emblem of what it means to be civilized, the reinforcement of whatever cultural rules or aspirations Italian-American Mafia families live by" (209). For Tony Soprano, the contradictions between family and brutality are manifested in his panic attacks, and he even comes to realize that food is the trigger for these attacks. In the pilot, he collapses while cooking meat on a grill, and through his therapy sessions with Dr. Melfi in the third season, he recalls the first time he saw his father cut off a man's finger — Mr. Satriale, the butcher and owner of Satriale's Pork Store ("Fortunate Son," 3.3). The brutality of this scene is juxtaposed with the family meal that night. While Livia cuts the roast, Tony's father dances with her, fondling his wife playfully. Here Tony has his first panic attack and collapses. As Melfi explains, "That's why you short-circuited. Puberty. Witnessing not only your mother and father's sexuality but also the violence and blood so closely connected to the food you were about to eat. And also the thought that someday you might be called upon to bring home the bacon. Like your father." The image of "putting food on the table" or providing for one's family is in constant dialogue with the bloodshed that Tony dishes out in order to secure his financial well-being. At some level, Tony's seemingly insatiable appetite for food parallels his greed as a mob boss— particularly his hunger for money and women.

Tony's message at that early family dinner is also undercut by the meal that they are eating. The Soprano family is consuming Chinese fast food — a Westernized distillation of Chinese culture. Though the series presents many scenes in which the family is eating Carmela's Italian cooking, this episode positions the Melfi family (the non-stereotypes) eating stereotypical food and the mob family eating stereotypical Chinese food — suggesting how they themselves contribute to a similar, prepackaged understanding of Italian-American culture. They are participating in the same type of clichéd understanding of ethnicity that Tony rails against: "Why would [Chinese] people who eat with sticks invent something that you need a fork to eat?" Tony uses food to claim some understanding of Chinese culture, while defending Italians from a similar kind of labeling.

Not surprisingly, Meadow will eventually use food as one of the ways to express her frustration with being a Soprano. The episode "Army of One" (3.13) culminates with Uncle Junior singing "Core 'Ngrato" ("Ungrateful

Heart") at an Italian restaurant, and during this scene, Meadow throws pieces of bread at him while singing lyrics from Britney Spears' "Oops, I Did It Again." Like Ed's act of tomato throwing in *Northern Exposure*, Meadow's behavior can be read metaphorically. The bread, which is also a slang term for money, suggests the money she is throwing back at her family ungratefully. Her disrespect reflects a growing struggle between her new identity as a college student at Columbia and her family roots. Her use of the Spears' song is also a rejection of family. It links her with teen popular culture, not with the Italian family traditions being promoted in this scene. Overall, Meadow's desire for both separation and solidarity continues to shape her development throughout the series—from rejecting her family when she first goes to college to accepting and even defending the New York mob boss Johnny "Sack" Sacrimoni to her fiancé in "Live Free or Die" (6.6).[14]

Conclusion

Both food and music encapsulate the need in Chase's fiction for social and cultural belonging. The music that characters listen to and the aromas of the dishes they eat speak to something visceral about identity, something that transcends words. Joel Fleishman has bagels flown in from New York, and Tony blames Indian food — not the meals at Artie Bucco's restaurant — for his food poisoning at the end of season two ("Funhouse," 2.13). These characters long for the familiar, and consuming regional/cultural food and music helps them assert their identity — as a New York Jew and as an Italian-American mobster in New Jersey, for example. Even Jim Rockford's penchant for fast food and the sound of his car parallel his itinerant nature and his place in a city crowded with fast-moving cars.

Like music, food is an essential part of the pacing in these shows. Sometimes, characters eat quickly and without enjoyment. At other times, they savor a glass of wine or the first bite of a meal — even Rockford partakes in an elegant meal once in a while. But *how* these characters eat always reveals something about their concerns, resentments, anxieties, and desires. *What* they eat also says a great deal about who they are in ethnic, social, familial, and professional terms. For Chase, the characters in his fiction tend to use food and music to negotiate and understand who they are. And ultimately, it reminds them of the broader forces that shape individual and communal identity.

Notes

1. Because of permission costs, the DVDs of *Northern Exposure* have substituted a number of musical pieces for those used in the original broadcasts. Many fans have

debated these changes on various websites and blogs. On one level, this debate is a testament to the powerful ways in which music helps shape one's memory of the visual. But it is also worth noting that some of the substitutions have been problematic. At the closing of "Survival of the Species" (4.11), for example, the production staff for the DVD has substituted an instrumental version of Leporello's aria "Madamina" from Mozart's *Don Giovanni* for Loreena McKennitt's "Tango to Evora." The text of this aria catalogues Don Giovanni's extraordinary sexual conquests, and this selection clearly undercuts the theme of female solidarity and community in the episode.

2. This interview was originally on the HBO website but has since been removed. It is also quoted in Kevin Fellezs's essay "Wiseguy Opera: Music for *Sopranos.*"

3. This translation comes from the liner notes for the Charles Dutoit recording of Fauré's *Pavane* in 1987 (London Records).

4. According to *The New Harvard Dictionary of Music,* a pavane or pavana is "a 16th-century court dance of Italian provenance. [...] The dance remained in vogue for most of the century, though its popularity abated somewhat in the last quarter of the period. It was restored and revitalized in idealized musical form" (615).

5. Jeannie Cusamano says this jokingly during a dinner party in the first season. She and her husband live next door to the Sopranos.

6. Tony and Carmela even discuss this in "Second Opinion" (3.7).

CARMELA: She's really learning [at Columbia]. [...] And if she passes us by —
TONY: If? She did that when she was fourteen.
CARMELA: Isn't that what you want for your kids?
TONY (sarcastically): No. I want them to be backwards and ignorant and sit around with their thumb up their ass.

7. This translation comes from the liner notes for the Cecilia Bartoli recording used in the episode. This recording was first released on her album *If You Love Me (Se tu m'ami): 18th-century Italian Songs* (1992). The translation for London Records is by Kenneth Chambers.

8. Certainly, the anguish of these women fits into one of Chase's broader goals with *The Sopranos:* "I didn't want to do a show about crime and punishment. I want to do a show about the crimes that people wreak on each other, psychic punishment, and psychic self-punishment. [...] I think if you watch *The Sopranos,* you're not seeing happy people there. [...] You're seeing largely tormented people" (Longworth 30–31). Both Tony and Carmela are tormented by the moral ambiguity of their choices. Tony seeks secular help (through Dr. Melfi and psychiatry), while Carmela yearns for spiritual guidance. But both of these avenues fail to inspire significant change. Tony and Carmela are stuck in a quagmire of crime, corruption, deception, and violence.

9. This sentiment returns in the final season when the mob is frustrated by its inability to shake down a similar chain in "Johnny Cakes" (6.8). Patsy, one of Tony's crew, laments: "It's over for the little guy. [...] What the fuck is happening to this neighborhood?" And in this same episode, Jamba Juice even buys one of Tony's properties — an old neighborhood poultry shop.

10. "What good is sitting alone in your room? Come hear the music play. Life is a cabaret, old chum. [...] Come to the cabaret. Come taste the wine. Come hear the band. Come blow a horn. Start celebrating. Right this way, your table's waiting."

11. Food also functions as an image for internal struggles in "Mr. Sandman" (5.12). In this episode, the Aurora Borealis is causing everyone in town to swap dreams — and the playfulness with dreams and psychotherapy here clearly bear the hallmarks of Chase's style. In this episode, Joel offers psychotherapy to Holling who suddenly finds himself unable to "stand the sight and smell of food." It begins with an aversion to milk and eggs on the morning that he is putting together a crib for his unborn child. As Holling

complains, "I can't eat anything." The therapy sessions, which include Maggie since she is having Holling's dreams of his father's cruel, harsh treatment of his son and wife, eventually enable Holling to come to terms with what it means to be a parent:

> Milk ... that's what started it all. Milk. [...] Mothers make milk. Milk is the very essence of motherhood. [...] My revulsion to milk ... that's the key, don't you think? [...] Pushing away milk, pushing away food, I was pushing her away. [...] I rejected her [my mother]. I thought she was weak because my father bullied and belittled her so. All this time I've been so fearful of becoming my father. But it doesn't have to be that way. No. I can be my mother. I can be kind and giving. I can be good to my child.

Food becomes an image for nurturing — of motherhood, the self, and family. It becomes an image for the kind of home that Holling wants to build.

12. For more on this, see Roseanne Giannini Quinn's "Mothers, Molls, and Misogynists: Resisting Italian American Womanhood in *The Sopranos*": "[In September 2001], representatives of the American Italian Defense Association (AIDA) were in a Chicago courtroom bringing forth a lawsuit against the producers and its pay-per-view network Home Box Office (HBO) for allegedly violating a dignity clause of the Illinois constitution. The suit, which was later dismissed by the presiding judge, presented an extensive argument that the program and its producers promoted and reinforced potentially damaging stereotypes of Italian Americans" (166).

13. Tony offers a similar lesson about Italian "history" to Anthony Junior in "Christopher" (4.3). As Native Americans protest Columbus Day, Tony, the rest of the mob, and other facets of the Italian-American community struggle to see Columbus and this holiday as a celebration of Italian heritage. "He discovered America is what he did," Tony tells A. J. "He was a brave Italian explorer. And in this house, Christopher Columbus is a hero. End of story."

14. Anthony Junior struggles with his identity as a Soprano and as an Italian American as well. In "Calling All Cars" (4.11), Carmela's father says to AJ during dinner: "You're not Italian if you don't like artichokes." AJ replies sarcastically: "I like rice ... maybe I'm Chinese." Here AJ rejects the ways in which food is associated with ethnicity. Like Meadow, he struggles for separation as he gets older, and by the sixth season, AJ can't escape being a Soprano — his friends and acquaintances at bar/club scene in New York primarily seem to spend time with him because his father is a mobster.

Works Cited

Anderson, E. N. *Everybody Eats: Understanding Food and Culture.* New York: New York University Press, 2005.

Chase, David. "Introduction." *The Sopranos: Selected Scripts fro Three Seasons.* New York: Warner Books, 2002: vii–x.

Fellezs, Kevin. "Wiseguy Opera: Music for *Sopranos.*" *This Thing of Ours: Investigating The Sopranos.* Ed. David Lavery. New York: Columbia University Press, 2002: 162–75.

Gabaccia, Donna R. *We Are What We Eat: Ethnic Food and the Making of Americans.* Cambridge, MA: Harvard University Press, 1998.

Lavery, David and Robert J. Thompson. "David Chase, *The Sopranos,* and Television Creativity." *This Thing of Ours: Investigating The Sopranos.* Ed. David Lavery. New York: Columbia University Press, 2002.

"Pavane." *The New Harvard Dictionary of Music.* Ed. Don Michael Randel. Cambridge, MA: Belknap Press, 1986.

Quinn, Roseanne Giannini. "Mothers, Molls, and Misogynists: Resisting Italian American Womanhood in *The Sopranos.*" *The Journal of American Culture.* 27.2 (June 2004): 166–174.

Rucker, Allen. *The Sopranos: A Family History.* New York: New Amsterdam Library, 2004.

Santos, Marlisa. "'Leave the Gun; Take the Cannoli': Food and Family in the Modern American Mafia Film." *Reel Food: Essays on Food and Film.* Ed. Anne L. Bower. New York: Routledge, 2004: 209–218.

"This Art's Kind of a Girly Thing": Art, Status, and Gender on *The Sopranos* and *Northern Exposure*

Kirstin Ringelberg

The first scene of the pilot episode of *The Sopranos* begins with Tony uncomfortably eyeing a work of art in his new psychiatrist's office. This encounter between the uneducated (but not unintelligent), hyper-masculine mob boss and a stylized, formalist work of art depicting a nude woman sets the tone for the whole series. Certainly there are things about the sculpture Tony surely "gets"—the perky breasts, for instance, and probably the role of "fine" art in such a chic setting.[1] But the look on his face suggests a limitation on his understanding—one that leaves little room for a visit to any psychiatrist, much less a strong, well-educated, female psychiatrist. This world of pseudo-modernist sculpture is not Tony's world; for all their money and power, in no episode do we see Tony and Carmela schmoozing with the Board of Trustees of the MoMA for some fundraising event or commenting with judicious approbation on the Zaha Hadid design for the new contemporary art museum in Rome. Yet despite this framing of the Sopranos, particularly Tony's lack of high-brow connoisseurship, the choice to start the pilot with an art encounter foreshadows the surprisingly regular and significant use of art in the series, as it appears in *Northern Exposure* perhaps more obviously.[2] In this essay, I will explore the role of art in these two shows—a role that is sometimes predictable but often complex, particularly given the deliberate framing of nearly all the main characters in both shows as uneducated in a traditional Ivy-League, "Great Masters" sense. In both shows, as in our own culture, a knowledge of and interest in art is equated with education and class superiority, so it is a useful tool in establishing such divisions among characters (and, on occasion, subverting them). But the creators of these series did not use art as a mere backdrop or tone-setter, as is so often the case in this supposedly visually "literate" culture of ours; to the delight of this art historian, there are deeper meanings established through the artworks and their makers in *The Sopranos* and *Northern Exposure* that are important to the larger understanding of the characters and their world.[3]

The way David Chase and his art directors and set dressers established the Soprano family as *nouveau riche*— all money and no taste — is masterful to the smallest detail. The restrained blond tones throughout their house, for example, are just those that might be recommended by an interior designer as a mark of subtle taste, but the materials and objects in which those tones are found are always just a little too ordinary. The use of plainly laminated pressboard furniture throughout the home shows a taste built on surface, not substance — image, not reality. If something can have gilded trim, it does, but that trim in such efflorescence begins to look merely brassy. For visual contrast, tune in to a re-run of *Sex in the City* and pay attention to Charlotte's apartments— dark wood, expensive fabrics, and the kind of subtle richness associated with "old money." The Sopranos are rich, but not rich enough; Carmela has just enough taste to put her above many of her circle, but Charlotte would immediately see the flaws in Carmela's taste.[4] The pitch-perfect interiors of the Soprano house of course required some references to classical art from the homeland, so I was prepared for the type of middle-to–High Renaissance painting that adorns the space above Tony and Carmela's bedroom dresser, to say nothing of the Ionic column that supports the television at the end of the bed. What is surprising, however, is the painting selected to serve as backdrop to the Soprano marital bed: *The Visitation* by Jacopo Carrucci da Pontormo (oil on wood panel, 1528-29).

What, you might ask, would be so surprising? The painting is by an Italian "master" from the 16th century, after all. It represents a subject not uncommon in Christian art: the moment when Saint Elizabeth, pregnant with John the Baptist, meets her cousin Mary, pregnant with Jesus (Luke 1:39–45). These things could certainly constitute a meeting of our expectations for a wealthy Italian-American Catholic family's decor. However, this particular choice, combined with its unusual presentation, is distinctive and clearly deliberate, even jarring. First of all, the original painting (this must be a copy, as we know the original hangs in the church of San Michele in Carmignano, near Florence) is from that brief stylistic period in art history known as Mannerism, in which artists took the "rules" of the recent High Renaissance (perfect proportions, clear organization of figures in rational space, subtle gradations of light and shade, harmonious colors) and bent them. Mannerism is deliberately a little weird, and intellectually so: by breaking the rules and still creating a successful work, the artist shows mastery of both the original, valued rules and the new, innovative style. Typical Mannerist works often include acrid, over-bold color palettes, figures compressed into space unnaturally, proportions extended to a physically dubious point. Pontormo's *Visitation* is a prime exemplar of the style. Along with the characteristics noted above, one of the most striking (and often commented-upon) aspects of the image is Pontormo's choice to have the two figures behind the Virgin and St. Elizabeth staring out at the viewer. Since the 15th century, the most typical way to represent anyone in the presence of the Virgin is to have him or her staring adoringly at her; this makes sense generally, as the painters and their patrons considered her the mother of God. In this painting, the Virgin is bearing the Christ child within her womb; she is essentially the embodiment of the coming of the Messiah, and thus all eyes should be upon her. In some such images, with which the artist would have been familiar, a peripheral figure might gesture out to the viewer, drawing him or her in to the scene with a physical gesture as if to say "look — here." Not only do Pontormo's onlookers ignore the titular visitation between the two women (and their fetuses), they stare disconcertingly out towards the viewer without any of the typical gestures of invitation to look or join in the scene. The Mannerist compression of space serves to amplify this experience, because these peripheral figures seem pressed upon Mary and Elizabeth in an uncomfortable way — we cannot ignore them to focus on the central story, nor could Mary and Elizabeth ignore such presences if the painting's space were to become "real." The painting's imagery is itself unusual, striking, and hardly typical fodder for home decoration.

Now to the placement of the work, first physically and then metaphorically: behind the bedstead of Tony and Carmela's bed. Not above it, not in place of it — *behind* it. The painting, which in its usual form is over 6 feet tall (202 cm × 156 cm), clearly could not be placed above the bedstead and still be shown in its entirety — the wall is not tall enough (itself a suggestion of class hierarchies, as tall ceilings are associated with more expensive and/or older houses). But it certainly demands comment that, rather than choose a different painting that would fit, or crop this painting and frame the cropped version, someone decided instead to make it appear as if 2/3 of this large painting is behind the bedstead. A close look reveals that in fact the painting's frame has been cut so that it is integrated into the bedstead.[5] To choose an unusual, even strikingly odd painting and then make its placement so deliberate clearly invites the television audience to consider its meaning in relation to the show.

What are the possible metaphorical interpretations of this choice — presumably made or approved by Carmela? As usual, there are several. Thinking about the subject of the image guides us in the direction of miracles, maternity, family ties, and the recognition of greatness. The importance of family connections is of course a clear thread throughout *The Sopranos*, where family ties make the difference between poverty and wealth, between life and death. The loving bond between Elizabeth and Mary is familial as well as based in the shared experience of a miraculous pregnancy. Both mothers, but particularly Mary, stand for the loving devotion necessary to any child, but particularly a child destined for great power and influence — a child whose power will ultimately leave him alone in a time of great need. The irony of this exemplary maternal devotion represented in Tony's bedroom, of course, is clear: Tony's mother certainly never cared for him as Mary and Elizabeth cared for their sons; it's hard to imagine Mary putting out a hit on Jesus. Tony's mother, doubtless a regular attendant at Mass, chose to ignore the *imitatio Mariae* that is expected of all good Catholic women — she does recognize her son's power and influence but finds these threatening to her own dominance. It is therefore unsurprising that in the episode "Proshai, Livushka" (3.2), the night Tony learns of his mother's death he is shown lying under the Pontormo, unable to sleep. The camera pans down steeply from a close-up of the painting to Tony's restless, troubled face — from the embrace of these adoring and serene mothers to a son whose own mother never showed such feelings.[6]

But Mary and Elizabeth meeting, and John the Baptist responding to Jesus, are seen in many more traditional images that could have been used as visual corollaries. First, why the choice of a Mannerist version of this scene? My description above might have alluded to a metaphoric connection: if Mannerists were marked by their ability to know the old rules but create new approaches to them, certainly this is also the position Tony finds himself in as he continually struggles to manipulate the traditionally accepted codes of his way of life in a new world. The more striking element of this particular image, however, is the audience — those witnesses/onlookers who look not toward the "action," but toward us. Both by looking (at us) and not looking (at the subject), these two figures remind us that looking is also the subject of this painting. What one sees and doesn't is the subject of any television show, given that it is a visual medium. In this painting, Tony might see ideal models for the kinds of relationships, maternal, familial, and power-based, that he has been socialized to value most — but that he largely lacks. The witnesses look out both to him and to us, as if to remind us that we need to look closely but not necessarily at the most obvious things. Indeed, in the first scene of the pilot, Tony looks intently and doesn't quite understand what the art is telling him.

In several episodes, art serves as a deliverer of messages, as a witness to Tony's feeling that things are not quite as they should be in his idealized vision. In "Denial, Anger, Acceptance" (1.3), the entire episode revolves around Tony's suspicion of the visual, particularly high art. Early in the episode, Tony is again waiting outside Dr. Melfi's office, but this time there is no sign of the nude sculpture.[7] Instead, Tony notices several impressionistic paintings of landscapes, including one depicting a barn that draws him in. Both he and we move closer, focusing in on the doorway of the barn. We see nothing unusual, but Tony claims later in Melfi's office to have seen a rotted-out tree that clearly disturbs him.[8] He angrily upbraids Melfi for having a "trick picture" meant to fool him. She establishes her difference from him in several ways — she selected the painting (from a "little gallery in Provincetown"), it doesn't disturb her, and she reads the image more accurately than Tony does. He, in turn, sees it as representative of her snooty intellectualism — an insult that reveals his lower status despite his greater power, both physically and in terms of influence. Tony can have people killed, but an impressionistic landscape is a threat. Later in the episode, we see the first full view of the Pontormo reproduction while Tony and Carmela talk in their bedroom. When Meadow's music grows too loud, Tony angrily bangs his fist on the image, ignoring it as both art and a sacred scene — it's just decoration to him, because it's not a "trick picture" — yet it is much trickier, as a picture, than Melfi's painting.

At his Russian girlfriend Irina's apartment in the same episode, Tony sees a David Hockney poster over her bed (note the same placement as his Pontormo). The camera first shows the whole poster, which depicts a modernist house's backyard and pool, an image typical of a certain portion of the British painter's oeuvre. Then it zooms in on a detail of the painted reflection in the fenestration of the house just behind a low director's chair placed on the patio. Again, Tony is somewhat troubled by what he sees in the details — and again, we see nothing unusual. He asks his *comare* what it means to her, and she replies: "Nothing, it just reminds me of David Hockey [sic]." This is a complex response. On one hand, she is aware of David Hockney and what is typical of his work, suggesting a greater awareness of fine art and taste than Tony has. On the other hand, however, she mispronounces the artist's name and the idea that it *reminds* her of him is confusing. She doesn't say "it is a David Hockney" or "I like David Hockney" or "it reminds me of California."

Clear differences in power are established when Tony's commissioned painting of himself toasting his racehorse, Pie-O-My, arrives after the horse's death ("Strong, Silent Type," 4.10). Unable to stomach the painting's reminder of his lost happiness with the horse, Tony orders Silvio to have the painting burned. As two underlings start to burn it, Paulie arrives and stops them: "Classy piece like this? Horse with the trees, wooden frame, 25 to 30 Gs at a minimum!" And then: "Be an honor to hang this picture at my house." A later scene in the episode shows Paulie hanging the portrait of Tony and the horse over his mantel, and after an initial satisfaction, Mr. Walnuts becomes troubled by Tony's unwavering gaze. He takes it to a frame shop (never a good sign in high art circles) and asks for someone to change the image to "Something classy [...] like a revolutionary war general. Napoleon and his horse. That kind of thing." The frame shop dealer suggests Tony is too fat to be Napoleon, and Paulie corrects him: "Not Napoleon exactly. *Like* Napoleon." The resulting painting actually shows Tony precisely as Napoleon — Tony in a Napoleonic uniform, but otherwise unchanged. Again, Paulie at first likes the painting, then gradually becomes unhinged at the constant gaze of his boss.[9] Throughout the episode, we see Paulie reemphasizing the notion of class; first by chastising the underlings for their lack of understanding of how classy the painting is, then by having it made even classier with the addition of historical referents. But we as the audience watch with the knowledge that the initial painting is less art than ego (despite its commissioning from a "real" artist who serves white wine in his studio in "Mergers & Acquisitions," 4.8), that the frame shop to which Paulie entrusts the improvements must be even lower on the high-art scale than the initial artist, and that Paulie's idea of "classy" art is one he has been socialized to see, not one he genuinely understands.

Tony finally finds art he's comfortable with in "Rat Pack" (5.02), when Jack Massarone, a snitch doing business with him, gives him a gift of a painting depicting Sammy Davis Jr., Frank Sinatra, and Dean Martin surrounded by Vegas iconography (the Sands marquee, a showgirl, four aces, a roulette wheel, dice, a bottle of wine, and a road sign for I-95 and 574). The painting is clearly intended to have a double meaning, as throughout the episode Tony considers it a symbol for his idealized vision of the Rat Pack as a happy, tightly knit group of undying friends; meanwhile, the man who gave it to him is selling him out to the Feds, and several other characters show their lack of loyalty in the episode. Surrounded by "rats," Tony dreams of the Rat Pack. Artistically, of course, we can go even deeper. When Tony first sees the painting, he says, "This is great! And I — I usually don't like modern art." Of course we can have a laugh at Tony's expense, because this is definitely not modern or fine art. Later in the episode, Tony gets drunk and puts the painting on the wall; not liking that placement, he moves it to the mantel in front of some tchotchkes. Looking at the other two framed images sitting on the mantel, an image of the Virgin and the classic American *Head of Christ* by Warner Sallman (1940) of blond, blue-eyed Jesus' head looking up, Tony flips them face down.[10] A contrast is established between the sacred images, however kitschy, and this image that is more sacred to Tony — loyalty among friends being placed above maternal love or religious devotion.

The power dynamics here deal not just with class or influence, but also with gender. In *The Sopranos*, the more difficult art (if there is any) is understood or embraced on some level primarily by women. It is Melfi's and Irina's art that unsettles Tony, and Carmela's that should. In "Amour Fou" (3.12), the episode begins with Carmela and Meadow meeting at the Metropolitan Museum of Art. They focus their viewing (as far as we are shown) in the rooms featuring Baroque European painting. Meadow instructs her mother on Paul Peter Rubens' propensity to depict the wives of wealthy merchants (clearly a stab at Carmela, who points out that Meadow's newfound educational gifts are not reflected in her grades), and Carmela stops short and begins to cry before Jusepe de Ribera's painting of the "*Mystical Marriage of Saint Catherine*" (entitled *The Holy Family with Saints Anne and Catherine of Alexandria*, oil on canvas, 1648). The Ribera is a convenient vehicle for Carmela to express remorse at her loss of innocence and increasing frustration with her marriage to Tony, as well as her feelings about the sanctity of maternity. Nonetheless, clear distinction is set up between the taste, knowledge, and leisure pursuits these women display and that of the male figures in the show. In fact, in the same episode Tony does have a moment of seeming art historical awareness when he describes his mistress Gloria's dark eyes staring at him as being "like a Spanish princess in one of those paintings, you know — a Goyim." The rest of the reference's acuity is lost in the final word's error (Tony should have said Goya), and then immediately followed up with an assertion that Tony's appeal for Gloria is probably his tough masculine heterosexuality. Furthermore, the pivotal pieces (in my view) are all of a type that in some way evokes gendered femininity: Melfi's nude sculpture, her Impressionistic landscapes, and the images of the Virgin and St. Elizabeth sharing their secret of childbirth or St. Catherine metaphorically (and chastely) marrying the infant Jesus. At his most comfortable with a picture one step away from an image of dogs playing poker, Tony wants his art to reflect his world: masculinist bravado and kitschy nostalgia for a clique of trustworthy pals. Paulie's revered general is "classier," but no less patriarchal in its meaning. Art in American culture is often linked with the feminine, particularly when it is being denigrated, and *The Sopranos* relives this idea that the "girly" images are tricky and artificial — not to be trusted much less loved and understood, like the women on the show.

Although for the most part the Sopranos all seem to share the same level of taste and artistic education, in "Everybody Hurts" (4.6), son AJ has a traumatic glimpse of his family's lack of class and status. An increasingly strong feeling that his new girlfriend Devin Pillsbury is his social superior is fully realized when he visits her house. Stunned to discover her parents have "real Picassos" while his family's claim to fame is merely Lladro, AJ decides he can't continue to date her. The twin themes of class superiority through art taste (this is, in fact, modern art — and real, not a copy) and emasculation through this power differential are made perfectly clear in this scene and AJ's inability to get beyond its implications.[11] The irony of a man feeling emasculated by a woman's possession of works by Picasso, famous for his representations of monstrous, threatening women as well as his dubious treatment of the actual women in his life, is doubtless lost on AJ, if not on the educated viewer.

Watching *The Sopranos* with an art history education allows certain viewers to recognize some of the artistic layers of the show, but it also allows them to maintain their own feelings of superiority as they watch people who may have more money and power. Many critiques of the show have primarily focused on whether or not it buys into negative, damaging stereotypes of Italian Americans as mobsters. Less has been said about how it consistently depicts these people as fundamentally *nouveau riche*, always clearly inferior in taste and education to those whose society they often emulate. Daughter Meadow, with her improved education, suggests a brighter future, but her artistic interests are more literary than visual, and her upbringing in a household where one 16th-century reproduction is overwhelmed by a sea of mediocrity doesn't bode well.

Northern Exposure, with its former Grosse Pointe and Manhattan denizens, logically contains both more accurate, educated references to high art and a more general acceptance of challenging avant-garde art. In fact, *Northern Exposure* functions somewhat as *The Sopranos'* mirror image — although many of the other characters are not traditionally well-educated, their folksy wisdom often includes knowledgeable high-art references as well as an acknowledgement (often lacking in arts institutions and academic circles) of the equally important art being created by local people. In Cicely, it is one's inner vision and the success in translating this to others that rates a work as successful — not how comfortably kitschy the work is.

In fact, in the first episode to feature art-making as a primary story arc, the one person in Cicely who seems to share Tony Soprano's troubled discomfort is Maurice Minnifield, the millionaire astronaut with otherwise high-brow tastes. Of course in both cases, art is something that, if it doesn't show a male hero on a horse, must be "girly"; and Tony and Maurice are both deeply fearful of any chink in their masculine armor. However, over the course of the series, even Maurice comes to appreciate some fairly avant-garde art, even if he remains suspicious of it.[12]

A primary source of much of the art discussion in *Northern Exposure* is due to Chris Stevens, Cicely's local radio D.J., resident philosopher, and occasional artist. I say occasional because Chris largely focuses his visual art skills on a single annual creation, putting more of his energy into philosophizing over the town's various happenings.[13] Two of the most significant art-referencing episodes are connected to each other both through titles and the subject to which the annual Stevens masterpiece responds: visual effects unique to the distant region in which the characters live. In "Aurora Borealis: A Fairy Tale for Big People" (1.8), we first see Chris' artistic endeavors. He builds a gigantic sculpture he calls *Aurora Borealis* during a full moon cycle. Showing no sense of selfish ownership over the work, Chris encourages his half-brother Bernard to work on it with him, and unveils it (as he does all later pieces) before the whole town. When they see it, everyone but Maurice loves it, oohing at the way the sculpture seems to abstractly represent the "real" atmospheric visual fireworks for which it is named. Maggie isn't sure she understands it but says she likes it. And Shelly, probably the most naïve and uneducated of the characters, clearly loves it. This episode paves the way for a fairly consistent treatment of art as a community experience, and one not dumbed down by the artist for ease of understanding. In "Northern Lights" (4.18), Chris again creates an annual sculpture for the entire town to enjoy, this time a cascading light sculpture that covers the facades of the town's main street during the darkest time of year. On this occasion, even Maurice enjoys the work, as does an itinerant "hobo" war veteran.

There are several consistencies in Chris' works in terms of style and approach. First of all, his pieces are nearly exclusively made from found objects he combines to create a new piece (he accurately describes his approach in 4.19 as "constructivist," meaning that he constructs his sculptures additively from parts to create a whole, rather than removing materials from a single object).[14] These parts often come from other people in town, and none seem to mind the hijacking of those parts, happy to contribute to the artistic project. Furthermore, the pieces are never realistic or representational in the traditional sense. Rather, Chris' work is consistently

avant-garde, pushing the boundaries of what the average *Sopranos* character would consider art. Although always avant-garde and constructivist, he
never creates two similar works in a row, an issue he discusses in "Northern Lights" when describing a sort of artist's block he's having: "Last year,
neo–Gothic ice palace, Lake Eagle. Year before that, metal cocoons. I took
an entire acre of spruce, and I wrapped it in tin foil."[15]

Also consistent is the support and knowledgeable response he receives
from the townspeople. In "Burning Down the House" (3.14), Chris decides
to do a performance piece, his only non-sculpture, by building a trebuchet
to fling a cow into the air. In the opening scene, Joel asks him if he understands that he will painfully kill the cow, and Chris defends his choice by
saying he intends to "create a pure moment." Joel responds: "I understand
the cathartic value of performance art. I was going to SoHo before it was
SoHo. [...] I was into Marilyn Jacovsky's inner landscapes before the Vorpal signed her. [...] But this...? A cow death?"[16] Although Joel is troubled by
the use of the cow, he is the only one in town who is, although later Chris
finds out from Ed that flinging a cow with a trebuchet has been done in the
Monty Python film *Holy Grail*. Becoming despondent, Chris rues the fact
that his idea was derivative, even if unintentionally: "Repetition. It's the
death of art." Maurice, of all people, persuades Chris to continue with his
vision, citing simultaneously Michelangelo Buonarroti's painting of the Sistine Chapel ceiling and fear of death in battle. Although Maurice maintains his manly anti-art stance, it is precisely manliness that is in question
for him with Chris' quitting: "This art's kind of a girly thing, Chris, but if
you don't want to lose your manhood completely you can't let this swallow
you up. Now I want you to go out there and fling something!"

This episode ends with the flinging of Maggie's piano, destroyed in a
house fire, and a speech by Chris in which he references Kierkegaard and
Descartes. Chris establishes himself not only as a constructivist and performance artist but as a process artist with his final statement: "It's not the
thing you fling, it's the fling itself." And his success impresses even Maurice, who wonders, "Well, I'll be!"

Chris is not the only visual artist in Cicely, and "Family Feud" (4.19)
revolves around Whirlwind family totem pole sculptor Leonard, who turns
the town upside down with his choices on the Raven clan totem he creates.
Choosing to depict one of the figures holding a fish, Leonard thus references an ongoing dispute between Raven and Bear clans about the true evolution of the Raven family ownership of a cannery. Leonard refuses to
change his totem pole, not wanting to compromise the work's integrity,
which he argues speaks through the materials and tells him what to sculpt.
Although Leonard, like Chris, is not academically trained as an artist, he is

revered throughout the community as a great artist whose work, like Chris', is unveiled in a town-wide gathering. Leonard is also shown to be art-historically knowledgeable, as when he and Chris discuss their work. Chris notes that Leonard is more "like Donatello [an early Renaissance sculptor] or [modernist sculptor Henry] Moore: one slip of the mallet and it's over." Leonard explains that he likes to reveal the essence of the figures trapped within the cedar, a statement which refers to a similar famous quotation from Michelangelo, and Chris immediately spots and names the reference. The artists share a respect for art ahead of compromise to please the viewing audience, so they come up with an alternative — a second totem that lacks the offending fish reference.

In *Northern Exposure*, we thus receive a quite different view of art, artists, and viewers than that presented by *The Sopranos*. The art we see is most often either avant-garde or Inuit, and in both cases that art is valued by most of the people in the community, whether they are educated and/or wealthy, or not. In fact, the art that is shown is thought in large part to be a community experience, both in the making (the parts and the stories come from everyone in town) and in the viewing (public unveilings are the norm). The only public unveiling of a somewhat kitschy representational work occurs in "Bumpy Road to Love" (3.1), when Maggie's commissioned bronze statue of her dead boyfriend is revealed. The realistic image, save for the somewhat incongruous propeller in the former pilot's hand, would make Paulie swoon, but it is an embarrassment to Maggie, who converses with Joel:

MAGGIE: You think it looks like a hood ornament.

JOEL: How'd you know?

MAGGIE: Because you would think a thing like that. And because, well, it does. It was supposed to be dignified and regal, and instead it looks like a....

JOEL: A hood ornament.

Although Maggie and Joel are probably the characters most likely to know what contemporary arts institutions would consider good art and also most likely to share those values, this is never established as a difference between them and the rest of the relatively uncultured townspeople. Instead, *Northern Exposure's* artistic knowledge is more democratic, allowing for intuitive sensibilities, open-minded appreciation, and a shared commitment to art as a natural part of daily life. Even Shelly, the teen beauty queen with a love of television shopping channels, comes around. In "Burning Down the House" (3.14), when she visits Chris' studio to see how the trebuchet is coming, Shelly tells him: "Wow! You can draw, too! I didn't even know what you were doing was art." Inquiring, from Chris' broad definition, if even slam dancing could be considered art, Shelly leaves the studio looking forward to the "transitory cow fling thing" she's going to get to watch.

Northern Exposure does not play as clearly into the gendered divide we find in The Sopranos, making fun of Maurice for seeing art as "girly" and establishing its most art-focused character, Chris, as a literal woman-magnet whose masculinity can be more flexible because his heteronormativity is never in doubt.[17] But again, the series toyed with such definitions of masculinity and femininity as part of its basic arc, with Maggie the airplane pilot (egad! how modern!) constantly tussling with her self-definition and Maurice occasionally raising the spectre of his potential queerness. With slightly more fluid views of masculinity and femininity, Northern Exposure presents a less rigid depiction of fine art as linked to tricky women. Or does it? Perhaps the most obvious reason why the linkage of art to the feminine doesn't occur so bluntly in Northern Exposure is because it can't: every artist represented in the show (even when we broaden our terms to include filmmakers, flute carvers, and illusionists) is a man. With men fundamentally in the driver's seat everywhere except Maggie's plane and Ruth-Anne's store, the realm of creativity is limited to masculine production. Recall that the one kitschy, bad artwork shown in the series is one commissioned by Maggie — her "hood ornament" memorial to her most recent dead boyfriend.

The enculturation of the various denizens of Cicely and New Jersey thus reverse our expectations: the rich, powerful family living a short drive from some of the most significant arts institutions in the country knows almost nothing about art, and that lack of knowledge is made perfectly clear, particularly to a knowledgeable audience. The more rag-tag group of misfits living in a tiny town in Alaska, on the other hand, are active participants in a thriving art community that includes fairly radical avant-garde art and local totem pole makers who easily reference Michelangelo. The deliberate quirkiness of Northern Exposure's characters, however, makes their manner of depiction fairly logical, as does the deliberate roughness of The Sopranos characters. Perhaps in the end we must acknowledge that it is open-mindedness, not wealth, training, or education, that makes a better art viewer. Both series deal in some way with a form of the American Dream, as the main character in each is a second- or third-generation immigrant with greater wealth, power, and prestige than their grandparents. Yet what is clearly established in both series is that money cannot buy taste or aesthetic understanding; rather, close attention to the visual is required. This is good news for television-watchers of all classes — but especially those without Fleischman money or Soprano money, much less Devin Pillsbury money.

However, in both series art is clearly presented as gendered, and in both cases the gendering favors the masculine. In The Sopranos, art is a tricky, destabilizing feminine force that must be controlled; it is connected to rats, *comares*, brainy Harvard women, and religion. In *Northern Exposure*, art is a wonderful, community-supported expression that is made exclusively by men. This type of gendering, as with the class concerns established previously, makes clear that in both series we can see identity issues being used in both stereotypical and non-stereotypical ways, but always in ways that clarify where the power is held: in the hands of the male main characters. Whether we see them as unfortunately in crisis or impressively intuitive, it is male characters who determine whether it matters to be art-knowledgeable or not, regardless of their class status or education. If it matters, it may be a "girly thing," but one to be mastered by tough men; if it doesn't, it's just a "trick picture," not to be trusted.

Notes

1. Although the work is doubtless intended to look like a modernist sculpture in the style of early modernist sculptors Aristide Maillol or Aleksandr Archipenko, the trained eye would see it less as stylized abstraction (and thus "fine" art serving a higher purpose) and more as a cheesy, too-perky variation on that theme.

2. Franco Ricci, in "Aesthetics and Ammunition: Art Imitating Life Imitating Art in *The Sopranos*" (in *Reading The Sopranos: Hit TV from HBO*, ed. David Lavery, New York: I. B. Tauris, 2006) makes a strong case for the relevance of looking at the art in that series that I won't duplicate here. Ricci's sweep is much broader than mine, briefly considering nearly all the artworks, both fine and popular, in the first five seasons of *The Sopranos*. Readers interested in the changing display of figurative sculptures in Melfi's office are particularly encouraged to read Ricci's essay.

3. Should the reader have moments of doubt, I wish to establish that as a writer and art historian I have an ambivalent relationship to issues of class superiority as established through knowledge of a given field. Art history itself is a largely elitist discipline, although this is slowly changing with the influx of practitioners devoted to the so-called "new" art history (now some 30 years old) informed by an emphasis on social context and identity politics. Ironically, even such class-conscious art history is often couched in the language of the über-educated and thus inaccessible to those outside of academia, itself a privileged arena. However, when speaking of "high" or "fine" art, I do not intend a personal valuation of art of a particular medium, origin, or cost. Rather, I am interested in the way such valuations are reified in popular culture, such that even as art history becomes increasingly less elitist, representations of it do not. I do not believe Tony is stupid because he doesn't have good taste in art, nor do I believe Chris Stevens of *NE* is particularly special because he does. But I do think how those attitudes are presented is telling of our culture — and how little some of our ideas on art have changed.

4. As does Henry James' Charlotte in *The Golden Bowl* (1904), wherein the difference between old (always European) money and taste and new American money and lack of taste is defined by the differing abilities of characters to see the flaw in the eponymous golden bowl. The suggestion that the American Dream mastered by mobsters and legitimate businessmen alike doesn't bring with it true taste has a very long history, and David Chase doesn't hesitate to walk in Henry James' shoes on that point.

5. The bedstead itself is a light Roman-arched structure with a prominent keystone

shape — fitting the Italianate theme and also emphasizing its structure and thereby reiterating the painting's odd placement.

6. Twice in the episode, Janice states that when she was younger she was known for her ability with the visual — an ability her mother did not nourish, but that Janice nonetheless feels flourished because of her mother's wisdom in not complimenting or supporting it.

7. This sculpture has been moved to Melfi's inner office, where it appears clearly behind her right side in 3.3. In "Second Opinion" (3.7), it has been moved back to the waiting room, where it is inspected impassively by Carmela, who tells Melfi later she loves the art "out there ... those country scenes? That statue is not my favorite." Carmela sees no trick pictures, and perhaps she dislikes the cheesy objectification of the female nude. But when she makes this criticism, Melfi shrugs as if to say, "You can't like everything" and Carmela seems to concur rather than get offended or try to argue her perspective as Tony does. Carmela is comfortable with art as a subjective taste in a way that Tony is not.

8. Later in the episode, Melfi calls him on the fact that there is no rotting tree in the painting. Again, her superior ability to interpret the paintings is pointed out.

9. Some internet chatter has suggested that Paulie's discomfort is due to his being an unrevealed snitch.

10. For more on the Sallman image, see David Morgan, *Icons of American Protestantism: The Art of Warner Sallman* (New Haven: Yale University Press, 1996).

11. If only his mother Carmela could have taught him about Pontormo — a more unusual and, in some ways, daring artistic choice — but perhaps the fact that it's a copy would still have the same effect.

12. Of course Maurice's sexuality is occasionally put into question, both invisibly for the viewer and visibly in his often overblown reactions to homosexuality (which are then usually defused by a somewhat unconvincing argument that he doesn't wish history to focus on sexuality over other forms of identity that signify "greatness").

13. In several episodes, Chris mentions that he feels his ultimate skill and interest is with words.

14. We are doubtless also being encouraged to make a link to Russian Constructivism, in which socio-politically motivated sculptors created large, often mobile sculptures out of metal; however, there are such significant divergences from their goals and outcomes that I don't wish to push that reading to include Chris' art. Most importantly, when the Russian avant-garde began their movement, gangly metal whirligigs meant to serve the workers were unknown and truly revolutionary. 70 years later, Chris can hardly claim to be staking out a new realm of useful proletariat dynamos for the small, independent, and generally proudly capitalist population of Cicely.

15. In this episode, he begins making a sculpture other than the light sculpture, but it isn't working for him. The sculpture he starts with is suspiciously akin in appearance to the Watts Towers in L.A., a famous work done by artist Simon Rhodia who, like Chris, had no formal training and made the work from found objects.

16. Marilyn Jacovsky is most well-known as the therapist/author of a mystery novel, *Irregulars* (New York: Permanent Press, 1999). She is almost completely unknown in the contemporary art world today. The Vorpal Gallery in SoHo was an active space in the 1980s and 1990s; interestingly, the word "vorpal," which hails initially from Lewis Carroll's poem *Jabberwocky* ("vorpal sword") has been used to describe the killer rabbit (or vorpal bunny) in the Monty Python film *Monty Python and The Holy Grail*.

17. The one hiccup in this presentation of Chris takes place only to be reaffirmed: Chris visits a monastery and falls in love with his Doppelgänger, a woman masquerading as a man so she can live a spiritual life without giving up her intense need for male companionship.

Narrative Ergonomics and the Functions of Feminine Space in *The Sopranos*

Susann Cokal

The Sopranos series opens with a shot of mafioso overlord Tony Soprano (James Gandolfini) caught between a woman's legs (pilot, "The Sopranos," 1.1). His round, fleshy face is staring forward, framed in a pair of shapely but greenish feminine gams that isolate him from the setting he occupies. He looks both puzzled and fascinated, and so is the viewer meant to be, until the camera moves enough to show that the legs belong to a bronze statue and that we are in the waiting room of some sort of professional's office: lawyer, accountant, doctor. The walls are paneled in wood, the chairs well cushioned, the magazines neatly arranged — a rather upscale professional's office at that. The camera pauses on a particularly fine pair of breasts before pulling back to show nearly the entire figure, which is posed in a manner both graceful and erotic. It's as out of place as, we will soon realize, Tony is.

Just as we've taken in the image, a door opens, and an attractive woman (Lorraine Bracco) calls Tony's name and invites him inside to sit down. She adjusts her glasses, looks at him expectantly, though not with the same open curiosity he showed toward the statue, and asks about his panic attack. He has gone to see a psychiatrist.

Kicking off the series with this sequence announces that women, or woman in general, will be an important framing device by which to understand Tony and his cohort, and that the series will use feminized spaces for defining and refining male characters. In this first sequence alone, women both confine Tony (tightly between the statue's legs) and allow him to expand (the therapist's invitation to speak). It is significant that the first woman shown is an artwork,[1] forever holding one pose: She is a construct that represents a frozen moment, a moment when any narrative in which she might have been participating has stopped. This narrative freezing will be typical of every feminized space in the series, as it enables a kind of reflection on Tony's larger life story. He stares at the statue in part to figure out why she is in the office, in part to figure out what she means, and most significantly to determine what she might mean to him — how she might fit into his own story.

On *The Sopranos*, the worst thing that a woman or man can be called is a cunt, but a cunt is also one of the best things to have. For men, it is a source of pleasure, and being able to command one is a sign of power; for a woman, it is the source of her power itself — however circumscribed that power, like all power, may turn out to be. (Tony's own power is somewhat limited, as his last name suggests: The only way a man can sing soprano is by being castrated at a young age.) Every goodfella needs one or preferably several women under him: some of them good girls, some not so good. They usually represent a momentary halt in the men's life narratives, a break from making money, forging alliances, and killing enemies; sex, therapy, and domesticity are the pauses that refresh. The men of the mob can move around their world fairly easily. Working under a boss such as Tony Soprano, each one in the system has a defined rank and job, but those jobs require (or allow) a wide range of activities: Some go into business for themselves (while giving a "taste" to the boss); others are regular "soldiers," performing routine errands and acts of violence at command; and most have some kind of domestic life shown onscreen. The majority also sample the girls at the strip club Bada Bing. They may guard their tongues a bit around the wives, but there is no space absolutely denied a male visitor.[2]

The women's world is less fluid. Most of those with whom Tony comes into contact have one role, associated with one kind of space. Aside from some transitional public areas such as restaurants and schools, there are three settings most often identified with and even dominated by females: Tony's home, run by his wife, Carmela (Edie Falco), who seems to spend most of her time in the kitchen; Dr. Jennifer Melfi's office, where Tony goes to analyze his problems in an often oblique way; and the Bada Bing strip club, where mostly naked girls gyrate on a stage usually kept in the shot's background. Each one of these settings serves a particular function in a series that uses space as ergonomically as Carmela's kitchen — that is, for maximum efficiency and viewerly ease of reference. The home represents Tony's emotional life, Dr. Melfi's office his intellectual processing of both professional and personal lives, and the Bada Bing a purely sexual outlet where women are only a backdrop to and temporary escape from the important male business at hand. Each of these spaces thus brings about a kind of comfort or release, yet each also introduces a set of problems that help structure the overarching story of a man struggling against what he sees as his (and his culture's) inevitable decline.[3]

As part of that struggle, and as a bit of a narcissist, Tony tends to view the women in his life in relation to himself, playing structured roles that should fit his expectations. When the show presents the women's point of view, as it does fairly often, we also see him in relation to them, as a moving force that disrupts the narratives they try to establish for themselves. In one of the series' earliest episodes, when Carmela expresses sorrow that she isn't a greater part of his life, Tony says, "Carm, you're not just *in* my life. You *are* my life" ("Pax Soprana," 1.6). It's a beautiful sentiment, but little that happens in the following years affirms it; it seems more likely that Tony is attempting to appease Carmela while molding her to a desired image. At the same time, we could reverse the terms of Tony's sentence and come up with a truism: *He* isn't just in Carmela's life; he *is* her life. So he would like to believe, anyway; he tries to think that he (and the home and children, which have been given to her by him) are enough life for her — to think that whatever story she might fashion for herself depends on him. And, in the male-dominated mob, it's true: When Tony lies near death in season six, Carmela begins to drop out of the system of respect and caretaking; as the men begin jockeying for Tony's position, they don't give her the money she's due — proving that without him, she wouldn't exist in this world ("Mayham," 6.3). And, in a neat reversal, he probably wouldn't recover if it weren't for her constant care and love.

As it is with Carmela, at least in Tony's mind, so should it go with the other women he encounters; he tries to enter their lives by entering their bodies, making his story their own, and letting his associates (and by extension the viewers) see them as his subordinates and his creations. Thus the series puts Tony between female legs again and again. But that space is not merely sexual: It's also for giving birth, and this duality complicates Tony's relationship to woman and to himself. Feminine space is both sacred and profane, an arena in which the modern-day gladiator has to prove himself in every episode. Tony demonstrates that he's a masterful cocksman, a real man, when he screws his mistresses or stuffs himself into a stripper's open mouth. Reimagining that space as a birth canal makes him feel often reverent, sometimes vulnerable, occasionally angry. That first shot, for example, emphasizes the roundness and pinkness of his head, which resembles a baby's; it shows he's vulnerable and open to change when he thinks about motherhood. Later, as he and Dr. Melfi unravel his relationship with his mother, the audience is forced to remember not only that Livia birthed him but also that psychiatric treatment is a kind of rebirth (in the DVD commentary, David Chase says the statue in the waiting room is called *Maternity*). Even when he's feuding with Carmela, he protects her from others' insults because she is the mother of his children. Sex may defile a woman, but its natural outcome, childbirth, sanctifies her again — and purifies the problematic space that she defines.

Whether she is sacred or defiled, each woman fits into an efficient, ergonomic system of references encoded in the few spaces identified with women; thus the house, office, and club streamline the series' storytelling by putting strict boundaries in place. Tony reinforces those boundaries any way he can, usually through his control of finances or, if even that fails, by wielding his sexuality as a weapon. But feminized space still helps define and drive the series' main narrative; even if the women themselves aren't accorded the power they might like to have, once entrenched, they do enable a certain form of storytelling. It's a move that's calculated to keep narrative flowing and to grant women a degree of subtle control, even as they submit to a system that tries to freeze them into statues.

Class, Morals, and "A Beautiful Home"

The home offers an efficient means of commenting on class, work, and masculinity. Though several critics have written of her as a feminist of sorts,[4] Carmela is a version of the Victorian angel in the house. She is the family's spiritual center, making a comfortable home for Tony, teaching the children morals and manners that her husband, who has inevitably been corrupted by the pressures of the outside world, cannot give them. As theorist Gwendolyn Wright points out, homes are metaphors, "suggesting and justifying social categories, values, and relations" (1); Carmela's interior design says everything about the Sopranos' history and aspirations. Decorated in hard-to-keep-clean pale colors, including off-white carpeting, this home positions the family in the upper middle class — but an arriviste version of that class: It reveals that its owners value money, comfort, televisual entertainment, and newness in all things. A large and showy McMansion, it boasts a formal dining room, a formal living room, and a great room where the family does most of its living. Visitors, particularly those with hostile or devious motives, frequently remark on the home that Carmela has created, as if this is the one comment to make about her: Gloria Trillo, Tony's mistress in season three, gives Carmela a ride home from the Mercedes dealership and says, "Nice house" ("Amour Fou," 3.12); the FBI agent who masquerades as Adriana's friend "Danielle" compliments her, "You have a beautiful home" ("For All Debts Public and Private," 4.1). Thus outsiders as well as insiders insist on identifying Carmela with the house and its appearance, thereby keeping her in her narrative place.

Carmela is associated not just with this house but with homes in general. She's genuinely interested in the open houses and housewarmings that she and Tony attend as a social matter of course. She has studied for a real estate license and tries to start her own business by building a spec house with her father (season 5).[5] When she becomes interested in Furio, the strongman Tony imports from Italy in season three, she channels her longing into giving him some home-decorating tips; and when she's depressed over Furio's sudden return to Italy, only Tony's offer of a beach house revives her ("Whitecaps," 4.13). The house is not really for sale, as it already has a buyer, but Tony exerts his influence to get the place for her, and Carmela perks up. It is ironic that this house helps her recover enough vigor to take a stand and demand a divorce when Irina violates her home with a phone call, as we'll see below.

The McMansion may be decorated by Carmela, but it is characterized to a large degree by Tony. He works hard to keep it and his family life in line with what his childhood trained him to expect. "Out there," he says, the world may be changing, "but in here it's 1954" ("Nobody Knows Anything," 1.11). Through his control on the purse strings, Tony tries to keep Carmela living in 1954, and she often seems content to do so. The 1950s were a time of conformity — and, following on World War II's relative empowerment of women in some jobs and the armed forces, of retrenching into older gender roles that kept women at home to care for the house and children. In the same era, technological innovations meant middle-class women had to spend less time cleaning and had more time for themselves; upper-class women still employed a maid, as Carmela is occasionally seen to do (for example, see "Denial, Anger, Acceptance," 1.3). Care for the house might be said to have replaced some care for the husband in her marriage; as she explains to Father Phil, "I could deal with the goomars— I knew I was better than them," and she has sometimes been grateful for the "masturbation" they provide for Tony while she is busy with the house and children ("Pax Soprana," 1.6).

It is Carmela's job to keep the entire home running smoothly, and thus in some sense it is all her space; but within the house there are certain places more closely identified with her than others. The great room where the camera lingers most often is a good example of the power dynamic within the family. A deliberately hybridized space, easily accessible from the echoing foyer, the room is a product of modernity, having become a popular feature in the 1970s and 1980s (thus, like the Sopranos themselves, it is fairly arriviste). This one combines a kitchen, an informal dining area, and an entertainment center with an enormous TV. Daphne Spain has written that spaces such as a great room bear witness to what we might call an egalitarian ideology: "Whereas Victorian housing reflected a concern that each function and member of the household have a designated place, housing designs of the late twentieth century reflect the concern that no function or family member be limited to a particular space" (132). She also maintains that "Architects did not set out to create more egalitarian environments specifically for women, yet the twentieth century was characterized by a gradual reduction in sexual spatial segregation and in gender stratification" (134). The hybridized space has inadvertently promoted gender equality and a kind of democracy within the family. But, in somewhat Victorian fashion, the Sopranos establish a compartmentalization within the great room, and the division is largely based on gender: The kitchen belongs to Carmela, the TV area primarily to Tony. When we see Carmela at home, she's usually involved in some kind of cleaning or cooking in the great room area — wiping down a counter, plumping a pillow, mixing up a sauce in what scholars love to point out is an ergonomic kitchen. That ergonomic aspect emphasizes Carmela's practicality; she may be bound to a kitchen, but it is one in which each cubic inch fulfills a function and her movements are conserved. It buys her time, as similar innovations did for the women of 1954.

Carmela's kitchen is actually quite small, occupying a surprisingly tight corner of the flowing great room. It is hard to imagine how the cabinetry on view can hold enough supplies for the elaborate Italian meals Carmela is constantly producing; perhaps she shops for groceries as often as her Italian forebears did in the era before preservatives and refrigeration. And the refrigerator is, even more than the stove, the *locus amoenus* of the Soprano household. Tony enjoys rooting through it to see what Carmela has left for him there (and his posture before it often looks comically sexualized). Next to his bulk, even a refrigerator looks small — and represents a space that, unlike the giant meat lockers at Satriale's, he will never be able to enter entirely. Instead, he can only attempt to consume everything within Carmela's refrigerator, to transfer the contents of that space into his own body. Perhaps afraid of that reverse-birth/death process as figured in the MRI, he expands his own body in compensation. It is fitting, then, that when they fight over Irina's phone call, Tony tries to get into the fridge and Carmela slams the door shut, cutting him off from the source of pleasure.

Once her space becomes ergonomic, the angel in the house may turn her thoughts away from the family's moral center and toward the outside world — but the narrative of *The Sopranos*, particularly the part controlled by Tony himself, keeps placing her back in the domestic sphere. The kitchen's efficiency gives Carmela time to devote to other activities at her church, the children's schools, and later (and somewhat disastrously) to property development. Following a separation in season five, Carmela agrees to reconcile if Tony not only gives up the goomars but also buys her a $600,000 vacant lot and helps finance a spec house she wants to build on it.[6] He agrees — but in season six, he repeatedly "forgets" to grease the right palms and the project is shut down. In the same episode, a senile Uncle Junior shoots Tony in (surprise!) Junior's kitchen ("Members Only," 6.1) and Carmela is thrust into the role of angel again — watching over comatose Tony's hospital bed, then his recovery at home. The spec house becomes unimportant when the family home claims her again. It is the one space in which she can control a narrative, the story of Tony's healing; but it is a narrative that is assigned by her culturally prescribed role. She, like her space, has a function to fulfill.

The function that Carmela's space serves in the series as a whole is a repetitious reinscription into a more standard American narrative of domesticity. Tony breaks with the law, with America's official cultural script, each week. By coming home, he seeks to escape the corrupting influence of the outside world and his work; he becomes like other TV-watching, big-dinner-eating workingmen. He tries to avoid talking about crime explicitly — in part from well-founded fears that the house is bugged — and if he needs to talk business, he brings visitors down to the basement, an unfinished domestic space used mostly for storage and washing dirty laundry. (The FBI will bug this basement but never get usable information from it, as Tony is careful to turn on noisy air conditioners to mask his conversations; the space remains doggedly domestic.) Moreover, as critics Kim Akass and Janet McCabe point out, "it is only through Carmela's understated but dominant position within the home that Tony's masculinity is determined as problematic; she defines the appropriate gendered behaviors" ("Beyond the Bada Bing!" 150). Their belief in Carmela's powers over Tony may be a bit too sanguine, but they make an excellent point about the arc that Tony is expected to complete and repeat — taming his more corrupt masculine impulses and sinking into feminized domestic space, inscribing himself into a more standard American narrative of homecoming that is constantly resisted through marital tensions and Carmela's desire for something outside the home.

A Look at All the Angles: Dr. Melfi's Office

Dr. Melfi's office offers Tony another kind of homecoming. It uses ergonomics to make the patient comfortable, if not the therapist, and gives visual clues that reinforce her authority while nudging the patient toward an intellectual processing of emotional material. It also establishes her as the kind of class figure Carmela might like to be, for the decor is chic, tasteful, and understated, even more so in the therapy room itself than in the waiting room we see in the first scene of the pilot. This setting presents Dr. Melfi as a no-nonsense but elegant person of refined tastes and mental acuity, and the space itself as one of self-evaluation and reflection. As Melfi enables and inspires Tony to tell his story, she also tries to make him think about what he's telling her and perhaps change the course that the narrative he's projected for himself might take.

The visual shorthand is perhaps stronger in this setting than in any other in the series. The office contains one light source, the window in front of which Melfi sits: she is there to train illumination into the narrative Tony provides. The slats of the vertical blinds in front of that window are always open, but they remind us that one can choose to close off illumination at will; they also perhaps recall the bars of a typical jail cell — the space Tony keeps trying not to occupy. Shiny surfaces reflect that light and invite Tony both to reflect on himself and to penetrate beneath the surface reflection: Dr. Melfi's chic rimless glasses, the glass over her diplomas, the clear glass of the round coffee table, the gleaming metal tissue dispenser. The clear surfaces suggest that Tony should look first at his reflection, then beneath the glass, where the real insights are. The opacity of the tissue box implies that someone who stops at reflection, feels sorry for himself, and weeps will never achieve complete illumination.

Melfi's space contains a number of angles and vertical lines that impute to her a kind of narrative authority perhaps even greater than what's conferred by that diploma from Rutgers. Tony sits in a padded armchair with rounded lines, but she takes a straight chair, upholstered but squared, with exposed wooden arms set at a needle-sharp acute angle. It is clear that she will be incisive, that she will hold her spine straight even as she crosses her shapely legs or, occasionally, giggles at one of Tony's jokes. In contrast to those sharp points, the room is set up something like a brain or womb; its walls appear to curve and cradle the two occupants, creating an enclosed and safe-feeling place where the main action of Tony's life pauses while he recaps and analyzes. The wood paneling is medium dark, broken by slots for recessed shelves on which books' spines stand up as straight as Dr. Melfi's morals. This invisible support integrates the books into the space as deeply and seamlessly as Dr. Melfi's education has been integrated into her life; it hints, also, at the kind of discipline that patients should adapt (and that Tony, with his explosive personality, never quite manages). In the office, Melfi speaks slowly and deliberately, as if reading from one of those books; she doesn't stumble over a word or burst into an expletive, as she sometimes does in her private life. Tony sometimes accuses her of being cold and rigid; perhaps he is reading the space more than he's reading her.

When she asks Tony about his first panic attack, Dr. Melfi deploys her education and mental acuity with deceptive simplicity. The question puts the series' narratives into motion and opens up its story space; the entire pilot is told as flashbacks, an idea that Chase considered and then rejected for the series as a whole. It is Melfi's job to ask questions that unfreeze Tony's preestablished ideas and help him establish relationships to the men and women in his circle, as well as to the mainstream and mob cultures that have produced him. It is a job crucial to the ergonomic narrative arrangement: If there were no Melfi, there would be no *Sopranos*, for Tony would continue to bottle up his feelings with Gary Cooper–like stoicism, and the show would stop at the shiny metal surface of a gun or knife, the crimes themselves, rather than the tissue box and the penetrable reflections in the office. Even when Tony quits analysis, or when he doesn't step into the office for an episode or two, he refers to his therapy by using phrases Melfi taught him or applying ideas she introduced. We are always aware of that office pressing on the narrative; we always expect Tony to return to the space of storytelling and reflecting, and so he never truly leaves it.

The pressures of business may be directly responsible for Tony's first panic attack, but over the next six seasons his therapeutic work with Melfi shows that the roots of his malaise go much deeper, even as far back as the 1950s: his relationships with his father and mother, his daughter and son, his wife, and his many mistresses and casual partners. The circular office with its jagged angles is thus a kind of reverse-birth canal, leading him into his past as well as deeper into his self. It's a journey he may resist — and he certainly resists some of Melfi's interpretations of it — but one that is also a conduit, for the viewer, into other parts of Tony's life. Psychiatric treatment's status as rebirth is made explicit through a dream sequence in season five: When Tony dreams that he tells his psychiatrist (actually his mistress Gloria Trillo, whom he first met in Melfi's office) that "what happens in here" is like "taking a shit," Gloria/Melfi says, "I prefer to think of it more like childbirth" ("The Test Dream," 5.11). Tony's interpretation, of course, brings to mind yet another orifice in the human body, one that allows men as well as women to bring something forth — something that produces relief but is itself of dubious value. Tony cannot be reborn on his own; he needs Melfi and her office to enable to process.

It is interesting that, early in season two, Tony's crimes put Melfi out of her space. She has to go undercover, meeting patients in a motel, because he's warned her that their association has put both of them in danger. That move indicates that, once he has entered her space, it will be branded by him; he may be killed, and she will be banished, if not killed herself. American culture and the show itself associates motels with sleazy sexuality and cheap hookups; she is in some sense reduced to sharing status with prostitutes, always a danger for the women of *The Sopranos*.

It is perhaps ironic that the office space identified so closely with an intelligent, empowered woman should also bear signs of 1954. The furniture, even that glass coffee table and acute-armed chair, bears a distinct stamp of the style called mid-century modern, which has become trendy again in recent years. Its clean lines and angles are as distinctive as the more exuberant geometry of Art Deco was, and they point again to the post–World War II era of conformity, retraditionalized gender roles, and rigid morality. It is a functional style requiring little dusting. Visually, Melfi's office hints that although she may be a modern woman, she will not be able to help Tony get beyond his mid-century modern ideas. Even at his most emotionally vulnerable, even after years of illuminating therapy, he'll still look longingly when he sees a Gary Cooper movie playing on a TV.[7]

A Backroom and a Stage: The Bada Bing

The series may present the doctor's office largely as a narrative pause for reflection and refreshment, and Tony may see it that way sometimes; but for true relaxation, it's necessary to go someplace where neither intellectual nor emotional activity, therapy nor domesticity, is the order of the day. There is one female-identified space that is all about sex: the Bada Bing strip club, run by Tony's consigliore Silvio Dante (Steven Van Zandt). The sign outside shows a naked woman arcing backward, overcome by the enormity of the exclamation point that emphasizes the club's name — a visual representation of the way a phallus overwhelms a woman, or a shock overwhelms a TV viewer.

Paul Levinson remarks that the strip club performs an important function for the series; as a major meeting place, he writes, it provides a "brilliant" justification for putting nudity onscreen (28). That nudity is usually kept in the background, and I'd say that within the series' ergonomic divisions of space, justifying nudity is perhaps the least important of the Bing's functions — after all, we see plenty of Tony's mistresses half-naked, Adriana

(Drea di Matteo) can always be counted on for an underwear shot, and even Carmela strides starkers across the screen after finally having sex with a new man (AJ's school counselor, who later accuses Carmela of using her "pussy" to manipulate him into helping her son ["Sentimental Education," 5.6]). The Bing's more important function is to provide or imply another sort of pause, to restore old gender hierarchies.

The Bing is a space truly out of time, an apparent counterpoint to the house and the doctor's office — except that it, too, could have teleported out of 1954. The venue probably hasn't changed much since the days of Tony's father: The bar/stage area appears grimy, with grainy searchlights trained on the naked bodies onstage, darkness everywhere else. The backroom in which Tony and his associates conduct their business is more private but no more clean and certainly no more modern; it holds a table, some filing cabinets, a messy desk, a checkerboard stained-glass window, and some pictures of naked or near-naked women on the walls. It doesn't look too different from the backroom at Satriale's pork store, emphasizing that the girls in this feminized space have the status of meat. When the meat comes backstage into the business area, it is to be consumed, most often in the subservient position of fellatio. This is a place of business or businesslike pleasure, not emotion or soul-searching.

Like any "gentlemen's club," the Bada Bing does contain a set of narratives of its own, repetitive ones that play out like the loops of old-time pornography stores. In one of the oldest mini-storylines imaginable, the dancers are there to seduce and tantalize. Showing sporadic energy at best, their gyrations and twirlings onstage and their casual toplessness while drinking with customers on the floor are signs of narrative exhaustion, a sense that the same story has been told over and over. It is an exhaustion that we might associate with the classic gangster movies to which the men delight in referring and quoting. The strippers' enactments are also boring; few of the made men actually watch the girls, rendering them truly a backdrop.

Those tired dancing girls are a type against which the more complex women are defined. Women such as Carmela and Dr. Melfi refuse to become exclusively sexual beings, but the Bing girls know that's their role and they play it; their passivity and willingness to occupy a background highlights the other women's more active narrative function, intensifying their roles by contrast.

Cindy Donatelli and Sharon Alward have a somewhat different opinion, suggesting that the Bing girls get a visual treatment is more empowering than the other women's: "Cunts that are publicly on display and are moneymakers are the only cunts who are granted a degree of autonomy that breaks free of the multiple burdens of 'family.' These women enjoy a range of camera angles which are closed off to the Soprano women, who are regularly shot in over-the-shoulder sequences" (70). Donatelli and Alward acknowledge that the dancers' fragmented bodies (we frequently see them without heads) and the lack of focus in their shots guarantees their anonymity. A strange kind of autonomy, this: It still depends on the men's desire to look at the female bodies and watch the old narrative replayed, but the mere fact that they are being looked at differently doesn't mean they're being looked at better, or even in the way they would want to be seen. Donatelli and Alward further suggest that the Bing girls triumph over the series' well-developed characters in the age-old beauty competition particular to women (71). It may be true that the other women would like to be considered as arousing as the dancers, but as we'll see below, the major female characters show a repeated desire for more narrative inventiveness and control than the dancers are allowed. Each one is, like the dancers, working within a small space in order to win herself a story.

"You Disrespect This Place": Ergonomic Boundaries

Thus the women of the series, and the spaces they occupy, are typed according to function, as a handy limited visual and emotional set of references telling us what Tony and the larger narrative need at a given moment. This does not mean that they won't step outside of their prescribed roles — in fact, such is the stuff of narrative, and there would be no story if they didn't act against type, if they simply accepted the limitations Tony attempts to impose when he tells Dr. Melfi, "I'm a man. You're a woman. End of story" ("Pax Soprana," 1.6.). Melfi is a psychiatrist precisely because she refuses to be categorized in a way traditional to Tony's world. As Regina Barreca puts it, "the women in Sopranoland are types who do not run to type. While they occupy familiar narrative positions around the male characters, and while they look exactly as you think they would, they do not talk, feel, or believe the way we anticipate" (36). The series may keep putting them back in their places, but they keep struggling against the system that identifies space with function, gender with role.

Some of the women cross from one physical or metaphorical space to another, often endangering Tony's shaky control of his own life narrative — while again demonstrating the women's ultimate inability to control their own stories directly. Tony does all he can to keep the spaces and aspects of his life compartmentalized: In season two, for example, a stripper called Tracee tries to make Tony into a father figure. He puts her in her place by having her give him a blow job ("University," 3.6). And as he says to his accountant in season four, "I'm supposed to make the money, [Carmela] takes care of the house. That's the way it should be. Carmela's a smart woman"—but, the episode shows, as a woman she still doesn't have a right to any control over the family finances ("Pie O My," 4.5). When they're facing divorce, Tony tells his friends that the house is more his than hers: "I paid for it" ("Whitecaps," 4.13). In short, she gets to take care of the house and decorate it as she pleases, but she is denied a larger say in the life of a family in which power is expressed in terms of dollars earned and distributed. Her attempts to make money are an incursion into Tony's territory, and he'll do all he can to keep her in the McMansion.

It's not just Tony who feels uncomfortable at seeing the assorted parts of his life overlap; he seems to have good reason to compartmentalize. When Dr. Melfi calls to cancel an appointment in season 1, Carmela answers the phone; she finally realizes Tony is seeing a female psychiatrist rather than a man, and she becomes furious ("College," 1.5). Dr. Melfi's voice has penetrated the sanctum of Carmela's home, and that penetration is problematic because she is "a girl"—a female overstepping the boundaries that a tacit pact has put in place. The innocent phone call makes Carmela realize that she herself is not, as she explains in the next episode, the only woman in Tony's life; or perhaps it is that she is not the only woman who plays more than a sexual role for him. Carmela envies Melfi's ability "to help you. To be a sort of salvation to you" ("Pax Soprana," 1.6). The angel cannot function with competition any better than she can without a house.

Two seasons later, Carmela steps into Dr. Melfi's space when she and Tony go in for couples counseling. At first Carmela is as uncomfortable with her own crossover as she is with Melfi's; she laughs ruefully and says, "Honestly, if you'd told me five years ago I would be sitting here today..." ("Another Toothpick," 3.5). She is uneasy not just at seeing a therapist (her religion has made her comfortable with confession, and she encourages Tony's therapy) but at seeing *Tony's* therapist. Melfi, however, appears to feel quite at ease with the overlap — because she is a professional who does not allow herself to get emotionally involved with a patient, certainly not to enter into a competition with his wife. Two episodes later, Carmela has an appointment with Melfi by herself. After Carmela complains about Tony and cries a little, Melfi shuts down her attempt at inscribing that room with her own narrative; Melfi says she can't treat Carmela because Tony is her patient, but she can give a referral to "a colleague in Livingston. An old teacher of mine" ("Second Opinion," 3.7).[8] Carmela is shunted off to an office far removed from Melfi's space.

When Carmela finally does decide to seek divorce, it's not because the Livingston psychiatrist has told her to, nor is it because of her unfulfilled (but not unrequited) love for Furio. It's because Tony's former goomar refuses to stay in her place. She calls the house and speaks to Carmela directly. "Is this Mrs. Soprano?" asks Irina. "I used to fuck your husband" ("Whitecaps," 4.13). Finally, Carmela snaps. Manlike, she threatens to kill Irina if she calls again, then begins throwing Tony's belongings out of the house that is, by now, an extension of her own body. Coming home, Tony drives over his own golf clubs—an excellent image of self-castration — then finds that Carmela has shut herself in the master bedroom, redefining the space where she used to sleep with him as uniquely her own. He has to knock on the bedroom door and ask what he did wrong.

When a woman either oversteps the boundaries of her own space or refuses to let Tony in for the kind of pause he desires, he tends to react in an absolutely physical way—thereby divorcing space from its metaphoric associations and converting it into a physical entity. He uses his considerable bulk and physical power for sexual dominance, so that each one of these narrative spaces becomes, at one time or another, as sexualized as the Bada Bing. A sexual object is, in his world, an easy one to control; if a woman needs a bit of discipline, Tony has just the stick to do it with. Thus he may identify Carmela with home, comfort, and mothering for his children, but when they fight he becomes physically violent and often takes a sexualized posture in relationship to her. Thus when Carmela explains why she's throwing him out of the house and filing for divorce, their argument devolves into a physical fight in which he bends her over the counter in a decidedly sexual position until she says, "I don't want you in my bed anymore. The thought of it makes me sick" ("Whitecaps," 4.13). Whatever his flaws, Tony has not been significantly violent toward Carmela before; Irina's transgression of the women's spatial boundaries has taken away some of Carmela's identity, and at that moment, whether in bedroom or kitchen, she becomes all body, like a stripper: expendable, physically punishable.

In a generous mood, or before receiving an absolute refusal, Tony may offer a few flowers or a diamond bracelet to ease the way. The gentle wooing is, of course, a less violent version of the near-rapes with which he tries to subdue his women. In such a mood, he plies Carmela with extravagant bouquets and kisses while insisting she can't make the financial investments she wants; in season two, after telling Dr. Melfi he dreamed he "fucked your brains out" ("Funhouse," 2.13), he plies her with compliments and says he's willing to stop therapy if she'll take him on as a boyfriend. The courtship stops if a woman refuses to let sex put her in her place: When Dr. Melfi rejects his advances, citing his occupation as a reason, Tony shouts, "Fuck you!" and "Fucking cunt!" ("Two Tonys," 5.1), becoming as verbally aggressive as he gets with his male underlings. By so doing, he brings their professional relationship back to a point it reached in season one, when Melfi charged him for a missed appointment. Tony threw the cash down, telling her, "I don't appreciate pouring my heart out to a fucking callgirl" and that she can take the money and "Stick it up your ass" ("The Legend of Tennessee Moltisanti," 1.8). He will retain the thought of Melfi as a callgirl and recall it as necessary, when he needs to feel he has more control over his life and its story. Every woman can be reduced to a cunt, and every space can become a Bada Bing, simply by activating the mental pole dance and reenacting an old sexual story.

A mostly younger generation of women attempts to step out of circumscribed roles and spaces and have it all, and they usually meet dramatic and violent ends. An older woman named Lorraine figures as a cautionary tale early in the fifth season. Tony's former partner in casual sex, she's now a collector who refuses to "kick up" to Johnny Sacks. We never see her as a functional, independent businesswoman, however; even her most masculine activities become sexualized as soon as they're presented. When her troubles start, she offers to fellate "all you guys" who have come to punish her ("Where's Johnny?," 5.3). A little later in the episode, Johnny calls her a "cunt" who has whacked a lot of men; there's never "enough body count for Lorraine." This may mean she's a killer, but metaphorically, it seems her cunt, not her gun, craves men's bodies. She's killed at home upon getting out of the shower, her rolls of middle-aged flesh flapping as she runs toward her younger lover ("All Happy Families," 5.4).

Others who attempt to guide their own narratives, blend roles, and have it all include Janice, who may be older but who lives her life as if eternally, and dysfunctionally, young; Meadow, who studies law, volunteers at a legal aid office, and cooks fabulous dinners in her new apartment; and Adriana. Long of limb and big of hair, with a body as curvaceous and firm as a Barbie doll's, Adriana is the series' official hottie. She shows no interest in men other than Christopher, however, and wants nothing more than to be his wife; she's happy to make him postcoital or post-argument eggs. Yet she doesn't deny her ancillary desires: She wants to be big in the music business, and she opens up a mob-financed nightclub called the Crazy Horse. The club name may echo that of a Parisian topless revue, and Adriana certainly puts her body on vivid display there; but she also handles the books, bosses the staff, and is genuinely in charge — subservient only when Tony and his crew show up needing her backroom and some drinks. So, although certain gender hierarchies prevail, Adriana has taken woman a step away from the Bing and the kitchen, into a more independent and rounded life.

But when the mobsters punish Adriana for overstepping bounds, they do so through a symbolic connection to the Bing. Toward the end of the fifth season ("Long Term Parking," 5.12), the FBI agents who have been pumping Adriana for information discover that she's covered up a non-mob murder at the Crazy Horse (essentially removing traces of masculine crime from her club). The best deal she can cut means telling Christopher about her yearlong involvement and asking him to enter the Witness Protection Program with her — to go into hiding for a woman's sake, essentially to enter a woman's space and be reborn as a civilian. There is only one thing to do, and we saw it happen to Big Pussy in season two: the squealer gets whacked. Adriana hasn't been privy to as many secrets as Big Pussy, but she has broken the rules and violated the mob code that makes any place in which business is discussed sacrosanct.

Tony delegates the responsibility to Silvio, who runs the Bada Bing and who disciplined Tracee when she came in late to work (though we rarely see him committing violence against men). This choice effectively makes Adriana into one of the bodies at the strip club, one of the women who fall under Silvio's control. Naively believing Christopher to be in the hospital after a suicide, and looking much older and more haggard after bouts with colitis and Christopher's angry fists, she gets into Silvio's car and rides with him into a forest — a place where little that's good ever happens in a gangster narrative. By the time she realizes what's been planned for her, Silvio is already dragging her out of the car and (in an ironic birth image) into the open, calling her a "fucking cunt" through that snarling heavy lip. The cunt meets Pussy's fate on the forest floor. Soon thereafter, we're back at the Bing, where Christopher is watching *The Three Amigos* in the backroom and using heroin to get over his heroine. The only way to cope with the loss of a cunt is to return to the business where cunts are kept in their places.

Adriana's symbolic rebirth as a Bing girl, and a dead one, alters the meaning of the forest as a space. The sylvan setting (and the name Silvio means "of the forest") has been used before as a place to kill or hide a corpse, and it is impossible to see the forest in this show without memories of the episode "Pine Barrens" (3.11) and the film *Miller's Crossing*; Adriana's execution reinforces that easily referenced identity. But this episode also complicates the now-feminized, Bing-ified site of violence when it shows first Tony, then Carmela, walking through woods that we naturally associate with the killing. It turns out, however, that these are not Adriana's woods; they belong to the vacant lot that Carmela wants Tony to buy for her so she can build her spec house: Once an overstepping woman has been reduced to a cunt and killed off, space is ready for domestication. As the camera pulls away and the music swells, we can only hope that Carmela's attempt at starting a business leads to more happiness than Adriana's has done ... and feel fairly sure that those hopes will prove unfounded.

"You Are *My Life":*
Feminine Space and Narrative Control

Because the feminized spaces represent pauses in the gangster master-narrative, some women are accorded a certain power. Using their own command of space, and sometimes their bodies, they might alter the course of those narratives, and they certainly evaluate Tony and his stories, determining what validity they should be accorded. This power is limited, and only certain women have it. Dr. Melfi and, to a lesser extent, Carmela manage to elicit narrative from Tony, and by asking questions and interpreting situations, using the head and the heart, they gain some power — though their alterations do not register strongly in the series' overarching system of plot arcs.

Let's start with the narratively disenfranchised, those who are purely cunt from start to finish. The women in the Bada Bing get no input, narrative or otherwise — they are only put into and put upon. As a backdrop to the main, masculine action, they might be present when Tony gets bad news; they might even interrupt the repetitive narrative of their tantalizing dances to come over and listen to his side of the phone conversation — but when one of them asks, "Is your mom okay?," Tony leaves without answering ("46 Long," 1.2). The Bada Bing girls have no right to guide his narrative, and they have no right to demand narrative from him; they are outside the story.

Even Tracee, the stripper and single mother who feels Tony has taken her under his wing, is just a body whose potential narrative he refuses. When she bakes him a loaf of date-nut bread, he tells her they have an "employer-employee relationship" and he has a family who will give him gifts ("University," 3.6). Later in that episode, Tracee and Ralph Cifaretto have an argument, and he beats her to death (her last words are "Does it make you feel good? Do you feel like a man?"); what bothers Tony most about the killing is, as he says to Ralph, "You fuckin' disrespect this place." It is the place, now defined as a space of masculine bonding, that matters, not the female bodies who facilitate the bonding. When Dr. Melfi notices Tony is sad a little later, he admits that he is mourning a "work-related death" — but he changes Tracee's gender: she becomes "a young man who worked for us." He does not allow Tracee to enter his life-narrative as a stripper or even as a woman; to justify his emotion, he leaves her cunt behind and reimagines her as a man.

The series' conversational and therapeutic narrative strategies are based on Tony's interactions with Carmela and Melfi. As Kim Akass and Janet McCabe put it, "It is through Carmela and Jennifer [Melfi ...] that we learn just how complicated Tony Soprano really is. [...] he is being represented within ambiguous narrative spaces defined by women whose attitudes towards him are profoundly morally confused and paradoxical" ("Beyond the Bada Bing!" 149). The gendered narrative practices are "allowing the male to speak about his problems and the female to listen and make sense of this information" (150). Tony is able to speak about his feelings and actions, however obliquely, because these feminized spaces are outside the sphere in which he acts— because they are afford him that pause in the action, that space for reflection. He rarely shares his feelings with his male associates, and then only in a truncated version.

In a later article ("What Has Carmela Ever Done for Feminism?"), McCabe and Akass argue for Carmela's narrative empowerment: "Tony may control the sixty-minute narrative but she takes control of the thirteen-episode arc that unsettles any authority he may think he has" (45). That may be overestimating Carmela's power — as we've seen, Tony manages to put her back in her place through his control of the purse strings— but it's true that Carmela's status as angel in the house does allow her some subtle narrative control. Outright demands are never successful with Tony, as Carmela discovers when she tries to get him to reorganize investments in season four,[9] and it is important to remember that a woman can be converted into a cunt when Tony deems it necessary. But her reaction to Irina's incursion proves that the home has given Carmela some power. Irina, who has said several times, "I am not a whore," has had no say in the main story; in season two, she tries to win Tony back by attempting suicide ("The Knight in White Satin Armor," 2.12)— but because she is only a cunt, Tony doesn't relent. More savvily, she phones Carmela, thereby violating the sanctity of domestic space and, in her transgression, asserting a momentary power. Irina has realized she can't get narrative control through her own body: To effect change and wield a little bit of influence, she had to contact someone with a voice that sways Tony's heart. Carmela is so firmly entrenched in the home that even Tony recognizes her right to throw him out of it — her right to interpret his behavior and redirect it. Her authority depends on the very space that has limited her.

Dr. Melfi is the series' chief representative of narrative principles. Her professional goals are to help patients effect change in their own lives; a psychiatrist should be a kind of puppetmaster, helping a patient to act appropriately within a culturally approved script. Jessica Baldanzi notes that the pressures on this particular therapist are intense: "Melfi is not just the non-gangster conduit into the show with whom so many of us identify. She is also a doctor, who must ensure that her patient travels mostly forward, rather than backward into an emotionally out-of-control narrative of revenge" (89). Melfi tries valiantly, but she is stymied at every turn. The demands of a television series mean that she sees relatively little progress in Tony; he's stuck in a narrative groove, unable to give up his notions of masculinity, femininity, and (most important to him) business interactions. At the end of season five, she expresses her frustration in firm terms: "Here we are, as always, back at square one" ("All Due Respect," 5.13). She even raises her voice slightly and allows herself to become emotional as she insists that Tony is getting sentimental, denying the hostile feelings he'd earlier expressed toward his cousin Tony Blundetto — thus regressing the therapeutic narrative as she sees it.

But she is seeing only part of what's going on. The viewer watches Tony go out to kill his cousin for an infraction that has brought his organization to the brink of war with Johnny Sacks's. So Melfi has had some impact on Tony's actions, though the legal constraints on the relationship mean she will never realize it — and, of course, she would be horrified if she learned that her narrative and therapeutic skills have been deployed in the service of murder.

The therapy is handicapped from the start, as the different laws that Tony and Melfi obey place strict limits on what can be said. In the pilot episode, he exclaims, "Look — it's impossible for me to talk to a psychiatrist!" (pilot, "The Sopranos, 1.1). To speak at all about what he does is to break a Mafia code of honor — and to put himself at risk by showing he's broken the code. Dr. Melfi, a blank slate with an impassive expression and a blandly tasteful tan pantsuit and turtleneck (it is more usual to see her in black), continues to question him. But, when he does begin to talk, she reinforces his sense of constraint by showing that for her, too, there are limits on what he can express in that office. If he — or any patient — tells her a story in which someone is going to be hurt, she must go to the authorities. There's a beat of silence and a small hand gesture; then, "Technically." She may add the last word so that he won't get angry and hurt her; that "Technically" reminds him that the limits on Tony's therapy are imposed not by her but by the law. She is clearly nervous about treating Tony; her stiff posture, occasionally quavering voice, and helpless hand gestures show that she wants both to hear what he has to say and to shield herself from unpleasant revelations. The space may be expansive, but the narrative capabilities are limited.

"Technically" also shows that Melfi is willing to be somewhat flexible about the treatment. She expects to learn of ill-doings but, as long as Tony can talk around them, she might be willing to obey the letter of the law rather than its spirit. She and Tony easily get around this restriction; in that episode, for example, he says he "had coffee with" a gambler who owed him money—a euphemism for a sequence of events that begins with Tony spilling the gambler's tray of takeout coffee as he and Christopher run the man down with a Lexus, then kick him. They develop a vocabulary that allows Tony to express himself—but, because this is a necessarily encoded speech, it reinforces the boundaries at the same time as it lets Tony hop over them. He cannot step beyond the limits of legal revelation.

If Carmela gains some power and authority through joining her life to Tony's, Melfi is bound to refuse such a tie. The series offers Melfi several opportunities to intertwine her own story with his, and she refuses. We know she's curious, as we've seen her climb onto a toilet to peek at his house from the next-door neighbor's; she's also attracted to him, as she admits to her own psychiatrist that she has found Tony sexy as a "dangerous alpha male" ("Two Tonys," 5.1). Perhaps the greatest example of those limits comes in the "Employee of the Month" episode, in which Melfi is raped in her office building's parking garage. Her attacker is released because the police failed to process his arrest properly, and she feels helpless and frustrated by the injustice ("Employee of the Month," 3.4). Tony notices she's upset and thinks it may be his fault; in a touchingly childlike moment, he offers to find another therapist (showing, again, the limits he feels placed on him in her office). When she begins to weep, he asks, "What? Do you wanna say something?" and she responds simply, "No." She won't tell him about the rape, won't activate the knight-in-white-satin-armor side of him in order to achieve justice for herself: Even in her distress, she keeps him and their discussion on the right side of the law, her life story from affecting and directing his. She also thus prevents sexuality from entering their relationship.[10]

Even more significantly, gentle as she may seem to the viewer, Tony frequently finds Melfi to be a bully. She may encourage him to let his feelings loose, but she insists on interpreting them, and the interpretations rarely suit Tony's sense of his due. She also interprets others' actions for him, sometimes arousing his anger: When she realizes Livia has allowed Junior to put out a hit on Tony, Melfi warns Tony that his life is in danger. Her reward is a stream of vitriol and a near brush with physical violence ("I Dream of Jeannie Cusamano," 1.13). He accuses her of failing to understand him and of trying to turn him against his family. She has intruded on his own thoughts and feelings, tried to shape them in a way that doesn't sit well with Tony. She has, in short, transgressed what he sees as a boundary held naturally in place by difference in their gendered bodies.

Tony has become a small part of Melfi's story, though she won't let him know it; she becomes part of his, though he can't let her know it. Together, they will feel constantly stalled and frustrated — but that is precisely why the space of the office works within the ergonomics of the series. It, like the home and the Bing, remains a place outside of time.

Conclusion: The Goddess in the Unconscious

A house, an office, a strip club: three spaces associated (in the case of the office, somewhat surprisingly) with women, three spaces that break up the male-dominated gangster narrative and problematize the emotional side of life. They give the series a handy system of references both visual and emotional within which the female body might also be divided up for maximum efficiency in its storytelling. Tony Soprano may experience these spaces as constricting, even as he tries to let himself grow to fill them either physically or metaphorically; but he does all he can to keep his women in their assigned places and to keep each space fulfilling its single function in his life. If all else fails, he or one of his henchmen can convert a space into an ersatz Bada Bing by reducing the woman who occupies it to a cunt.

This does not mean women are absolutely powerless, however. Michel Foucault has written that every member of a power system, no matter how apparently weak, is participating in that system.[11] Thus, although they may struggle, these women are helping to reinforce the structure that keeps Tony in his own position at the top of the heap. They do so perhaps by the very act of thinking about these spaces with different functions; as long as they believe that business, home and family life, and hedonistic sexuality are different functions, the divisions that keep them relatively powerless will endure.

The Sopranos presents one dramatic exception to the rule, a woman who cannot be reduced to a cunt although she uses hers, or the suggestion of it, to her advantage. Introduced in season two, she haunts the series as an example of the best a woman — or even a man — can become. When Tony and a handful of his men arrive in Italy ("Commendatori," 2.4), they meet with an old boss whose wheelchair is steered by a curvy nurse with wild dark hair (Sofia Milos). She oozes sexuality, and Tony is instantly attracted. It turns out that this woman is not just Don Vittorio's nurse; she is also his daughter. And she is not just his daughter — she is also the acting boss, Annalisa Zucca.

Hard to believe, yes, but also alluring. Tony falls under Annalisa's spell. Her sexuality makes her irresistible, and her position of power makes her dangerous. She is the one woman, besides Tony's mother, who really could have him whacked; the aged father in his wheelchair seems to be testimony to her power to emasculate and infantilize. As he does with other women who cross the boundaries of their defined roles, Tony tries to sexualize her; he fantasizes about penetrating her on a balcony and is his most charming in real life. She rejects his loverly advances—but not those he makes as a businessman. By exerting himself, Tony manages to make a deal with her that includes her gift of Furio, who comes to America and charms Carmela, thereby emasculating Tony to a degree. We won't see a full scene with Annalisa again. But the memory of the female boss lingers in the series' unconscious, informing Tony's negotiations with Carmela, his analysis he Dr. Melfi, perhaps even some of his trysts with purely sexualized strippers.

As to why *The Sopranos* allows this woman to be daughter, cook, nurse, and boss, the answer is beautifully simple. She lives not in New Jersey but in old Italy—the mother country that seems, in its modernizing of female roles, to have circled back into a past in which women could be goddesses of war as well as of wisdom and love. The possibilities found in the classical past are emphasized by the fact that Annalisa is wearing a toga in Tony's fantasy. Life in New Jersey has made the Italian setting almost irrelevant; it remains a cultural touchstone, yes, but the American mafia has all but broken away from the Italian one, and the Italian mobsters don't set narratives into motion, only react to Tony's initiatives. Accordingly, Annalisa holds herself apart, as another woman whose personal life and limbs do not entwine with Tony's. She exerts no narrative power in the overarching series, but she remains a sign of women's ability to manipulate their fathers, or their lovers.

Thus Annalisa Zucca also contributes to the ergonomic arrangement in the series, efficiently demonstrating that in the main narrative of the New Jersey mobsters, there is no real feminism, no permanent empowerment—rather, a representation of narrative potential within a space whose boundaries may be large but are still unbreachable.

Notes

1. The fact that the first image is of a sculpture, not a life cast or photograph, proves that any narrative truth produced in the office will always be a construct, an artist's interpretation—in the same way that a TV show is. Tony will later comment on other artwork—for example, what he sees as a rotting tree in a painting of a red barn ("Denial, Anger, Acceptance," 1.3)—but he doesn't ask about the bronze woman. In fact, she disappears, drops out of the narrative. Or perhaps we could say she gets subsumed in it, as the nature of womanhood and the arts that transcend the physical female body are always an implied topic, so that first archetypal female figure and the space she creates for Tony between her legs gets swallowed up in the individual stories that the series tells.

2. For example, in the season five finale, Johnny Sack invites Tony to come to his

house to discuss the near-war that's raging between their organizations. When Tony demurs, Johnny asks if he really thinks he's likely to get killed with Ginny, Johnny's wife, right there in the house ("All Due Respect," 5.13).

3. In the early episodes, Tony laments that he's come in "at the end of things" (pilot, "The Sopranos," 1.1), and he and other characters are constantly decrying the dilution of Italian culture and decline of mob work ethics.

4. For an analysis of Carmela's feminist traits, see Ellen Willis, who calls Carmela Tony's "emotional equal" (3), and Janet McCabe and Kim Akass's article "What Has Carmela Ever Done for Feminism?," which argues that Carmela is part of feminism's third wave, embracing ambiguous roles (43).

5. For an example of Carmela's enthusiasm at open houses and housewarmings, see "Denial, Anger, Acceptance" (1.3), in which she and Tony visit Artie and Charmaine's new place; Carmela exclaims, "I couldn't wait — I had to see the new house." For the home-decorating discussions with Furio, see "Christopher" (4.3), "The Strong Silent Type" (4.10), and "Eloise" (4.12); for Furio's housewarming, at which he and Carmela dance romantically, see "The Weight" (4.4) and "Watching Too Much Television" (4.7).

6. Given her role as angel in the house and guardian of morals, it is perhaps surprising that Carmela focuses not on Tony's crimes but on his mistresses. Her life is one of constant moral compromise, and the morals she instills are always relative.

7. For example, when Carmela allows Tony to move back into the house in season five, he watches a cowboy movie while she takes care of the dishes on his first night back ("Long Term Parking," 5.12).

8. The name Livingston might remind viewers of "Dr. Livingston, I presume?" — a manifestation of exaggerated politeness within a spatial heart of darkness; it also reminds us that Carmela, like Tony, is trying to live in this town. That Livingston doctor tells Carmela she should get a divorce, something she won't be willing to do until the end of the next season.

9. Tony does have a change of heart, but it comes only when, unknown to Carmela, a dream makes him feel guilty over Gloria Trillo's suicide ("Everybody Hurts," 4.13).

10. In an earlier scene in the same episode, Carmela and Tony attend Johnny and Ginny Sack's housewarming in New Jersey. When Carmela says, "Oh my god, this house," Tony says, "You already have one"— demonstrating her relationship to houses in general and showing that he wants to keep her confined to the family home, still in the role of housewife: He keeps Carmela in her assigned role even as he repeatedly tries to talk Dr. Melfi out of hers.

11. See *The History of Sexuality*: "Power comes from below; that is, there is no [...] duality extending from the top down and reacting on more and more limited groups to the very depths of the social body" (94); and, "Where there is power, there is resistance, and yet, or rather consequently, this resistance is never in a position of exteriority in relation to power" (95).

Works Cited

Akass, Kim, and Janet McCabe. "Beyond the Bada Bing!: Negotiating Female Narrative Authority in *The Sopranos*." Ed. David Lavery, *This Thing of Ours: Investigating The Sopranos*. New York: Columbia University Press, 2002. 146–161.

Baldanzi, Jessica. "Bloodlust for the Common Man: *The Sopranos* Confronts Its Volatile American Audience." Ed. David Lavery, *Reading The Sopranos: Hit TV from HBO*. London: I. B. Tauris, 2006. 79–89.

Barreca, Regina. "Why I Like the Women in *The Sopranos* Even Though I'm Not Supposed To." Ed. Regina Barreca. *A Sitdown with the Sopranos: Watching Italian American Culture on TV's Most Talked-About Series*. New York: Palgrave Macmillan, 2002. 27–46.

Donatelli, Cindy, and Sharon Alward. "'I Dread You'?: Married to the Mob in *The Godfather, Goodfellas*, and *The Sopranos*." Ed. David Lavery, *This Thing of Ours: Investigating The Sopranos*. New York: Columbia University Press, 2002. 60–71.

Foucault, Michel. *The History of Sexuality, vol. 1: An Introduction*. Trans. Robert Hurley. New York: Vintage, 1978, 1990.

Levinson, Paul. "Naked Bodies, Three Showings a Week, and No Commercials: *The Sopranos* as a Nuts-and-Bolts Triumph of Non-Network TV." Ed. David Lavery, *This Thing of Ours: Investigating The Sopranos*. New York: Columbia University Press, 2002. 26–31.

McCabe, Janet, and Kim Akass. "What Has Carmela Ever Done for Feminism?: Carmela Soprano and the Post-Feminist Dilemma." Ed. David Lavery, *Reading The Sopranos: Hit TV from HBO*. London: I. B. Tauris, 2006. 39–55.

Spain, Daphne. *Gendered Spaces*. Chapel Hill: University of North Carolina Press, 1992.

Walker, Joseph S. "'Cunnilingus and Psychiatry Have Brought Us to This': Livia and the Logic of False Hoods in the First Season of *The Sopranos*." Ed. David Lavery, *This Thing of Ours: Investigating The Sopranos*. New York: Columbia University Press, 2002. 109–121.

Willis, Ellen. "Our Mobsters, Ourselves." Ed. David Lavery, *This Thing of Ours: Investigating The Sopranos*. New York: Columbia University Press, 2002. 3–9.

Wright, Gwendolyn. *Moralism and the Model Home*. Chicago: University of Chicago Press, 1980.

Crooked Reading: Postmodernism and *The Sopranos*

Ann C. Hall

MEADOW: I read, Mom. Probably half the canon.

CARMELA: The canon. Okay, what is that now?

MEADOW: Now? The great books? Western literature? Dead white males? Who even in their reductionism have quite interesting things to say about death and loss. Maybe more interesting than what you have to say.

CARMELA: Is Mary Higgins Clark a part of that group, 'cause that's what I saw you reading every time I passed by the pool.

— *The Sopranos,* "No Show"

In Jacques Derrida's influential *Writing and Difference*, a collection of essays outlining the processes of signification and deconstruction, he aligns signification with violence. Competing ideologies, theories, meanings, and interpretations must battle for expression, privilege and power, in a manner very similar to the relationships depicted in David Chase's blockbuster television series, *The Sopranos.* Like the structuralist movement which preceded deconstruction and which in some ways gave rise to its rival theory, the Mafia brotherhood seeks to obliterate rivals, obstacles, and conflicting interpretations. Of course, the problem with either method, on the theoretical or practical level, is that nothing is ever "erased" completely, there is always something left over: for deconstructionists it is "play" or "differ-ence"; for the mob, body parts, nightmares, and maybe even twinges of guilt and fear. So what is a critical theorist or mob boss to do? In this early iteration of his philosophy, "Structure, Sign, and Play," Derrida offers a not surprisingly paradoxical statement about human existence embedded in a linguistic system, a point that is frequently overlooked by both his support-ers and his detractors:

> There are thus two interpretations of interpretation, of structure, of sign, of play. The one seeks to decipher, dreams of deciphering a truth or an origin which escapes play and the order of the sign, and which lives the necessity of interpretation as an exile. The other, which is no longer turned toward the origin, affirms play and tries to pass beyond man and humanism, the name of man being the name of that being who, throughout the history of metaphysics or of ontotheology — in other words, throughout his entire history — has dreamed of full presence, the reassuring foundation, the origin and end of play [292].

We yearn for security and conclusive interpretations, but we also yearn for something more, the possibility of another interpretation, another option. Further, we yearn for certitude, know that there is ambiguity, but we must make judgments. Our interpretive and even existential castles are built upon sand, but build them we must. The job and perhaps the joy for the deconstructionist, and in this case, David Chase, then, is not destroying the castle and constructing a relativistic nightmare, but instead, pointing out the sand, reminding us all not to take ourselves too seriously, not to become too attached to rigid interpretations and institutions.

Called "postmodern" mobsters, David Chase's *The Sopranos* illustrate this deconstructive strategy in very humorous ways at times in order to remind us all that existence is insecure at best and our personal power fre-quently a vain delusion.[1] Through numerous episodes, it becomes clear that placing faith in certitudes, even in rigid interpretations of deconstruction, is akin to a mob hit. It appears to solve the problem and in certain instances, it is unavoidable, but there's always the problem of body disposal, that play of signification.

Surely the mutability of existence is nothing new, so taking a decon-structionist stance on something like popular culture or the David Chase series might seem like many of the hits illustrated on the series — overkill. The series, however, is a reflection upon, a representation of, and the prod-uct of postmodern culture, a culture which simultaneously gave rise to deconstruction and which is shaped by deconstruction itself. Though a bit convoluted, the "reality" of the situation leads to several issues. First, decon-struction not only points out the chaos of the universe, but the price our attempts to order that universe exacts, a price that many would like to pretend does not exist. Second, the claim that Derridean philosophy is relativistic is not only based upon misreadings of deconstruction but also irrelevant here. We know that we are entering a morally relativistic universe when we watch *The Sopranos*. We do not expect the ethical high ground; these are mobsters after all. So, if there are any qualms about entering a postmodern world or entertaining a postmodern epistemology, they are alleviated by the context, a willing suspension of disbelief which reduces any resistance to the postmodern agenda on the part of the audience.

Some have argued that it is precisely the transgressive nature of the mob that attracts viewers. As early as the 1930s, Robert Warshaw argued that the mobster films challenged the American status quo: "the gangster speaks for us, expressing that part of the American psyche which rejects the qualities and demands of modern life" (qtd. in Grieveson et al. 2). Films such as *Public Enemy* (1931), one of Tony Sopranos favorites, as well as *Bonnie and Clyde* (1967), *Thelma and Louise* (1991), the French *The Professional* (1994), and the British *Sexy Beast* (2000) celebrate antisocial behavior, perhaps illustrating its international and timeless appeal. In other instances such as the successful television series, *The Untouchables, Dragnet, Law and Order,* and *CSI* our enjoyment springs from seeing the criminal, representing the chaotic, uncontrollable, primal, even id-like, elements in society, caught, tried, and punished — all within a thirty to sixty minute time frame. Admittedly, there is a kind of "play" or "difference" in these works as a result of the long-running nature of many of these televisions series. One criminal may be behind bars, but, like Ulysses's Myrmidons, more keep springing up, but since they are always caught, tried, and punished, the repetition provides the illusion of stability and security, not ambiguity and ambivalence.

The Sopranos, clearly, offers no such security. David Chase manages to use the show's longevity to complicate simplistic interpretations and conclusions. People reappear, vendettas are eternal, nightmares persist, memories are long, and the federal government is always watching. In the end, it will be interesting to see how he concludes the series, a series characterized by its postmodern, open-ended, structure.

While the end is still a few months off, Tony is clearly a postmodern everyman. He appears to have everything. The famous opening credits, for example, represent him as the ultimate self-made man, the living embodiment of the American dream, moving from working poor to upper-middle class, all in the matter of minutes. He has it all, including the big car and the big cigar.[2] But more episodes than not show him completely adrift, vulnerable, and lacking, far from self-sufficient. During the early episodes of the latest season, "Join the Club" (6.2), for example, Tony is hospital-ized as a result of Uncle Junior's delusional shooting. Tony and his family, then, must rely on his underlings for financial security and payments. His two closest allies, Paulie and Vito, hold on to their monies just a little bit too long, indicating Tony's dependence. Further, once he returns, he notes that his men are beginning to question his authority, which his psychother-apist, Dr. Melfi, indicates as natural, a sense of turf-testing. Tony trans-lates her sociological/anthropological observations into mob culture which results in his brutal beating of an innocent but incredibly strong bystander in order to establish his power ("Mr. and Mrs. Sacrimoni Request," 6.5). Nowhere is the postmodern so clearly illustrated. Tony's power comes from oppression and violence. Because we have gotten to know Tony, however, he is not just a mobster anymore; he is our guide through this underworld, and what we see is not as alien as we would like to believe. We, too, have our own illusions about personal power, and we too are vulnerable in ways we would rather not admit.

The series begins by establishing Tony's likeability. He is a self-made man, powerful, and in control, behind the driver's seat, all the clichés of American, masculine power, but he is also sentimental. He is fascinated by a family of ducks that have taken roost in his palatial swimming pool in the series pilot episode. The episode illustrates that he is a man out of his ele-ment, perhaps a man who still longs for the simple connection to the earth his Italian ancestors had but is denied such connection as a result of this meteoric rise in class and postmodern culture. Even when he returns to his Italian roots in Season Two ("Commendatori," 2.4), he is disenchanted: you can't go home again, though Tony manages to bring back an Italian strong arm, Furio, who ends up falling in love with Tony's wife, Carmella. Clearly, Tony has no control over his life, and he is alienated and lost. He is no victim, however. In a word, he wants his duck and eat it, too. He wants the security of his family, but he persists in meaningless sexual encounters and long-term affairs with unstable women.

The ducks' departure may trigger Tony's panic attacks in the first episode but his lifestyle has been contributing to his stress and sense of loss for a lifetime. And like all good Americans who feel discomfort, Tony turns to psychotherapy for an answer. Of course, anyone who has been in ther-apy knows, the journey is far from straightforward. Dr. Melfi is particu-larly fond of the non-directional Socratic method, asking Tony questions, probing him to make draw his own conclusions, and assuring her a long tenure on the series. Early on in his treatment, she prescribes Prozac. Tony immediately feels better, presuming that the drugs have taken effect. When

Melfi tells him that it is not the Prozac but the "talking cure," Tony is momentarily surprised, perhaps by the paradox: by discussing fears and insecurities, he feels better, more complete. Violating the mafia's codes of silence brings relief. By admitting his lack, his needs, and his dependence, he can be strong. The converse is also true, and to this date, Tony still struggles with therapy sessions, presuming he feels better and therefore does not need the treatment.

In "The Legend of Tennessee Moltisanti" (1.8), Tony tries out the "cure" at a picnic, only to reach comic ends. He tells his friend Artie, whose restaurant has been burned down to prohibit a mob hit, to talk about his feelings. The plan backfires, Artie whines and Christopher, Tony's young nephew, throws a tantrum. It is only when Tony shouts out orders and reassures Christopher that the future will be bright that equilibrium in the family is restored. Tony must pretend to have it all together, to be the patriarch, the "subject-supposed-to-know," in the words of postmodern psychoanalyst, Jacques Lacan. Later in "I Dream of Jeannie Cusamano" (1.13), Tony confesses his therapy sessions to his crew. Christopher leaves, asking only one question: "Is that like marriage counseling?" But Paulie confesses that he went to a therapist for "issues." Later, however, Paulie confesses to Silvio that he basically lied about his therapy sessions so that Tony would feel better. Nothing is as it seems. All is dynamic. All is perilous.

While Dr. Melfi asks a lot of questions, she appears to know more than she is telling, particularly about Tony's relationship with his mother. For awhile, she becomes the "subject-supposed-to-know." Casting a female in this position violates Freudian psychology's origins which was based upon Freud's treatment of some of Vienna's most hysterical women. And here, Tony seeing a woman to talk to, to violate the code of silence, not for sex? Forgettaboutit.

Despite the pleasure we might gain from this inversion of the male-female hierarchy in patriarchy, the show's postmodern process undercuts Melfi's power as successfully as it undercuts Tony. A mere inversion of the status quo is not the postmodern process. Dr. Melfi is not invincible. Not only does she herself see a therapist, but her family life is fragile. Her ex-husband is controlling and bossy, and listening to the two of them interact underscores the nightmare of living with two psychologists. In "The Legend of Tennessee Moltisanti," for example, her ex-husband and son basically take Dr. Melfi to a therapist for family counseling because they do not approve of her treatment of a "made guy." In a classic scene more akin to Woody Allen than Francis Ford Coppola, the couple spout off psychiatric jargon, while the son appears surprisingly well-adjusted. Perhaps to underscore the true vulnerability of Melfi, and us all, the series includes her rape and, most importantly, her temptation to tell Tony in order to exact revenge upon the rapist. Once again, violating the traditions of psychotherapy, the "talking cure," it is silence that offers her redemption, not further disclosure. She heals and carries on, but it is one of the most series most terrifying episodes.

Major social institutions which were created with high-minded principles and good intentions are also subject to corruption, change, and plain old-fashioned incompetence. Nowhere is this more apparent than when the FBI attempt to plant a bug in Tony's basement in "Mr. Ruggiero's Neighborhood" (3.1). With the Dunn theme playing in the background, the FBI swoop down on Tony's house like bees. With a surveillance camera in place, they watch the basement, and while doing so, their relationship to the Soprano family is highlighted. They are like one another. There is not that much difference among them, and the relationships here are solidified by that great American equalizer, shopping. One of the agents notes that he has the same piece of equipment as Tony. Another notes the water heater and warns that it will explode, which is precisely what happens during of their later visits, as they try to place an audio recorder in the house. Eventually, they do place the audio surveillance in a lamp, but after all their trouble — the episode is pretty much devoted to their breaking and entering — in a subsequent episode, Meadow, like all good college students, takes the lamp from her home for her dorm room. Serendipidity thwarts the agents in this case. As Douglas L. Howard notes, "for all the FBI do on *The Sopranos*, for all the bugging and the wiretapping, for all the coercion and pressure, for all the family members they flip and the information they get, for all the undercover agents that get on the inside and for all the busts they make, their plans almost never work out, or, at the very least, they never turn out the way they intended" (169).

The FBI, however, is not incompetent, and they are not portrayed as buffoons. In "Mr. Ruggiero's Neighborhood," lunchtime at the FBI and lunchtime with the mob are juxtaposed. The FBI, of course, eats and works. Their table is littered with fast food containers, as they watch and comment upon the video surveillance of the Soprano basement. In the very next scene, we see Tony and his crew having lunch. In this case, the men are cooking, enjoying fresh bread, homemade pasta, salad — a dinner most of us would kill for. Paulie, however, enters, stoops down, ties his shoes, and then washes his hands. This action prompts the ridicule from his compatriots. He explains in graphic terms that his shoelace was probably untied when he used the men's where he walked on urine soaked floors. By the time he is finished, the beautiful meal the men have before them is inedible. The Italians may have the beautiful food, but in this case, they do not enjoy the meal.

The FBI, moreover, successfully captures and incarcerates mob boss Johnny Sack in "All Due Respect" (5.13), and though the family helps to make his stay comfortable, he has to do the time and beg for permission to attend his daughter's wedding. Further, it is the FBI, not his family or crew, that tells Tony his own mother and uncle are plotting to kill him ("I Dream of Jeannie Cusamano," 1.13). Tony discovers the plan that his uncle Junior and his mother Livia have planned. Tony disguises his feelings, but it is clear during this revelation that the agents feel for him, and they are hoping to channel what they hope will be justified rage against the crime family. Ironically, the fact that he is seeing a therapist enables Tony to retain his control during a situation that could leave him open to the FBI's manipulations.

"University" (3.6) illustrates the vulnerability of all women in the Soprano world. In this episode, a needy young woman, Tracee, tries to befriend Tony, but instead, ends up with Ralph Ciferatto. When the relationship falls apart, she argues with him, and he out of a deadly combination of idiocy and cocaine, brutally beats her. Though annoyed by the girl, Tony is enraged by Ralph's actions. He punishes Ralph, and a feud smolders between the two men. This is not the only plot development in this episode. Juxtaposed between the scenes between Tracee and Ralph are the scenes between Meadow and her new boyfriend, Noah. Tony has summarily dismissed Noah because of his ethnic background, but it becomes clear as the episode unravels that Noah is just as much a predator as Ralph. In a glance, Chase makes that point clear, while the next episode, under the direction of another writer, makes the point explicit. In both cases, however, it is clear that existence is insecure at best. Here is a more serious way, elsewhere in more humorous ways.

On a practical level, the series also challenges our expectations about certitude through its casting, as well as its storytelling. Important actors are cast in important roles, only to be killed off, thereby violating some of the cardinal rules of television — never kill the famous. They may be the guilty parties as in the classic television *Columbo* or *Murder, She Wrote* series, but they must remain alive for the entire show or series. Not so with *The Sopranos* — even the famous are whacked.

The production of the television show also violates the usual production practices in a postmodern way. Most films and series are released, almost magically. Their status as products is elided, made invisible. We enter a world, a seamless, self-contained entertainment world, and we are lulled into a sense of complacency and expectation — life is like this, whole and complete, ready made. As David Chase himself observes:

> I think the first priority [of network television] is to push a lifestyle. I think there's something they're trying to sell all the time.... I think that they're try-

ing to sell that everything's OK all the time, that this is just a great nation and a wonderful society, and everything's OK and it's OK to buy stuff. Let's just go buy stuff.... There's some indefinable image of America that they're constantly trying to push as opposed to actually being entertaining [qtd. in Lavery 5].

The Sopranos's production is always creaky; we see not only the people behind the scenes, but the writers, those important and frequently invisible creative artists who are responsible for much of what we see and view in the entertainment industry. Such exposure reminds us that we are dependent on others, on writing, and on artists, that entertainment is a product and process—it does not occur magically. By exposing the machinery of production as effectively as the series exposes our tenuous existence, the series once again supports the postmodern agenda, as well as questioning the society that presumes to control. At the same time, Chase exercises final artistic control over the series. Other writers create episodes, but he oversees the revisions and the final scripts in his own uniquely "countercultural" way. As David Lavery and Robert J. Thompson note in their essay on David Chase and the creation of *The Sopranos*:

> By retaining his role as the final rewriter of every *Sopranos* script, but farming out most of his episodes to other writers, Chase has chosen a dramaturgical model that may be the most effective one for telling artistically mature stories in a continuing series. *The Sopranos* is enriched by the subtly different voices that various writers bring to the series. Chase's refusal to hog all of the scripts himself provides a degree of multivalent complexity to the universe he has created. At the same time, his stewardship assures that the show takes advantage of the unique ability of a television series to tell stories that develop characters and accrete detail over long periods of real and narrative time [22–23].

This process of production insures meaning, through Chase's authority, but "play," as well, through the interaction and contributions of other writers. In effect, the two interpretations of interpretation — not chaos and relativism as some critics of deconstruction would argue, but decisions made with humility, collaboration, and a realistic sense of the dynamic nature of existence, writing, and the entertainment industry.

In this way, the series and its production remind us that power is illusory. Again, as Chase himself reflects:

> What Tony Soprano shows, I guess, is that rarely is anything black and white in life. Life is difficult, messy, disappointing. Things don't work out the way we'd like — our kids make bad choices, our parents are a burden, our friends disappoint or betray us.... What *I* love most when I'm watching something is a feeling of strangeness, suspense, poetry — things happening that you can't predict [x].

Existence is tenuous, and we must live it accordingly, asking questions, revising assumptions, reassessing, laughing at time, enjoying the ride, and then settling on some interpretation we can live with until another option challenges us to revise again. Or David Chase writes more episodes.

Notes

1. In her wonderful essay "Investigating the Sopranos," Ellen Willis calls the series a "postmodern *Middlemarch*" (3), as well as concluding, albeit hyperbolically, "the richest and most compelling piece of television — no popular culture — that I've encountered in the past twenty years." It is a "meditation on the nature of morality, the possibility of redemption, and the legacy of Freud" (2). Her essay, however, focuses on the psychoanalytic elements of the series and its commentary, concluding, the show's appeal is based upon the unconscious: "the murderous mobster is the predatory lust and aggression in all of us" (8). Clearly, the relationships among postmodern psychoanalysis and philosophy are close. Jacques Lacan, for example, argues that the unconscious is structured like language, so the linguistic and psychoanalytic examinations are close. In this paper, however, I would like to build upon Willis's observations to demonstrate exactly how the postmodern is expressed in the Chase series.

2. David Johansson offers a close reading of the opening scene, noting that it is a "'road movie in miniature'" showing us the "American landscape as an urban, sterile place, deprived of natural wonder yet possessed of all the danger of the jungle" (31).

Works Cited

Chase, David. Introduction. *The Sopranos: Selected Scripts from Three Seasons.* New York: HBO Productions, 2002.

Derrida, Jacques. *Writing and Difference.* Trans. Alan Bass. Chicago: University of Chicago Press, 1978.

Grieveson, Lee et al. "Introduction." *Mob Culture: Hidden Histories of the American Gangster Film.* New Brunswick, NJ: Rutgers University Press, 2005. 1–10.

Howard, Douglas. "Tasting Brylcreem: Law, Disorder, and the FBI in *The Sopranos.*" *Reading the Sopranos: Hit TV From HBO.* Ed. David Lavery. New York: I.B. Taurus, 2006. 163–178.

Johansson, David. "Homeward Bound: Those *Sopranos* Titles Come Heavy." *Reading the Sopranos: Hit TV From HBO.* Ed. David Lavery. New York: I.B. Taurus, 2006. 27–36.

Lavery, David. "Introduction: Can This Be the End of Tony Soprano?" *Reading the Sopranos: Hit TV From HBO.* Ed. David Lavery. New York: I.B. Taurus, 2006. 3–14.

_____ and Robert J. Thompson. "David Chase, *The Sopranos*, and Television Creativity." *This Thing of Ours: Investigating the Sopranos.* Ed. David Lavery. New York: Columbia, 2002. 18–25.

Willis, Ellen. "Our Mobsters, Ourselves." *This Thing of Ours: Investigating the Sopranos.* Ed. David Lavery. New York: Columbia, 2002. 2–9.

Wackos in the Wilderness vs. Getting Whacked in Newark: Dueling Family Models in *Northern Exposure* and *The Sopranos*

Mardia J. Bishop

In November 1995, President William Clinton proclaimed the fourth week of November of that year "National Family Week." President George W. Bush made a similar proclamation in November 2001. While the purpose of their pronouncements was the same — setting up that particular week in November to encourage citizens and local governments to honor families in "appropriate" ways, their rhetoric diverged dramatically, exposing Clinton's and Bush's different definitions of family and family values and, consequently, their approaches to domestic and foreign policies. Using family values or the emphasis on family as a political strategy certainly wasn't invented by the Clinton or Bush administrations. In the past one hundred years whenever there have been "problems" in society, the supposed breakdown of the family is cited as the cause. The most recent endeavor in highlighting family values as a political strategy was ushered in by then Vice President Dan Quayle in a 1992 speech in which he condemned the television character Murphy Brown for getting pregnant and having a child out of wedlock.[1] According to family and marriage historian Stephanie Coontz, Quayle's remark about Murphy Brown "kicked off more than a decade of outcries against the 'collapse of the family'" ("For Better" 1). When delivered in 1992, Quayle's comments created public and media scorn and damage to the Republican presidential campaign; yet, ten years later, his comments very much align with the current Republican party platform. The change in perception of Quayle's comments is indicative of the nature of the term "family values"—a vague social and political concept to be sure; as such, its definition is determined by how a particular group uses it. Since social and political organizations' philosophies change due to changing economic, political, and cultural trends, the definition of "family values" changes as well. What we see in the Clinton and Bush definitions of family reflects a shift in dominant political and cultural trends and philosophies.

During the same time periods, David Chase was involved with two of television's most critically acclaimed programs—*Northern Exposure*[2] and *The Sopranos*. Both programs portray families that are dramatically different from each other, but representative of their era's definitions of family. Using the work of linguist George Lakoff and the family speeches by Clinton and Bush, it becomes clear that the Chase television series serve as both a reflection and an analysis of the eras' presentations and articulations of family values. In various reviews, *The Sopranos* consistently has been identified as satirizing both "family" and "values" in response to today's political preoccupation with "family values" and *Northern Exposure* has been recognized for espousing the 1990s notion of the global village where cultural diversity is appreciated.[3] Yet by using Lakoff's work, the political subtext of the shows can be interpreted in a different way — as keys to understanding contemporary moral politics. In light of today's political climate, which is entrenched in "values" discourse, a dualistic mentality, and strict partisanship, Lakoff's work is extremely appropriate because it gets at the core of why liberals and conservatives think and act as they do and why, despite the use of sometimes similar language, they cannot understand each other. Lakoff untangles the "family values" web by arguing that the family is at the center of American moral politics and that each side's definition of family dictates its moral code and worldview. Consequently, by using his work to analyze the families depicted in *Northern Exposure* and *The Sopranos*, we can move beyond political assignations and acquire a sense of what liberals and conservatives hold dear and how their moral politics affect the American family.

Clinton on Family

William Clinton began his two-term presidency in January 1993, a presidency highlighted by multiculturalism, feminism, gay rights, a push for universal healthcare, economic prosperity, and the emergence of the United States as the primary leader in global diplomacy. The predominant theme of Clinton's presidency was multiculturalism. As Francine Kiefer points out, "This is the diversity president speaking, a man who sees nearly every issue — at home and abroad — through the prism of multiculturalism. [...] Clinton the Communicator has returned again and again to his theme that people need to overcome their fear of one another [... and] learn to live with one another" (1). Clinton's multicultural prism can also be seen in his perception of the family.

When examining Clinton's speeches on families, five characteristics emerge. First, Clinton sees the nuclear family as "society's most basic unit" ("Proclamation 6852" 2028), where people first learn to conduct relationships. Second, Clinton consistently fails to specifically define the composition of the nuclear family, which he refers to as the "literal" family ("Remarks at Sons of Italy" 968). Whenever discussing it, he automatically talks about the diversity of families. For example, he begins his proclamation for National Family Week in 1995 with "Blessed with an extraordinary diversity of people from every culture and nation around the globe, the United States has always drawn strength from our citizens' shared commitment to the importance of family life" ("Proclamation 6852" 2028). Third, Clinton consistently places any comments regarding the nuclear family as a precursor to a wider definition of family. In his speech to the Sons of Italy Foundation Dinner, Clinton states: "I want to talk about family in the literal sense and family in the larger sense and what it means to our future as a country as part of a bigger family — a global family that is composed of many cultures, ethnicities, politics, races, sexual orientations, and religions" (968). Clinton sees the role of the family as a crucial one in "developing the character of our collective communities — on the local, national, and global levels" ("International Year of the Family" 38). Fourth, Clinton sees the nuclear family as being responsible for raising children to be respectful of difference. He comments that families have to teach children

> to be proud of themselves and what is special about themselves without thinking people who are different are lesser than they are — they may differ in race, or ethnicity, or religion, or politics, or sexual orientation, or just what they like to do. [...] We have to prove to our children — by the way we live, and what we say, the way we conduct ourselves — that we think every decent person has a home in America and that they're all part of our family ["Remarks at Sons of Italy" 970].

Because of his emphasis on teaching children tolerance, whenever Clinton talks about protecting families, his emphasis is on protecting children. "[T]he most important job of any society is not the creation of wealth but the creation of richness and wholeness in the lives of the children" ("Remarks at Sons of Italy" 968). Finally, Clinton identifies the family in positive ways, as a structure "providing the acceptance, love, and reassurance that enable each of us to flourish and succeed" ("Proclamation 6852" 2028). Ultimately, Clinton sees the nuclear family as a diverse, loving place that should teach tolerance — it is the training ground for the family that Clinton is more interested in — the global family.[4] And Clinton's vision for the global family is one in which everyone gets along and respects one another no matter what differences are present.

Bush on Family

Inaugurated in January 2001, George W. Bush ushered in not only a new century, but also different approaches to family and politics, which are highlighted by a strongly polarized political climate, unilateral diplomacy, slow economic growth, rampant corporate corruption, and the emergence of the religious right as a major lobbying force. When examining Bush's speeches regarding family, five characteristics become prevalent. Similar to Clinton, Bush identifies the nuclear family as the key social unit and a place where values are taught. He states: "The family is the foundation of this society. [...] It is where the character of our Nation is shaped and where values are forged" ("Remarks on Promoting Safe and Stable Families" 83). Unlike Clinton, however, whenever Bush talks about family, he always identifies family as the American family. Here he is not referring to America as one big family, as Clinton did, but an America insulated from the rest of the world — he never associates it with a global community. Second, as opposed to Clinton's somewhat evasive rhetoric on family, a definition of family does emerge from Bush's rhetoric. Although he recognizes that "[m]any one-parent families are also a source of comfort and reassurance, a family with a mom and a dad who are committed to marriage and devote themselves to their children" ("Proclamation — National Family Week" 1705) is best. Third, the nuclear family has a greater purpose. Instead of being the key to a global family, for Bush the family is the key to American society — "our strong Nation is built on strong families." According to Bush, when children have a strong family, "they will grow up to be confident in their self and loving toward others. She'll make her community stronger and her Nation better" ("Remarks on Promoting Safe and Stable Families" 83–84). Fourth, like Clinton, Bush identifies family in a positive way. He comments, "Families provide us with comfort and encouragement, compassion and hope, mutual support and unconditional love" ("Remarks on Promoting Safe and Stable Families" 83). Yet, as a fifth characteristic, Bush continually mentions that families need to be strengthened (Clinton instead talks about protecting families, primarily through helping children). Bush insists that government should promote policies that "help strengthen the institution of marriage" ("Proclamation — National Family Week" 1705) and that "We must work to strengthen families in America" ("Proclamation — National Family Week" 1705). Ultimately, Bush defines the nuclear family as one composed of married heterosexual parents and their children whose purpose is to teach "values" and build a strong American society.

Obviously, what Bush and Clinton clearly have in mind regarding family isn't evident from their speeches, as they speak in vague terms that can be defined differently depending on the listener. Bush's comment "[families] are the primary source of strength and health for both individuals and communities across our Nation" ("Proclamation — National Family Week" 1705) can be interpreted in a number of ways, such as families should take care of the less fortunate by providing food and healthcare. In the same vein, Clinton's comment that "the most important job of any society is not the creation of wealth but the creation of richness and wholeness in the lives of the children" ("Remarks at Sons of Italy" 968) spawns many interpretations depending on the listener's definitions of "richness" and "wholeness." Yet, while Bush's and Clinton's words can be interpreted differently, their word choices serve as linguistic clues to very different views of the family and the world. George Lakoff's work on linguistics will help untangle the rhetoric and mystery surrounding these statements on family or the lack thereof. Lakoff's work, for example, points out that Bush's continual use of the word "strong" ("our strong Nation is built on strong families") is indicative of conservative political discourse just as Clinton's use of "diversity," "protection," and "caregivers" is indicative of a liberal one (30–31). To acquire a better understanding of their definitions of family, the next part of this essay uses the work of Lakoff to further explore Clinton's and Bush's definitions of family.

Lakoff's Strict Father and Nurturant Parent Family Models

In *Moral Politics: How Liberals and Conservatives Think*, George Lakoff argues that liberals and conservatives have different moral systems and different discourse forms (word choices and reasoning modes). In his analysis of how Americans conceptualize morality, he asserts that Americans do so through metaphors.[5] After examining the various metaphors that liberals and conservatives use, he concludes that each group has a different moral system and, most importantly, that moral system stems from a specific image of the ideal family. In his research he clearly defines each group's ideal family and the moral metaphors that each group prioritizes. He labels the conservative family model as the Strict Father and the liberal one as the Nurturant Parent. Basically, he argues that these two very different views of families provide the moral systems for conservatives and liberals. The connection between definitions of family and political worldview is due to "one of the most common ways we have of conceptualizing what a nation is, namely, as a family. It is the common, unconscious, and automatic metaphor of the Nation-as-Family that produces contemporary conservatism from Strict Father morality and contemporary liberalism from Nurturant Parent morality" (13).

The Strict Father family model begins with the premise that life is a struggle and the world is dangerous. Consequently, according to this model, the best way to overcome the struggle, succeed, and stay safe is to adhere to the Strict Father model, which is

> a traditional nuclear family, with the father having primary responsibility for supporting and protecting the family as well as the authority to set overall family policy. He teaches children right from wrong by setting strict rules for their behavior and enforcing them through punishment. The mother has day-to-day responsibility for the care of the house, raising the children, and upholding the father's authority. Children must respect and obey their parents [...] because by doing so they build character, that is self-discipline and self-reliance. Self-discipline, self-reliance, and respect for legitimate authority are the crucial things that a child must learn. [...] Survival is a matter of competition, and only through self-discipline can a child learn to compete successfully [66].

Accompanying this model is a set of prioritized moral metaphors that a family adhering to the Strict Father model will inherently believe in and follow. Lakoff identifies Moral Strength and Moral Order as the metaphors with the highest priority. Moral Strength says that in order to be morally strong one needs to have self-discipline to deny the internal and external temptations that continually challenge us. Moral Order establishes a hierarchy of moral authority that seems "natural," consequently, legitimizing the Strict Father's authority and traditional hierarchical power relations (99–100).

Lakoff defines the Nurturant Parent family as being composed of

> [P]referably two parents, but perhaps only one. If two, the parents share household responsibilities. The primal experience behind this model is one of being cared for and cared about. Children become responsible, self-disciplined, and self-reliant through being cared for and respected. [...] The obedience of children comes out of their love and respect for their parents and their community, not out of the fear of punishment [108].

It is a family model where parents must communicate with their children, explaining their disciplinary decisions, and children are encouraged to question their parents. The principal goal "is for children to be fulfilled and happy in their lives." (34). Similar to the Strict Father model, there are moral metaphors prioritized within the Nurturant Parent model. The top two are Morality as Nurturance and Morality as Empathy. Morality as Nurturance says that it is moral to help any person who needs help. Morality as Empathy asserts that it is moral to feel what another person is feeling and to want that other person to experience a sense of well being.

Based on Lakoff's work, Clinton's definition of family with his emphasis on diversity, acceptance, community connections, and taking care of people fits the Nurturant Parent model. Whereas Bush's definition with his emphasis on the American nuclear family, a heterosexual, two-parent household, and a purpose of building a strong America fits the Strict Father model. While the words of both Clinton and Bush seem positive and healthy for families, in light of Lakoff's research, are their definitions really positive and healthy? An examination of the families in Chase's television programs exposes the strengths and weaknesses of these definitions of family.

Strict Father Model as Depicted in The Sopranos

Superficially, the Soprano family fits the Bush/Strict Father family model — Tony is the breadwinning father and Carmela the stay-at-home mother who has raised Meadow and A.J. according to Catholic values. Yet, upon closer examination of the families in *The Sopranos* (both Tony's biological and mob families), the superficiality of the model becomes apparent and several problems emerge. First, while this television family is fiction, so is the family model. It is a myth based on erroneous information and selective amnesia of "the good old days." The Strict Father model is the model of conservatives who consistently champion a return to the "traditional" family as a way of solving all social ills. The "traditional" family refers to a 1950s view of families, which included a breadwinner father, a stay-at-home mother, and obedient children. As pointed out by family historian Stephanie Coontz, however, this "traditional" family model did not stop perceived social ills of that time. She notes that although marriage and fertility rates increased in the 1950s and divorce rates fell, most Americans did not experience the idealistic image of family life. Poverty was more widespread, juvenile delinquency increased, rates of unwed childbearing tripled, segregation was a way of life, women couldn't get loans in their name or serve on juries in most states, and spousal rape was legal ("The American Family" 2–5).

In addition, using the term "traditional" has problems. The 1950s male-breadwinner family model was not in existence very long. According to Coontz, the American male-breadwinner family didn't exist until the mid-nineteenth century and the majority of Americans did not participate in this family model ("The Family in Upheaval" 2–3). Instead, the term "traditional" would more appropriately refer to polygamy — the marriage model that has been most widely accepted "through most of human history and in most cultures" ("Just Which" 1).[6] Moreover, the Strict Family male-breadwinner family is not realistic. "Many families today require two incomes just to meet basic living expenses" since thirty percent of jobs filled by people in the prime family-raising years don't even pay poverty-level wages (Coontz, "Uncle Sam" 3). In addition, the societal changes that have occurred over the past forty-five years cannot be reversed. For example, women are a large part of the paid-work economy and currently more women than men attend college. As argued by Coontz, our concept of marriage has changed. In the 1950s, women had very few rights and marriages were controlled by husbands. Although stereotypical gender roles within the home still prevail today, marriage is approached more equally in terms of division of labor, finances, and emotional attachment.

With *The Sopranos,* Chase shows us a family that fits the model, but in the process points out the weaknesses and inaccuracies of the model. Tony Soprano is the breadwinning father who sets the rules, protects his family and adheres to Strict Father morality in terms of Moral Order and Moral Strength; yet, he beats up and kills people, operates illegal businesses, and cheats on his wife. By having this "strict father" perform what would be considered immoral acts by both conservatives and liberals, Chase points out that the "traditional" family model is just that — a model, and as such, can be manipulated in numerous ways.

Chase also shows us that the model doesn't work, especially for children and marriages. A.J., despite being raised in a wealthy home with two heterosexual parents who "follow" Catholic morality, is messed up. He does drugs, vandalizes his school, gets expelled, and can't keep a job. Tony's and Carmela's marriage also demonstrates that the Strict Father model doesn't work for marriages. Both are miserable in the marriage. Following her Catholic faith, Carmela believes in the sanctity of marriage and through the first few seasons agonizes over her marriage, Tony's infidelities, and his illegal activities. In the first season, she consults a priest (a symbol and agent of Strict Father morality) who tells her she is partially responsible for Tony's problems and encourages her to be faithful to her marriage vows and try to reform Tony. The priest then suggests she confess her sins and take communion. Chase, of course, undercuts all of this advice by having the priest get drunk and make a pass at Carmela. By the third season, Carmela has become so depressed with her life and marriage that she sees a therapist. This time, however, the therapist tells her to get out of the marriage because as long as she is in it, she's Tony's accomplice in his illegal activities. Ironically, it is the secular therapist, not the priest, who points out greater moral issues than just her marriage. Yet, from the Strict Father mindset, the therapist is not to be trusted because therapy is a sign of weakness—people don't need therapy if they have enough moral strength. By the end of the fourth season, Carmela has become so frustrated with and humiliated by Tony's infidelities that, despite her faith, she kicks him out of the house.

The marriage doesn't work for Tony either. Tony believes since he is the male-breadwinner and the authority of the household, that he can live his life the way he desires, which includes having numerous affairs. Most of the time, he thinks he can control Carmela by simply appeasing her with a monetary show of affection—a fur coat, a jade ring, a donation to Meadow's school. Despite enjoying the comforts Carmela brings by being the homemaker, he still is most attracted to the seemingly independent businesswoman, such as the Mercedes Benz saleswoman Gloria Trillo in season three.

On the other hand, the marriage does work for both of them on some level. In the fifth season, during their separation, Tony has a difficult time not being at home and the intimacy between them becomes very apparent when Tony calls Carmela from his hotel in the early morning and they discuss mundane, but comforting things. Despite his many affairs, Tony finds some level of fulfillment in being with his stable Carmela in their home. And as miserable as Carmela is, she still remains loyal and genuinely likes some parts of Tony. In addition, she gets the economic and social lifestyle she wants. Yet, while this marriage appears to be appropriate, according to the Strict Father family model, appearances are deceiving—the individuals are miserable in their marriage and commit acts in violation of their marriage vows.

Finally, Chase depicts what happens to people who try to live by the Strict Father ideal or live by a model that doesn't reflect reality. Coontz comments that people who try to live according to "traditional" values often set themselves up for failure. For example, the Bible Belt has the highest divorce rate in the U.S., and in research conducted by the National Longitudinal Study of Adolescent Youth, 88 percent of the teens who had pledged sexual abstinence during the 1990s had broken their vow. Of even more concern is the fact that the majority of the 88 percent admitted to engaging in unprotected sex ("For Better" 6). In the real world, trying to live a life that is not based in reality or no longer exists sets you up for failure, which we see in *The Sopranos*.

In addition to trying to live his life as a "strict father" in his nuclear family, Tony tries to live his life as a "strict father" in his other family. Tony longs for "the good old days," the days when gangster life was more like the Corleone's in Mario Puzo's *The Godfather*. John Cawelti describes *The Godfather* world as one of a "tribal closeness" with the Don as "its theocratic center. He is not only the boss, but king, judge, and priest ... the tribe-family ruled by the Don is a patriarchy with absolutely clear roles and lines of authority" (as qtd in Fields 617). Tony longs for things to be the way they used to be — but they don't exist anymore, if they ever existed.[7] His mob family doesn't have the same commitment to loyalty, honor, and respect shown in *The Godfather* and his nuclear family doesn't either (Tony's mother continually questions his authority in his mob family and even contracts to have him killed, while Tony's children and wife challenge his authority at home). Consequently, Tony's desires for the romanticized mob family and nuclear family leave him frustrated. He feels "that the best is gone, that I came in at the end" ("Pilot," 1.1). He suffers from panic attacks, horrific demonstrations of anger and violence, and feelings of inadequacy — "I got the world by the balls and I can't stop feeling like a fucking loser" ("The Happy Wanderer," 2.6). He ends up seeing a psychiatrist and taking Prozac. What Tony shows us is that trying to live a romanticized life based on selective amnesia of "the good old days" is impossible and leaves one open to never ending frustrations and feelings of inadequacy.

A second problem with the Strict Father family model is its Moral Order metaphor. George Lakoff explains that this metaphor is based on a folk theory of the natural order, which claims that the order of dominance seen in nature — God over man; man over nature — is the "natural" order of dominance that occurs in the world. The Moral Order metaphor takes this folk hierarchy of natural power relations and transforms it into a hierarchy of moral authority: God has moral authority over people; people have moral authority over nature; adults have moral authority over children; men have moral authority over women (81). What this metaphor is doing then is legitimizing power relations, making them seem natural and, more importantly, moral. Therefore, according to the Strict Father model, fathers and paternal authority figures are naturally and morally superior to everyone else. Any social movement, such as feminism, that questions the hierarchy or even people who don't fit it are seen as inferior and even immoral. Ultimately, then, according to the Moral Order metaphor, the most moral are rich, heterosexual, white males. Wealth characterizes the Strict Father moral system because in order to become rich one has to have self-

discipline, self-denial, and self-reliance, which are the highest moral characteristics one can possess. White and male because the hierarchy of natural order demonstrates that men are superior to women and Caucasians are
superior to people of color. Heterosexual because natural order demonstrates
that successful, moral mating is composed of one man and one woman.

Although the Moral Order metaphor legitimizes white, heterosexual
male authority, for the purposes of this essay, I will only concentrate on the
how the Moral Order metaphor legitimizes gender relations. How does the
metaphor work for women? Obviously, it places them in the position of
"Other" in which they are seen as unequal and inferior. Historically, we can
see the tangible results of the metaphor in social expressions such as a lack
of suffrage. But how does the metaphor operate in contemporary society
and in the contemporary television family of the Sopranos?

Adhering to the Moral Order metaphor, the majority of the women in
The Sopranos are in subordinate positions to men, servicing men in a variety
of ways. Most of the women portrayed on the show are wives, girlfriends,
or sexual conquests/objects. On the surface, the women in the show fit gender stereotypes or even archetypes. There are whores, mothers, wives, and
daughters. First there are the whores—Tony's numerous mistresses, call
girls, and occasional secretary. Their purpose in Tony's life is to be "fucked."
Few have more than a name. The staging and camera position used for most
of these sexual encounters further emphasizes these characters' role. For
example, in the second season when Tony is advised by his attorney to
spend time at his legal business, Tony starts going to the Barone Brothers
Sanitation office every day where he is extremely bored and desperately
wants to get back to his illegal pursuits at his strip club, the Bada Bing.
When we first see one of the office secretaries, who is young and attractive,
she is introduced as a nice, Christian girl. Later in the episode, we see her
being "fucked" by Tony. He is sitting in a desk chair entering her from the
rear. As the camera shows her moving her body up and down to accom-
modate Tony, he is sitting behind her with a bored look on his face. What
the shot tells us is that she is simply there for Tony to use sexually. His bored
expression tells us that his sexual encounter is meaningless, something to
do to pass the time. Her greater involvement, both physically and presumably pleasurably based on her facial and vocal expressions, indicates that
the encounter has more meaning for her and that it is her job to please him
sexually—to do more work. We see the whore archetype again whenever
the action is filmed at the Bada Bing. Actually, one way the camera lets us
know we are at the Bada Bing is that it pans the bare-breasted, thong-wear-
ing pole dancers of the club. As soon as we see women writhing against a
pole, we know where we are.

Another archetype we see is the wife/mother. Through most of the seasons, Carmela does not work outside of the home; instead, she recognizes that it is her job to make a happy home. She cooks fabulous Italian dinners, arranges with the housekeeper to keep the house clean, decorates the house, hosts family and business dinners/parties for Tony, and looks after the family's religious interests through her involvement with the Catholic church and other volunteer activities. As a mother, she helps Meadow with her college admission procedures and with her boyfriend issues in other seasons. In the first few seasons, she is sensitive to A.J.'s issues and tries to fix them — seeing A.J.'s school counselors, researching different school options. She loves her children and wants the best for them. Carmela knows and accepts her role, and the role of all the women in the family, although that role is a source of great dissonance in her material and spiritual world. When Angie, the widow of a slain captain, takes over her husband's business and ultimately his role in the world of organized crime, even the older, wiser Carmela of season six is moved to state, "she's one of us, now it's like she's one of them" ("Live Free or Die," 6.6).

Although the women are in stereotypical positions, they still have some power and very rarely simply submit to Tony and wait for him to take moral or any other type of superiority over them. Over time, Carmela asserts herself around Tony. She confronts him about his mistresses, leaves for a trip to Paris when she needs a break from him, and kicks him out of the house when she's had enough. Although she stays out of Tony's business, she runs their household, telling Tony what to do to be a better husband and how to be a better parent.

Tony's mother Livia, who dies in the third season, is the antithesis of the mother archetype. From her behavior at family dinners, we see her as an acid, rancorous force for discord in the family, and aggressively detrimental to Tony's power as father and son. Through his sessions with Dr. Melfi we find out that his mother was consistently abusive and emotionally absent. For example, she gave Tony's dog away and threatened to put a fork through his eye. In the first three seasons, she joins with Uncle Junior to undermine Tony's authority as Boss and puts a hit on him. Even after she dies in the third season, her presence is felt strongly through Tony's fantasies, his psychotherapy, and his near-death experiences in the sixth season.

Tony's sister Janice is also very determined, constantly doing things her way. She insists on a big funeral for their mother and managing her estate. She joins forces with Uncle Junior and Richie to undermine Tony so that she gets a bigger cut. In season five, she manipulates recent widower Bobby Bacala into marrying her. And in season six, we see Janice in the full blossom of her Livia-like role of manipulative mother and wife and watch her fall completely apart in the most histrionic ways when the putative source of her strength as a "Daddy's Girl" — Tony — is on death's door.

Although Chase depicts some assertive women and gives them some power, their power is limited because it's not legitimate. In the Strict Father model, men control the public sphere of employment — making decisions, making money. Women are relegated to the private sphere of home management. In *The Sopranos* what we see is what happens to women when they are stuck in their stereotypes and stereotypical positions. Tony's mother and sister buck the system and they do it the only way they know how or can — working behind the scenes to undermine male authority. To the audience they come across as manipulative, self-absorbed, cutthroat, and cruel. The same adjectives can be applied to Tony's gang, but because his gang is "legitimate" according to the Strict Father model, those adjectives are more attractive and seen as necessary for them to survive.

The most interesting male/female relationship on the show, that of Tony and Dr. Melfi, tears apart the Moral Order metaphor. Dr. Melfi is a woman, yet she works outside of the home, financially supports herself, and is successful in an educated, professional position. As Tony's psychiatrist, she is not only his equal, but often his superior. She is the one who prescribes Prozac for him and whom he embarrassingly has to notify of the sexual side effects that it causes him. In addition to knowing about his sexual inadequacies, she also knows about his other weaknesses. Even being in the position of helping him with his panic attacks puts her in a superior position because in therapy sessions Tony has to act against his perceived notions of masculine behavior and talk about his feelings. She is his educational superior, often providing historical or philosophical references for him. When he complains about A.J.'s flirtation with existentialism and Nietzsche, she explains what existentialism is. She consistently provides advice to Tony, who, if he doesn't use it in his emotional life, uses it in his professional life.

As a final jab at the Moral Order metaphor, she often is morally superior in that she challenges his behavior and his illegal activity. "Why don't you just give it up?" ("For All Debts Public and Private," 4.1) she asks him directly when he complains about the lack of future for men in his business. His response is, basically, that he can "handle it" — that his plan for his future will allow him to avoid all the unpleasantness of prison or assassination. And whenever Tony tries to help her using his connections, she refuses because they are illegal. After she is raped and her rapist gets off on a technicality, Tony offers to provide "justice," but she refuses "justice" that doesn't come from the legal system. Often, Tony tries to get the upper hand with her by sexualizing their relationship, telling her off, threatening to quit their therapy sessions, but he keeps coming back even though he doesn't have the upper hand. Although he is physically attracted to her, he ultimately respects her intelligence and cares about her. In their relationship we see one that is more equally balanced; consequently, Tony has to work harder — he can't rely on his monetary gifts or demonstrations of power to appease and/or attract women. Instead he has to give in other ways — of his feelings, of his patience, and he has to communicate with her as honestly as he can. Interestingly, because of Melfi, he finds himself most attracted to intelligent, career women.

In *The Sopranos* David Chase interrogates the Moral Order metaphor, showing what happens to families that live by the Moral Order. In the show, the majority of women are not included in legitimate positions of power and are confined to stereotypes. As a result, they're miserable and so are the men. The healthiest relationship in the show is the one that defies both masculine and feminine stereotypes, tearing apart the Moral Order.

A third problem with the Strict Family model is its prioritization of the Moral Strength metaphor. Applying characteristics from the physical domain to the moral domain (such as "Being Good is Being Upright"), this metaphor asserts that people are born morally weak (Lakoff 72). In order to become morally strong, people have to develop, either through teaching or punishment, self-discipline and self-denial. Then, they can fight the internal evils of lust or drug addiction and the external evils that challenge Strict Father morality. This metaphor entails that the world is strictly good or evil, that to ruthlessly attack evil is moral, and that the views of one's adversaries need not be understood or respected because they are immoral. Such a strong dualistic view of the world has several ramifications. Most problematic of the ramifications is that it does not allow for any gray.

As pointed out by Lakoff, a cognitive scientist, such strict constructs are "out of touch with real minds" (376). Basically, the human mind doesn't operate on a strict, dualistic level and neither does reality. Consequently, people who try to live by strict constructs create their own reality to make the constructs work. In *The Sopranos* the line between good and evil has no reality — doing good in the world of Tony Soprano is being the best criminal you can be. Yet, both families are set up around a Strict Father model, so they have developed their own reality or own code in order to adhere to the dualistic good vs. evil construct, thus producing the central dramatic conflict of the series. For someone in the world of the Sopranos, the moral high ground is in being upright *as compared to everyone else*. A man must be more "moral" than the next guy. The "Father" of the crime family is generally removed from the actual violence, the commission of crimes, the collection of protection money. He is a *better* father, a better provider, a better drinker, lover, eater and friend. Only by being more upright than the men surrounding him can he retain his position in the moral structure and his position of Moral Strength.

According to Lakoff, self-discipline and self-denial are the keys to moral strength and are learned through obedience to superiors. Those characteristics are central to the efficient running of the crime family, as well — but are defined by the guy at the top. Therefore, we see obedience exhibited by everyone *not* the boss — and disobedience is punished swiftly and mercilessly. Disobey too many times, and your chance to disobey again is removed permanently.

Christopher Moltisanti, Tony's cousin, has shown his tragic flaw to be an almost complete absence of Moral Strength — much to Tony's disappointment. Tony perceives himself to have given Christopher all the guidance, discipline, punishment, encouragement he might need to become a "father" for the family — grooming him to take over as head, primarily because he is "blood." "You've got to exercise impulse control," Tony advises when Christopher allows a brokerage firm he was supposed to be running to descend into chaos ("Guy Walks into a Psychiatrist's Office," 2.1). Time after time, Christopher shows himself incapable of learning or even trying. He has none of the moral strength required to sustain the structure — he is a victim of his weaknesses — bad judgment, addictions, and lack of insight.

A.J. is perhaps the saddest victim of the inadequacy of the Moral Strength metaphor. He has watched his demented grandmother, his dysfunctional parents, and his extended families struggle to make sense of a morality that shifts constantly to keep its center. When Tony was A.J.'s age, he had already been introduced to the business — watching his father at work. A.J. is protected, purposefully, not only from learning the business and thus becoming an active part of the ersatz moral structure, but from ever being involved in what has made his family what it is for generations. As he matures, he has no sense of personal history, no sense of right and wrong, no work ethic, no direction. His perceptions of what a "man" is — moral or not — he has had to create from intermittent threats and guidance from a father who never practices what he preaches.

Ultimately, Chase interrogates the Moral Strength metaphor. By showing how a family tries to adhere to a dualistic mentality, he shows a family that has to make up the rules to fit the dualism. Consequently, everything is a mess because dualism doesn't exist, yet in trying to fit the prescription, good and evil are defined to suit the powers at be.

Nurturant Parent Model as Depicted in Northern Exposure

Similar to Clinton's approach to family, *Northern Exposure*'s emphasis is not on the nuclear family, but on the diverse community or global family.[8] The emphasis on the community family, however, is appropriate for the Nurturant Parent model because this model emphasizes an individual's responsibility to community — "A fulfilling life is [...] one committed to family and community responsibility" (108). In describing the Nurturant Parent family model, Lakoff comments that the goal of parents is to raise their children to be the "right kind of people" (112);[9] that is, people who can

> take care of themselves, be responsible, enjoy life, develop their potential, [...] and become independent-minded. They also learn to empathize with others, develop social ties, become socially responsible, communicate well, respect others, and act fairly toward them [111–112].

The *Northern Exposure* family is filled with the "right kind of people." Chris, Maggie, Holling, Shelly, Ruth-Anne, and Ed take care of themselves, are responsible, enjoy life, and promote social responsibility. Typical scenes in the show include Ruth-Anne managing her store, Chris and Ed enjoying the great outdoors, Ed working on his potential, first as a movie director, then as a Shaman, and all of them working together to develop community activities that will promote social responsibility, such as a blood drive.

They are also expert communicators. Common scenes include the characters helping each other out by talking out individual and group problems. Maggie and Joel are famous for their abrasive communication style; yet, it works for them and they are able to articulate what they need from each other. In "Up River" (6.8), Maggie and Joel try to cohabitate. By the end of the episode, due to the stress of trying to live together, Maggie tells Joel that they need a break from living together.

MAGGIE: Joel, what I'm trying to say is ... you exhaust me.

JOEL: I exhaust you.

MAGGIE: There's just too much of you, you know? And it's always working so hard [23].

Despite the fact that Maggie dissolves their relationship, the two are very good at expressing their needs and understanding what the other is saying.

Other characters in the show don't communicate in such a direct style; yet, their style is still successful. Marilyn, Joel's office manager, uses the stories from her heritage to make her point. In "Bolt from the Blue" (5.14), Ed is struck by lightning and is experiencing much angst because he can't figure out why. He asks Marilyn, "Is it a nihilistic universe with no meaning, oh, other than survival, or does the enlightenment view prevail? Does the Creator have a master plan, and if so, what is it?" Marilyn responds by telling him the story of a warrior who had a fine stallion. The warrior experienced good things and bad things that could be tied to the stallion. Each time something happened people told him he was either lucky or unlucky. And each time the warrior's response was "Maybe" (25). It is not until he listens to Marilyn that Ed is able to relax and realize that sometimes things just happen.

The characters' communication is also intelligent and complex. They aren't afraid to go beyond surface pleasantries, exploring topics such as the meaning of life, the function of art, the consequences of behavior. They are not only intelligent, but they recognize the need for community to figure out life's big questions. In "Up River," Chris hires a contractor to remodel his trailer. Living in chaos has Chris uncharacteristically short-tempered and anxious. As he tries to figure out what happened to him, he explains to Joel: "Thing is, Joel, what's a house? It's a metaphor, right? For the mind. Isn't that what it's all about? You gotta tear down the old before you can build the new, you know? You gotta lose your mind before you can find it" (21).

Verbalizing his conundrum makes the situation clear to Chris, and he is able to regain his equilibrium. The characters tend to speak metaphorically on a consistent basis, yet they understand each other or at least try to. For the most part, they are respected for their analytical and verbal abilities because the community is a nurturing one that accepts each other, encourages independent thinking, and encourages people to fulfill their potential.

Joel, although abrasive and abusive in much of his communication, recognizing the importance of communication/social skills, even teaches an inept communicator how to talk to people. In "Bolt from the Blue," Joel reluctantly befriends Stan, a national parks employee who has spent the last twenty years patrolling on a fire tower. When Stan is transferred from the tower duty, he has difficulty adjusting to being around people. He is a horrible communicator in that he tends to discuss at great length everything. Joel, in his characteristic abrasive way, tells Stan he babbles ("Stop. See you're doing it right now. I didn't ask for an explanation about speech disorders. You understand? It's like, Ruth-Anne didn't ask about the taxonomy of tubers") (21). Later, Joel teaches a devastated Stan how to communicate and make friends.

JOEL: I want you to tell me something, and not from a book or something you've read or heard, okay? I want you to just tell me about your life.... I'll tell you something about me, and then we'll try to have a conversation.... Favorite food, or sports?

STAN: I like Franco American spaghetti....

JOEL: (laughs) Okay, I actually have a special fondness for Chef Boyardee ravioli. Beef [24].

Despite differing communication styles, the characters consistently communicate their needs and help each other through listening and speaking.

Finally, the characters in the show are the "right kind of people" in that they empathize with others and respect and treat others fairly. After Lakoff explains what the "right" kind of people are according to a Nurturant Parent model, he describes what kind of world is needed for these people "to develop and thrive." That world has to be as "nurturant as possible [...]. It must be a world that encourages people to develop their potential and provides help when necessary. [...] It must be a world governed maximally by empathy [... and] governed as much as possible by bonds of affection, respect, and interdependence" (112). Predominating in Lakoff's description of the "Nurturant" world are the model's top two moral metaphors—Morality as Nurturance and Morality as Empathy, both of which *Northern Exposure*'s family adheres to.

Morality as Nurturance means that it is moral to care about all people and take care of all people even if one has to make sacrifices to do so or if one disagrees with those people's differences. In *Northern Exposure*, the characters take care of each other, whether it's teaching someone basic social/communication skills as Joel does for Stan, buying someone a beer at The Brick so he/she can vent frustrations, or giving someone a place to sleep because his/her house burned. In "Shofar, So Good" (6.3), Eugene is organizing a house-raising for Hayden Keyes, who burned his own house down by smoking in bed. Most in Cecily plan to participate, except Joel. Joel refuses to help because he feels Hayden brought the problem on himself and "refuses to help himself." "Do you not see that by indulging him in this way, you are basically giving tacit approval to this deeply embedded pattern of incredibly negligent behavior? You let him spend a night out in the cold, and then maybe he'll realize that he brought this on himself, and he's gonna have to get himself out of it" (4). Here, as well as in most of the show, Joel demonstrates elements of the Strict Father moral system. According to that moral system, it is not moral or appropriate to help people who refuse to help themselves. People who refuse to stop smoking when their doctor has told them to and then burn their own house down by smoking in bed, do not have self-discipline and are therefore immoral and undeserving of help. Joel proposes a tough-love solution to Hayden's problem, which is a Strict Father disciplinary approach. Yet, although Joel is the knowledgeable physician, by the end of the episode he realizes his tough-love approach is the wrong one. This episode uses a Dickensian framework to help Joel see the error of his ways. On the eve of Yom Kippur Joel is visited by the "ghost of the present" in the form of Rabbi Schulman who takes Joel for a walk where he encounters a frostbitten, coughing Hayden who has been left out in the cold to learn a lesson. Then in his visit by the "ghost of the future," Joel sees Hayden's grave. Upon awaking from his dream, Joel immediately signs up for a full day of work on Hayden's new house.

In another episode "Zarya" (6.6), Ed cares for Marilyn by helping her heal the pain in her leg. Ever since the pain appeared Marilyn has been dreaming of one of her grandfather's stories. Ed believes that the pain and the story are connected, but since Marilyn can't remember the ending, he decides to film her telling the story and perhaps the film will tell the ending. Ed spends hours caring for Marilyn in this way, healing her leg and giving her back a piece of her family history because in the process of telling the story, Marilyn learns more about her grandfather.

The other important moral metaphor that the Cecily community family adheres to is Morality as Empathy, which means that it is moral to feel what another is feeling and to "act so as to promote a sense of well-being in that person" (114). *Northern Exposure* is filled with examples of characters living the Morality as Empathy metaphor. In "Shofar, So Good" (6.3), Holling is depressed because he feels his adult daughter Jackie's problems in life are his fault for being a bad father. Although he never knew about her existence until she was an adult, he still blames himself: "I created a hole in the world that I can't repair" (10). Ed aches for Holling and wants to heal his hurt. So Ed decides to act as a "scape goat" (or fox in this case because Ed is also going to be the fox for Maurice's fox hunt) where Holling places his "sin" on Ed and Ed bears it away. Holling thinks the idea is foolish, as well as dangerous, but Ed is willing to make sacrifices to make his friend feel better. Although Holling was reluctant about the idea, by the end of the hunt he becomes grateful to Ed and seems to have more of a sense of well-being.

Chris also is consistently empathetic to the other characters. In "Fish Story" (5.18), Holling is depressed because he feels his paint-by-number painting is not art. Although he had been feeling good about his paintings, Maurice criticizes them as "therapy for the artistically challenged [... and] what they prescribe for cretins in dayrooms" (8). When Holling confesses to Chris that there is no joy in painting anymore and he wants to hang up his brushes, Chris explains that art is a process, not a product, and that he'll help Holling "get your ego out of the product and put it back in the process" (10). Chris's solution is for Holling to burn his latest painting in order to "liberate the art from the artist" (18). Holling doesn't quite understand, but he places his painting in the incinerator and by the end of the episode he's back to painting and according to Shelly, "It's even closer [to a photographic likeness] than last time" (25).

The two metaphors work together to create a respect for diversity and difference. Morality as Nurturance insists that equal priority or fairness is given to all "and since children necessarily have differences among them, all those differences have to be respected and toleration is required. Moreover, each child has something different to contribute to the family" (Lakoff 228). Morality as Empathy insists that when having empathy for others, one must understand their values and viewpoints—not judge them, but try to have empathy for them from their perspective and act from their perspective. Cecily is inhabited by a diverse bunch of people who, for the most part, treat each other fairly, respect each other's differences, and try to learn from those differences. Rabbi Schulman once again appears to Joel in a dream and admits he's having difficulty embracing "gender-free" services. "It's no longer correct to refer to the Lord as a masculine presence, as in 'blessed by his name.' Now it's 'blessed be his or her name'" ("Fish Story" 13). But he acknowledges that he probably was too harsh on Emily, his replacement, and that gender-free services aren't such a bad idea and that he's starting to embrace gender-free language. The characters also try to nurture each other by acting empathetically from the other character's point of view. For example, in "Fish Story," Maggie, who was raised Catholic, wants to surprise Joel by having a Seder. She has been sensing some type of sadness on Joel's part and thinks he misses the Jewish traditions with which he was raised. She admits she's been reading up on Passover and tells him she is "trying to give you [Joel] a part of your [his] culture" (2). Another example is Ed trying to heal Marilyn's leg pain by approaching the healing from her perspective — she has to find the ending of her grandfather's story in order to heal her leg.

In addition, the characters' respect for diversity makes it possible for their world to be governed by nonhierarchical interdependence (Lakoff 112). According to Lakoff, the Nurturant Parent world is one that is interdependent, where people are equal, and where authority comes out of wisdom, judgment, and empathy, not dominance (113). *Northern Exposure*'s characters are equally powerful. Although Joel has the degree in medicine, Marilyn's and Ed's holistic remedies are sometimes just as good. Gender norms are challenged in that the female characters hold non-stereotypical positions — a bush pilot and storeowner/motorcyclist — and aren't merely relegated to the private sphere of domestic management. In the last season, Maggie even becomes town mayor. Moreover, there is no direct authority figure in the town (although Maurice and Joel try to be). Instead, the characters are interdependent, asking for and giving advice to each other. Chris is sought out for advice on religious or philosophical angst; Ruth-Anne for basic relationship issues; Maggie for mechanical problems; Holling for basic common sense.

Northern Exposure does not create perfect people or ideals; people do have problems. Asking questions, working things out can lead to self-absorption. For example, Chris, who often is the spiritual advisor for the group, occasionally shows that he can think only of himself. When Ruth-Anne runs off in "Fish Story" because she's overwhelmed by customer demands and Maurice wants to force open her store, Chris at first defends her right to control her own store. Yet, once he realizes he is almost out of beer, he quickly rescinds and is ready to storm the store. In "Up River" we see him lose his temper, fire his contractor with extremely harsh words, and not show up for work because he is stuck in the chaos of home improvement.

There are also characters who don't fit the Nurturant Parent model; instead, they represent a Strict Father approach to life. The show's original main character, Joel Fleishman,[10] is an urban, educated, Jewish doctor from New York who reluctantly comes to Cicely to practice medicine in exchange for the $125,000 he borrowed from the state of Alaska to pay for medical school. Joel arrives with many preconceived notions about everything. A common source of tension in the series is Joel's arrogance and inability to accept other ways of doing things. For example, he dismisses Ed's holistic healing abilities because they aren't part of his scientific and American Medical Association prescriptions. He continually disparages over his assistant Marilyn's relaxed approach to managing his office. Time and time again, he insists on Strict Father discipline — Hayden should sleep outside in the cold until he learns his lesson — and Strict Father respect for his authority: "I'll write the prescriptions, and you take the medicine. That simple enough? Something that pea-size brain of yours can handle?" ("Thanksgiving" as qtd. in "Shofar, So Good" 13). Time and time again, however, Joel is proven wrong. Not until the fifth season does Joel finally admit that he is a Cicelian and we see him acting more according to a Nurturant Parent model.

Maurice Minnifield, a former astronaut and current self-perceived town power broker, also adheres to the Strict Father model. Maurice has difficulty with almost anyone who is different than he is — a conservative, wealthy, white, heterosexual, male entrepreneur. When he learns he has a son from a tryst he had during the Korean War, he wants nothing to do with him because he isn't "white." In addition, Maurice goes to great lengths to avoid Ron and Erick, a gay couple, and their wedding. Maurice perceives himself to be better than everyone else and more moral because he had the self-discipline to work hard and make money. He refers to Cecily as a special place where he wants "to maintain the quality of life. We do not want refugees [...] pushing shopping carts up and down the street" ("Bolt from the Blue" 11). Maurice, like Joel, however, eventually learns to accept those who are different than he. Yet, he remains arrogant and likes to remind people that he has power and money. By having these two characters become more nurturing and by positioning them to be ridiculed when they are not nurturing, the show ultimately tells us that the Nurturant Parent behavior is best.

And is the Nurturant Parent family model and moral system best for the *Northern Exposure* family and for society in general? The characters in *Northern Exposure* are certainly happier than the characters in *The Sopranos*. Despite the vicissitudes of life, the characters of *Northern Exposure* seem to feel fulfilled — they have the ability to grow and change, have positive views of themselves, communicate well, and live in a crime-free community. But is this kind of family ideal workable in our world today, which is being run according to a Strict Father model. When people are working longer hours for less pay, poor health insurance, and limited daycare options, is it easier to yell and use punishments as a discipline approach than have the patience to engage in an open dialogue with children? Is it possible to emphasize cooperation instead of competition in our world today where raising children has become the latest way to "keep up with the Jones'" and parents compete to have the smartest, most athletic, most creative child on the block.[11] In addition, is it possible to use this model when the majority of families still operate on a Strict Father model? One thing the characters of Cecily learn is that they may have a wonderful community family, but they can't run away from their Strict Father nuclear families — they keep appearing or influencing them in some way. But, the characters also learn to make peace with their nuclear families, learn what they can from the process, and move on with their lives. So even if it's not easy to follow a Nurturant Parent path, the outcome is surely more attractive than the outcome of the Strict Father model as depicted in *The Sopranos*.

Conclusion

According to Lakoff, the definitions of family and family moral systems provide the moral worldviews in contemporary politics, influencing national and international policies; consequently, it's worth taking a look at how the nuclear family definition works in national politics. After examining *The Sopranos* as an example of Bush's Strict Father definition of family, it is clear that there are numerous problems with it — it's based on errors, it's unrealistic, it has horrible repercussions for marriage, children, women, gays, and people of color. If Bush's approach doesn't work for the nuclear family, why would it work for the national family? Ultimately, what *The Sopranos* demonstrates is that Bush's family moral system, in the name of "morality" and "national strength," promotes violence, racism, sexism, homophobia, xenophobia, and moreover, is one that can be manipulated to support those in power. Furthermore, the dualistic us vs. them mentality of the Moral Strength metaphor allows moral relativity where evidence of weapons of mass destruction is lied about and personal liberties are stripped away all in the name of fighting the enemy,

Perhaps it is a case of selective amnesia, but the Clintonesque/Nurturant Parent days of the 1990s, when diversity was important, women's equality was important, intelligence was valued, and as *Northern Exposure* demonstrated — people tried not to judge each other, but value and take care of each other, looks much more appealing. The lack of violence and warfare in Cecily, Alaska, is really attractive. The *Northern Exposure* characters live in peace. *The Sopranos* characters desperately want to live in peace, but they can't because the family model they embody and admire is so limited. There is no doubt that *The Sopranos* is brilliantly written and directed, but ironically, it advocates a "culture of death," all the while espousing traditional family values.

Notes

1. In his speech Quayle blamed the Los Angeles riots on the breakdown of family values. In commenting on how popular culture contributes to the breakdown, he stated "it doesn't help matters when primetime TV has Murphy Brown — a character who supposedly epitomizes today's intelligent, highly paid, professional woman — mocking the importance of fathers, by bearing a child alone, and calling it just another 'lifestyle choice'" (2).

2. I will concentrate comments regarding *Northern Exposure* to its fifth and sixth seasons (1994–1996) because those are the years that David Chase was consistently at the helm as executive producer.

3. Most notable reviews of *Northern Exposure* are Frank McConnell's "Follow That Moose," in which he identifies the show as a "pastoral" or a "myth of the Special Place" with Cecily being a global village (18–19), and Taylor's and Upchurch's *Northern Exposure* and Mythology of the Global Community" in which they argue that *Northern Exposure* features the global village — "an ideal place where we can find unity in cultural diversity, individual freedom in community cooperation, and individual growth through social participation" (76). Patrick McCormick's "Family Night Gets Whacked" is one of numerous reviews that comment on how *The Sopranos* satirizes the American family.

4. During the early part of Clinton's administration, Hilary Clinton made famous the expression "global village" through her "It Takes a Village to Raise a Child" campaign, which emphasized that every citizen had a stake in raising healthy children.

5. Morality as Empathy is an example of a moral metaphor, in which "[E]mpathy is understood metaphorically as the capacity to project your consciousness into other people so that you can feel what they feel." Language that demonstrates this metaphor includes: "I know how you feel. I feel for you" (114).

6. As for Christian marriage traditions, it wasn't until 1563 that the Catholic Church mandated that ceremonies had to be performed in order to make marriage legitimate. Before, people were married in the eyes of the Church if they simply exchanged "words of consent." And it wasn't until 1754 when governments tried to control or define marriage with England's requirement of a license in order for a marriage to be considered valid ("Just Which" 2).

7. The romanticized view of the mob as popularized by *The Godfather* is very similar to today's conservative view of the family—a patriarchal one with clearly defined rules, roles, a strong code of loyalty and service. In an excellent article on social politics and gangster narratives, Ingrid Walker Fields, discusses Tony Soprano's infatuation with Don Corleone and the frustrations Tony experiences from his failure to live up to his romanticized image of how he thinks his life should be.

8. Despite its emphasis on the community family, the show's nuclear family of Holling, Shelly, and baby Miranda is an example of the Nurturant Parent model in that this family is composed of two parents who "share household responsibilities" (Lakoff 108). Both Shelly and Holling take turns running their bar The Brick and caring for their daughter.

9. Lakoff comments that Strict Father parents want to raise their children to be the "right kind of people" as well. The difference between the Strict Father and Nurturant Parent goals is how they define "right."

10. Rob Morrow, who acted the role of Fleishman, reduced his appearances in the fifth season and was absent from most of the sixth season.

11. A recent article in *Newsweek* addresses the problem of high-stakes, competitive learning at the first-grade level brought on in part by Bush's No Child Left Behind legislation. Many educators are seeing burnout in elementary school students, as well as parents choosing to send their child to school a year later so that the child can be ahead of the game and in the top of his or her class (Tyre, et. al. 34–44).

Works Cited

Bush, George W. "Proclamation — National Family Week, 2001." *Weekly Compilation of Presidential Documents* 37.47 (2001): 1705.

_____. "Remarks on Signing the Economic Growth and Tax Relief Reconciliation Act of 2001." *Weekly Compilation of Presidential Documents* 37.23 (2001): 858–859.

_____. "Remarks on Signing the Promoting Safe and Stable Families Amendments of 2001." *Weekly Compilation of Presidential Documents* 38.3 (2002): 83–86.

Cawelti, John. "The Mythology of Crime and Its Formulaic Embodiments." *Adventure, Mystery, and Romance.* Chicago: University of Chicago Press, 1976. 51–79.

Clinton, William J. "International Year of the Family." *Children Today* 22 (1993/1994): 38.

_____. "Proclamation 6852 — National Family Week, 1995." *Weekly Compilation of Presidential Documents* 31.46 (1995): 2028.

_____. "Remarks at the Sons of Italy Foundation Dinner." *Weekly Compilation of Presidential Documents* 35.21 (1999): 967–972.

Coontz, Stephanie. "The American Family." *Life Magazine* Nov. 1999. 22 August 2006
    <http://stephaniecoontz.com/articles/article10.htm>.
_____. "The Family in Upheaval." *Philadelphia Inquirer* 19 June 2005. 22 August 2006
    <http://stephaniecoontz.com/articles/article17.htm>.
_____. "For Better, For Worse: Marriage Means Something Different Now." *Washington Post* 1 May 2005: B01. 22 August 2006 <http://www.washingtonpost.com/wp-dyn/
    content/article/2005/04/30/AR20050400018.html>.
_____. "Just Which 'Traditional' Marriage Should We Defend?" 5 July 2006. *Council on
    Contemporary Families* 22 August 2006 <contemporaryfamilies.org>.
_____. "Uncle Sam Should Give Working Families a Hand." *Newsday* 7 September 2005:
    A33. 22 August 2006. http://pqasb.pqarchiver.com/newsday/access/892739981.html.
Fields, Ingrid Walker. "Family Values and Feudal Codes: The Social Politics of American's Twenty-First Century Gangster." *Journal of Popular Culture* 37 (2004): 611–33.
Kiefer, Francine. "Why 'Togetherness' Is a Cornerstone for Clinton." *Christian Science
    Monitor* 20 May 1999: Op 1.
Lakoff, George. *Moral Politics: How Liberals and Conservatives Think.* 2nd ed. Chicago:
    University of Chicago Press, 2002.
McConnell, Frank. "Follow That Moose: *Northern Exposure*'s Pedigree." *Commonweal*
    5 November 1993: 18–20.
McCormick, Patrick. "Family Night Gets Whacked." *U.S. Catholic* June 2006: 42–43.
Quayle, Dan. Speech to Commonwealth Club of California. 19 May 1992. Transcript
    available at "Quayle's 'Murphy Brown' Speech Still Rings True." <www.mfc.org/
    pfn/95-12/quayle.html>.
Taylor, Annette and David Upchurch. "*Northern Exposure* and Mythology of the Global
    Community." *Journal of Popular Culture* 30 (1996): 75–85.
Tyre, Peg, Julie Scelfo, Catharine Skipp, Nadine Joseph, Paul Tolme, and Hilary Shenfield. "The New First Grade: Too Much Too Soon?" *Newsweek* 11 September 2006:
    34–44.

Northern Exposure

"Bolt from the Blue." Season 5, episode 14. Teleplay: Jeff Melvoin. Dir.: Michael Lange.
    CBS. 24 January 1994. Transcript available at <http://members.aol.com/duvelle.html>.
"Fish Story." Season 5, episode 18. Teleplay: Jeff Melvoin. Dir.: Bill D'Elia. CBS. 14 March
    1994. Transcript available at <http://members.aol.com/duvelle.html>.
"Shofar, So Good." Season 6, episode 3. Teleplay: Jeff Melvoin. Dir.: James Hayman.
    CBS. 3 October 1994. Transcript available at <http://members.aol.com/duvelle.html>.
"Up River." Season 6, episode 8. Teleplay: Andrew Schneider and Diane Frolov. Dir.:
    Michael Fresco. 14 November 1994. Transcript available at <http://members.aol.com/
    duvelle.html>.
"Zarya." Season 6, episode 6. Teleplay: Andrew Schneider and Diane Frolov. Dir.: Jim
    Charleston. CBS. 31 October 1994. Transcript available at <http:members.aol.com/
    duvelle.html>.

The Sopranos

"For All Debts Public and Private." Season 4, episode 40. Teleplay: David Chase. Dir.:
    Allen Coulter. HBO. 15 September 2002.
"Guy Walks into a Psychiatrist's Office." Season 2, episode 14. Teleplay: Jason Cahill.
    Dir.: Allen Coulter. HBO. 16 January 2000.
"The Happy Wanderer." Season 2, episode 19. Teleplay: Frank Renzulli. Dir.: John Patterson. HBO. 20 February 2000.

"Live Free or Die." Season 6, episode 71. Teleplay: David Chase, Terence Winter, Mitchell Burgess, and Robin Green. Dir.: Tim Van Patten. HBO. 6 April 2006.

"Pilot." Season 1, episode 1. Teleplay: David Chase. Dir.: David Chase. HBO. 10 January 1999.

Defense-of-Family Acts: Queering *Famiglia* in *The Sopranos*

Lorena Russell

The Sopranos plays out in a state of tension between the everyday and the extraordinary. The quotidian of the bourgeois existence that the Soprano family enjoys stands in stark contrast with the violence of the mobster Soprano *famiglia*. While the show displays a predictable normality through its presentation of family, it simultaneously undermines any sense of stability though the close proximity and chaotic potential of mob-world violence. In *The Sopranos,* Family and *famiglia* are not always distinct, and throughout the series the two worlds come together in unexpected and disturbing ways.[1] While the home would seemingly mark a space made recognizable by its comforting familiarity, it is rather made strange by the broader field of violence that marks the mob's world.

Because of these uncanny aberrations and the constant threat that the violence of the mob will overcome that of the home, family in *The Sopranos* is charged with functioning as a defender of normality. As such, it becomes quite significant how narrowly and how fiercely it gets framed. Family is staged throughout the series as a kind of social bulwark, a comforting retreat to traditional values, but then this conservative gesture is repeatedly undercut through the violence, cruelty and thoroughgoing criminality of the *famiglia*. The resulting irony becomes part of the way that the show sets itself against the ideology of the normative family. As Anthony Rotundo points out, the value system that drives the Soprano's violence is paradoxically linked to their concept of family: "these homicidal rages also attack the fundamental principle of family on which these men have staked their integrity" (68). Practically with every episode, the show presents its viewers with routine and normalcy only to undermine these concepts through violence and hatred.

This paper explores the way that *The Sopranos'* ironic approach to "family values" opens up spaces for questioning conservative social politics. Through its critique of conservative values, *The Sopranos* challenges viewers' concepts of heteronormativity,[2] and lays bare the inconsistencies of a set of principles that on the one hand claims high moral ground and on the other condones violence. Tony Soprano's world view is one that is based on an assumed cultural hierarchy, one that draws from an imagined past to privilege a narrowly defined sense of family that is in turn bolstered by an abstract set of values ("loyalty," "honor," etc.). This combination of nostalgic entitlement and universal values creates a world where violence and deceit are the norm, even when playing against the recognizable and everyday.

The queer potential in this critique of family is made most explicit through the show's treatment of homophobia. The show's final season, Season Six, contains a major plot line that uncovers much of the complexity in the series' treatment of homophobia. But even here, Vito Spatiore's outing and subsequent murder only forms one part of the show's established homophobic worldview. And while the show's focus is on the rarified [and fictionalized] world of an Italian-American crime family, the lessons the audience is invited to consider clearly relate to the broader system of values informing late twentieth and early twenty-first century America. As Fred Gardaphé notes, "What makes *The Sopranos* worth watching and worth talking about is the way that Chase uses Tony Soprano's actions to speak to contemporary life in the United States" (91). Furthermore, Jay Parini argues that the violence in the show reflects the violence that is a part of everyday American life, and that the violence itself stems from a complex cycle of repression that is "part and parcel of bring male in America at the dawn of the twenty-first century" (Parini 87). Through its ironic treatment of family and the related concept of "family values," the show offers its viewers unique insight on the complexities of homophobia in America.

Martha P. Nochimson considers the way that the show ironically displaces family as it leads viewers towards a consideration of human connections: "it is also about the otherness of body and family to American corporate culture, and, above all, it is about the undying connections human beings have to each other..." (185). Nochimson places her discussion in the context of the gangster film genre, noting that *The Sopranos* plays within the conventions and extends them as well. The inclusion of therapy offers an opportunity to make explicit "its displaced investigation of the American family" (189). For Nochimson, the show challenges viewers to reconsider our pleasures in what she characterizes as "the infantile innocence of the gangster" (191). For me, the displacement of family functions equally as a comment on homophobia.

The Sopranos' treatment of family has always been central to the show's humor. The very first season establishes the ironic interplay between family and *famiglia*. Tony Soprano may rule supreme in his work world, but he is no match for his mother and sister. Despite the fact that his mother is a monster who schemes with Uncle Junior to have her son killed, Tony holds to a system of morals where outdated ideals of family loyalty reign supreme. No matter how cruelly his mother taunts him (a sarcastic "Poor you!" becomes one of Livia's trademark phrases, a derision picked up and echoed by numerous characters even after her death), Tony tries to please. It's only at the end of the season that he loses control and nearly smothers her in bed. This broad treatment of a classic dysfunctional family points to the inadequacy of Tony's traditional outlook, and uncovers a shallow morality based on "family values," one that is grounded in delusional "ideological projections" that are "holograms of a past that never was" (Hipsky par. 14).

Tony Soprano may operate via murder, lying, cheating and assault, but when it comes to family, he starts talking like a conservative Christian. When his children speak openly of sex in the first season, Tony cuts the conversation short: "No talking about sex at the breakfast table. The 1990's are out there. In here it's 1954" ("Nobody Knows Anything," 1.11). Of course part of what is "out there" is a world of violence where Tony is challenged to kill one of his own, Big Pussy. "In here" is best maintained as another world, but the distance becomes less and less tenable as the series progresses. In part this happens through the way that the violence of the mob world is seen as inextricably linked to the dysfunction of the family.

And while most families measure their dysfunction in terms of verbal and physical violence, both of these markers are writ especially strong in The Sopranos. Tony's mother Livia remains one of the most compelling, believable, and most horrifying characters of the entire series. She is irrepressibly negative, selfish, ruthless and manipulative, and does not hesitate to turn her powers against her family. Her destructiveness is at the heart of Tony's dysfunction.

Tracing the pattern of his relationship with his mother between the first and sixth season reveals the persistence of this theme. In the final season opener, Dr. Melfi reminds him "you cannot accept that you had a mother who did not love you." At the end of the first season, Tony struggles to accept the obvious, that his mother tried to have him killed for putting her in a nursing home. ("I Dream of Jeannie Cusamano," 1.13). The season ends with a powerful father/mother confrontation in the hospital aisles. Despite her recent stroke, Livia manages a telling smile, an implication that she has indeed been manipulating the strings behind his recent "carjacking." Throughout the series Tony moves in and out of denial about his mother's complicity. At one point, Dr. Melfi quietly recites the characteristics of Borderline Personality Disorder in an attempt to push him towards recognition of his mother's complicity in having him killed. He reacts my throttling her and reminding her "That is my mother you're talking about!" By Season Six he continues to maintain his ethic of family values, rewriting history when it comes to his mother's experience in the nursing home, and earnestly claiming that one can still depend on family (6.1). The episode ends with Tony nearly dying from a fatal shot from his demented Uncle Junior, a piece of dramatic irony that again points to the impossibility of creating "safe space" within the home, or of maintaining the nostalgic innocence of "family values" as drawn from the 1950s.

Tony is not the only character to struggle with family and the complexity of family ties. In Season Six, Paulie Walnuts' value system is shaken to the core when his assumptions about kinship are challenged. He learns that his erstwhile aunt is really his mother, and the discovery throws him into an existential crisis. It comes as little surprise that this undermining of kinship would shake up his world view. The notion of blood as a bond of kinship is built into the ritual initiation where the newly "made" literally blend their blood to create *famiglia*. Paulie is disgusted by what he considers to be a violation of blood and trust: "Family. In the end they fuck you too." His invective against family contrasts with Tony's optimist claim several shows earlier that family is all you can trust, and again calls into question the uncertainty of basing a value system on kinship.

The *famiglia's* dysfunction often becomes apparent through its perverse investment in a narrowly-defined heterosexual masculinity. The memorable treatment of cunnilingus in Season One's "Boca" (1.9) centers on this dynamic. When Uncle Junior is "outed" as a master of the sexual art, his position is the family is immediately threatened and his heterosexuality questioned. As Junior tries to explain: "They think if you'll suck pussy, you'll suck anything." Seemingly, this deviation from reproductive sexuality comes to represent a slippery slope to fellatio, and helps to exemplify the way normative sexuality in *The Sopranos* is closely defended and narrowly defined.

As with so many things in *The Sopranos,* the privileged forms of gender identity and sexuality are those that loosely translate to those positions that confer authority or represent power. In his analysis of "Boca," Joseph S. Walker notes how

> [d]espite clearly being a heterosexual act, cunnilingus threatens the sexual identity — and thus the complete identity — of the man who performs it. It is not difficult to speculate on the psychological underpinnings of this reasoning; to perform the act is to surrender the self, giving up even the ability of speech, of self-assertion, in the name of female pleasure. It is a privileging of the feminine, a muffling of the male [117].

The episode thus not only reflects the sexism of the *famiglia,* but it also makes an explicit link between the narrow framing of masculinity and homophobia and their relationship to power. For Walker, such a dynamic points to a conservative underpinning in the show: "For all its revisionary moves, *The Sopranos* cannot help but celebrate that most powerful of mythic figures: the male as coherent subject, the male as the self-validated hero of his own story" (Walker 121). My reading of the episode differs at this point. While I agree that the aversion to cunnilingus is linked to a perceived threat to masculinity, I think the show stages this dynamic ironically. Moreover, as with most things in the show, it is the association of the act with weakness that fuels the misogyny and its associated homophobia. As Rob White in his reading of the episode puts it, cunnilingus "suggests weakness. It's too intimate, too submissive" (12). By making explicit the underlying psychology of sexism and homophobia, I maintain the show ironically questions the normative stance that would align cunnilingus with fellatio. The episode invites us to consider the illogical and destructive mechanism of "homosexual panic," whereby the mere implication of sexual deviance threatens to collapse Junior's authority and power, an authority precariously dependent on a specious construction of masculinity/power.[3]

Another example of "homosexual panic" occurs in Season Two. The episode "Knights in White Satin Armor" establishes ironic narratives that juxtapose homophobia, masculine anxiety and family values. With its focus on masculinity and femininity and its broadly ironic look at the institution of marriage, this episode exemplifies the show's intricate framing of gender and sexuality. The opening sequence is highly disorienting: viewers may wonder if they are watching *The Sopranos* at all. The scene begins with a shot of an empty but brightly lit upper-middle class home: familiar in its type, but clearly not the usual Sopranos domestic setting. The ambient music, which borders on generic Muzak, further disorients. *The Sopranos* prides itself on its clever use of source music: rather than scenes that are scored to elicit an emotional effect from the viewer, the show typically incorporates the source of the music into the scene itself.

And while most shows use music to highlight or exaggerate the emotional mood of the scene, *The Sopranos* often finds tunes that comment ironically on the moment at hand. In either case, it is very unusual to have generic music playing in the background, seemingly removed from the scene (Chase in Bogdonovich interview). When an unfamiliar couple dancing sweep into the scene, the music is explained, but their identities are unknown. It's not until we see Janice that we realize the couple are in fact her fiancée's son and his dancing partner. When Tony enters the scene, he is quick to mock Richie Jr.'s gender expression and sexuality, which contrasts with the more acceptable forms of male behavior modeled by Rich Senior's nephew Jackie and his gang of cigar-smoking, football-watching friends. From the beginning, the episode establishes that there is a "right way" and a "wrong way" of being a man, as it ironically contrasts the light and breezy world of ballroom dancing with the male venue of junior gangsters. Moreover, the disorientation of the opening scene highlights how out-of-place ballroom dancing (with its privileging of pristine femininity) seems in the macho world of *The Sopranos*.

Alongside this questioning of masculinity, the episode develops from the concept of Janice and Rich's impending marriage to further critique normative social roles. The narrative undermines iconographic representations of the institution with the realities of the character's lived experiences. When Janice tries on her wedding dress, for example, we watch her and Carmela go through the motions of the ritual. Carmela tries to tow the party line ("Oh, this is so exciting!"), despite Janice's confession that she "is only doing this for the presents." As Carmela dreamily recalls her own wedding, Janice calls her bluff. Carmela's advice boils down to the fact that Janice had better enjoy the wedding rituals, as she will need to accept the fact that her husband will take up with a mistress ("goomah") in the next year or so. Janice then divulges that she and Richie play with a gun during sex. The scene begins with a convention of traditional marriage, and then quickly sets the irony in play by posing the dress fitting against the complexities of the "goomah" tradition and Janice's dangerous fetishes.

This episode comes to a climax when Janice shoots her fiancée at the dinner table. Given Richie Aprile's propensity for violence and generally nasty behavior, the murder is an oddly gratifying moment (Tony is simultaneously struggling with the question of how to get rid of the increasingly troublesome Rich when his sister settles the problem for him). At the same time, it stands as one of the most unexpected and violently upsetting moments in the show. Most viewers remember this moment when Janice dispatches Richie, but few actually recall that the violence between the couple is sparked by homosexual panic.

Like the dress scene, the opening plays on wedding traditions. Janice is cooking, Rich opening wine, while Janice seeks his advice about the rain date for the ceremony. Rich quickly devolves into complaints about his son, and is especially annoyed with Janice's use of the diminutive "Little Ricky." He wants his son to be known as "Rick" or "Richard," something suitably masculine and less suspect. When Janice defends ballroom dancing as "a legitimate art form," Richie mutters about his son's effeminacy and possible homosexuality. Janice fatefully challenges Rich's homophobia: "Just because he's a ballroom dancer, you think your son's gay. And what if he was gay? What difference would it make?" This question is enough to incite Rich to punch Janice squarely in the face. While Rich begins his dinner, reading *New Jersey Bride,* Janice fetches the family gun and shoots him multiple times. He is quite dead.

When Janice breaks off the engagement by shooting her fiancée, we have a clear example of mob violence interrupting attempts at building family and normality. Even before the violence totally subverts the scene, the traditional values conveyed by the dinner preparation (Janice cooks; Rich opens wine; they chat about wedding plans) are undermined by the family's own "perverse" ways of operating (Janice has slipped her mother Nembutal so that she and Rich can have sex; the gun with which Janice shoots him was likely the same one that they used in their sex play).[4] When Rich lashes out at Janice, the power of the punch surprises, but given Rich's capacity for violence and his building aggravation, it does not seem totally unexpected. That he reacts following Janice's "outing" of Ricky is consistent with the show's pattern of a masculine identity that depends on a repudiation of male homosexuality. Interestingly, when Janice calls his son's sexuality into question, it threatens Rich's own sense of masculine entitlement. The homosexual panic precipitates violence, but this panic comes from Rich's shame of having a gay son. The excessive violence of the scene thus shows both the superficiality of heteronormative values—the way that these repeated rituals let people go through the motions of acceptability—alongside the fierceness with which they are defended.

Season six picks up another ironic take on weddings with "Mr. & Mrs. John Sacrimoni Request..." (6.5). Here the kitsch and excess of the wedding rituals are posited against an ending that reveals Vito's secret life at gay bars. When Vito is unexpectedly discovered by a couple of wise guys, he has little choice but to leave his family. As his life crumbles and he kisses his sleeping children goodbye, we hear "All the Chapel Bells Were Ringing." The banal and traditional music creates an ironic space through which to read the pathos in Vito's situation. As he settles down in a low-rent motel room and looks down at the gun by his bed we realize that suicide remains a real possibility.[5]

Allegra Sacrimoni's wedding is over-the-top by any standard. Tony asks Johnny how much he had spent on the reception and is told that it is almost half a million dollars. The episode serves as an important reminder of class privilege and its central role in *The Sopranos'* "family values." The show has long established the ways in which relationships are sustained through elaborated gift giving. Tony is consistently buying Carmela's favor. In Season Five he literally buys her back and ends the threat of divorce with a spec house. Part of the corruption of *The Sopranos* is signaled through their implication in consumer culture. They represent an extreme of exploitation. Not only do they steal and extort, they consume a disproportionate amount and seem to be tied into a pattern of conspicuous consumption. Gifts don't concur with real feelings, but according to the codes and conventions of consumerist culture. In season six Paulie and Vito chafe at the idea of sharing their profits with Carmela when Tony's survival is in question. They eagerly make their offering when he regains consciousness. It is not that they genuinely care for Tony's family, but rather that they understand how to use money to portray an appearance of love and loyalty. Once again, what looks like family affection is revealed as window-dressing. It is the underlying power relationships that count.

Attempts in *The Sopranos* to narrowly define sexual behaviors always backfire. First there's Junior with his cunnilingus, and then Janice with her fetish. In season three, we learn that Ralphie has alternative sexual proclivities. Janice tells Tony: "He doesn't fuck me. Something's very wrong with him." Tony reports to Dr. Melfi that Ralphie does not engage in "penissary contact with [Janice's] Volvo" ("Amor Fou," 3.12). While Ralphie is ostensibly killed because Tony blames him for his racehorse's death, the fact that he was not sexually normative certainly didn't help his case.[6] As Gibson puts it, Ralph is marked as queer and weak by his non-normative sexuality: "Ralph's private sexual submission to women, exemplified by his queer gender-switching when he has Janice screw him from behind with a strap-on dildo ('Christopher'), makes him seem an impotent, passive liar to Tony..." (201).

In all these incidents, gender and sexuality get defined against narrow and outmoded cultural norms. When things don't fit, they are overcorrected with a violent response. The excessiveness of the violence not only reflects a surface level dedication to those "family values," but further implies an underlying anxiety about their lack of substance. Like class privilege, male privilege and white privilege, heterosexual privilege is supported by a vague and potentially specious set of identity claims. This anxiety about identity politics is compounded by a sense of the inherent weakness of any forms of sexual behavior that are marked by femininity or surrender: "effeminacy and homosexuality, in Tony Soprano's world, mean an utter erasure of tough-guy, 'made man' masculinity — it *is* death" (Gibson 199).

Mob identity for the *famiglia* is frequently formulated in direct opposition to things queer and effeminate. In "Fortunate Son" (3.3) Dr. Melfi asks Tony to articulate what it might be that makes him attractive to Gloria (a current mistress), Tony makes it clear that his primary sense of self is drawn in terms of his heterosexuality, or, even more poignantly, in opposition to "all those cry babies and fags." In an exemplary moment of struggle with language he states his identity in negative terms followed by an ellipsis: "Whatever I am I'm not...." After a momentary struggle with words he settles on the euphemistic "Captain Industry," which Melfi translates into "a tough guy." His statement of identity follows directly from a repudiation of [an unstated] homosexuality to reiterate a sense of self closely linked to power and traditional masculinity.

Week after week we witness the inadequacy of *The Sopranos'* moral universe. When Tony boasts to Dr. Melfi "I don't know about morals, but I do have rules" ("Mergers and Acquisitions," 4.8), we are offered one way that the code of ethics is almost guaranteed to dysfunction, and ultimately does. In the first season of the show, Tony must kill his closest friend, Big Pussy, because he has violated the code of secrecy by becoming a double agent for the FBI. In the final season, Tony is similarly challenged to kill another faithful soldier, Vito, because his sexuality has become public knowledge. This is a rule-bound and reactionary sexual ethics, one based on unexamined codes of loyalty and honor that inform the shaky artifice of "family."

The Sopranos' family values not only include a fiercely guarded masculinity and chauvinism, but also depend upon a deep-seated racism. If, as Kocela convincingly claims, Tony's hold on whiteness is tenuous, haunted by a repressed memory of his lost ethnicity, his hold on heterosexual privilege is equally at risk (Kocela). These are parallel anxieties. When Tony dreams of a water bird winging away with his penis, this symbolism of phallic dismemberment signals much more than a perceived loss of manhood. The loss of the phallus is at its base a loss of privilege and of power. And power is multivalent in its expression in late-twentieth and early twenty-first century America, split, as it were, between competing claims on normalcy and majority that are at once patriarchal, white, and heterosexual. Tony's racist anxieties are closely linked to his sexism and bound to his homophobia. Kocela notes the way that the family dynamic in the show relates to racist anxieties: "every domestic scene is framed by racial conflict or by the threat of such conflict" (Kocela par. 26). The phallic anxiety that motors Tony's behavior draws from fears regarding sexuality as well as race.

Gibson somewhat awkwardly aligns Tony's racism and homophobia in slightly different terms, linking the complex dynamic of the monstrous mother with the inadequate model of masculinity his culture affords: "Tony's homophobia is an attempt to mask his fear of mother-driven, castrating effeminacy and his anxiety about his sole patriarchal endowment of panic attacks in an effort to maintain the facade of his simplistic, phallic, mob boss masculinity" (202). While I would not underestimate the complications of Livia's legacy, I think the anxiety of privilege Kocela outlines offers a more likely scenario, one that links his sexism, homophobia, class aspirations and racism to a similar place of anxiety, one based on the weak claims to privilege Tony actually can claim in terms of his whiteness, his class status, his gender and his sexuality.

A scene in season four's "Eloise" exemplifies the link between class and racist anxiety. When Tony and Carmela visit Meadow at her new apartment, they find her friends are upper class. References to family homes and ski resorts skip off of their tongues. Tony and Carmela are notably quieted by the class display, awkwardly put in a position of feeling inadequate to this group of young adults. Their sense of isolation builds as the talk turns to the possibility of reading Hermann Melville's *Billy Budd* as a "gay book." The students make an articulate argument (Meadow referencing the critic Leslie Fiedler), and Carmela and Tony are left with few defenses aside from a vague conspiracy theory ("Maybe she's/he's gay," Carmela offers about Fiedler and the teacher Mr. Wegler),[7] and a complaint that "this gay stuff" is "pervading our educational system, not to mention movies, TV shows...." Carmela's rhetoric articulates a familiar complaint of late twentieth- and early twenty-first century conservatives: the specter of the traditional family under siege by a broad conspiracy of gay social forces.

Vito Spatafore's story-line in Season Six was drawn from a real-life case, and goes beyond the specter of the "pink canon" to exemplify the deadly result of being gay in America. Apparently a New Jersey mobster, wiseguy John D'Amato, was killed in 1992 when he was outed as gay.[8] Viewers first learn of Vito's sexuality in Season Five, when Meadow's boyfriend (and subsequent fiancée) catches him going down on a security guard at the construction site ("Unidentified Black Males," 5.9). Word doesn't actually hit the *famiglia* until a couple of colleagues spot him at a gay bar, fully decked out in Village People regalia. News of Vito's sexuality prompts a virulent but comically ignorant outpouring of hate speech as the group struggles to accept the possibility that one of their *famiglia* might be gay. The blatant homophobia helps to assure the group of their own heterosexuality and assumed superiority, and in some ways guards against the pollution that Vito's gayness threatens.

In late twentieth-century/early twenty-first century America, homo-phobic rhetoric is often associated with the politically conservative Chris-tian block as a part of the ideology of "family values." *The Sopranos* plays off of this association, and Season Six's episode "Live Free or Die" (6.6) ironically uncovers the virulence of the gang's homophobia against the back-drop of legislated adultery (the system of "goomahs" is referenced repeatedly throughout the episode) while the scene at the "The Bada Bing" undercuts the high moral ground of their hate speech.[9]

When Christopher and his AA acquaintance arrive with news of Vito's recent spotting at a gay bar, the first response is denial. Paulie Walnuts pro-tests that Vito is a married man "with a goomah," as if the presence of a mistress would counter any possibility of sexual deviance.[10] As the group explores the possibility of Vito's gayness, the volatility of the secret becomes apparent. Christopher claims to having known all along, and the rest chime in with a history of suspicions. In some sense the group is as threatened by their inability to correctly "read" Vito as they are by his apparent homo-sexuality. The problem of definitive knowledge emerges as Christopher asks, "So what do we have to do, Tony? Actually see Vito take it in the ass?"

As Christopher's crude reduction of Vito's sexuality implies, the group's attempt to come to grips with the "meanings" of Vito's sexual identity inevitably falls short. They have no shortage of homophobic epitaphs, but ultimately are ill-equipped to understand what his sexuality really means to the group. In fact, the group has stumbled upon one of the more trou-bling implications of sexuality: it's notoriously difficult to correctly "read" another's orientation. Furthermore, this is a form of knowledge that is formed around a cult of secrecy not unlike the oath of loyalty that secures the brotherhood. The "love that dares not speak its name" is not unlike the code of silence that marks the spaces of the mob. As Eve Kosofsky Sedg-wick notes, a good deal of cultural anxiety about homosexuality circulates around the impossibility of sexual "knowledge," a complexity driven in part by the possibility that homosexuality identity is driven by desire rather than some essential essence. Accordingly, anyone with sexual desire could be gay. As the group at the Bada Bing struggles to make sense of Vito's iden-tity, some seem to be reacting to the question, "If him, why not me?" Once again, the homophobia in the show seems to relate back to the tenuous nature of heterosexuality and the privileges it confers.

In the middle of this homophobic confusion the audience is exposed to a range of responses verging from the lenient ("doesn't really matter to me") to the violently excessive and racially charged ("I'd drag him behind my truck"). In the midst of this fast-moving and volatile outpouring Tony comes forward as the voice of reason ("a man's reputation is at stake"), resisting the quick calls for violence and blood. When he later meets with Dr. Melfi, he is clearly in conflict about the expectation to whack Vito solely on account of his sexuality. The audience, along with Dr. Melfi, is invited to consider if this "kinder, gentler" Tony might signal some basic change in his character. Has therapy in fact made some progress with his deep-seated issues around masculinity and femininity? If so, it seems only natural that this change would manifest through a softening of his attitude towards homosexuality.

Season Six offers viewers a brief look at Vito's attempted "straight" life as part of a same-sex family. He goes on motorcycle rides, kisses in an open field, plays hero at a house fire, cooks meals for his lover, and even tries working a regular job. The simple pleasures that he enjoys with Jim contrast with the material-driven heterosexual relationships that the other mobsters call marriage. Through juxtaposing the hurtfulness and superficiality of socially condoned marriages against the modest yet genuine appeals of same-sex love, the final season fleshes out *The Soprano*'s critique of the heteronormative family.

While Vito's story line in season six marks an obvious space for considering homophobia, the integrity of the "tough guys" in the show has consistently depended on repudiations of homosexuality. Homophobia has always marked a volatile fault line in the show, and its repudiations offer a way to maintain a stable sense of self in a world that is repeatedly perceived as out-of-synch with the traditional values of the mob. When Tony mourns for Gary Cooper (see 1.1 and 4.3) or the simpler life of the 1950s (1.11), part of what he is asserting is the value system of white, bourgeois, heterosexist family values. Yet the ironic distance the show maintains not only calls Tony Soprano into question, but his entire system of conservative family values as well.

The show thus becomes a microcosm of cultural tensions within the early twenty-first century United States, where conservative legislations like the "Defense of Marriage Act" seek to protect the idealized American family, and where homophobia and sexism parade as family values. In the nation as in fiction, the ideology of family supersedes its real value, and rather than face the changes and their own corruption, conservative proponents, like the rigidly conservative Wise Guys in *The Sopranos*, simply blast away at a perceived enemy.

Notes

1. For an elaboration of the persistent double bind of "good" and "bad" family representations of Italian-Americans, see Pellegrino D'Acierno, "Cinema Paradiso," *The*

Italian American Heritage: A Companion to Literature and Arts (New York: Garland, 1999).

2. I define heteronormativity as a set of mutually informing beliefs and assumptions that assert the superiority and naturalness of reproductive heterosexuality. According to my usage, certain sexual behaviors between men and women (e.g., fetishes or SM and BD sexualities) would be considered "deviant" from a heteronormative position, and hence qualify as potentially queer.

3. Following Eve K. Sedgwick, I use the "homosexual panic" as an analytical term to signal a manifestation of homophobia on either an individual or on a broader social level. For a general discussion on the uses and abuses of the term, see Eve Kosofsky Sedgwick, *Epistemology of the Closet* (Berkeley: University of California Press, 1990), 18–21.

4. For this latter detail, I'm indebted to Maurice Yacowar, *The Sopranos on the Couch: Analyzing Television's Greatest Series*, 3rd ed. (New York: Continuum, 2005), 116.

5. Earlier we had seen Vito speculating about Eugene Pontecorvo's suicide: "He may have had to come out as homosexual and killed himself. It happens," he suggests to a skeptical Meadow as the family waits in the hospital for word of Tony's condition.

6. Consider as well the point that Tony's rage against Richie is also equally informed by his rage at his unnecessary murder of Tracee, the "stripper with a heart of gold" from an earlier show ("University"). Here, Tony's affection for the girl is confused with his love for his daughter, Meadow.

7. A further irony emerges in the fifth season when Carmela has an affair with the same Mr. Wegler, who in that case recommends she read the classic text of heterosexual adultery, *Madame Bovary*.

8. See Michele McPhee, "TV's Wisegay 'Sopranos' Fella Hits the Other Way," *New York Daily News* 3 May 2004 for details on the story.

9. This is not the first time, nor the last, that the "Bada Bing" functions to ironically undermine the easy espousal of family values. In Season Six "The Ride," the commentary by Terence Winter notes the ironic backdrop of the stripper working the pole at the "Bada Bing" while Christopher waxes on the rightness of family values. The show is deliberately shot to create a contrast between the righteous solemnity of Christopher's confession and the sleaze just behind him.

10. This logic supports Rob White's claim that heterosexual sex "is significant only to the extent that it shores up relationships between men."

Works Cited

Chase, David. "Peter Bogdanovich Interviews David Chase." DVD. HBO-Time-Warner, 2000.

D'Acierno, Pellegrino. "Cinema Paradiso." *The Italian American Heritage: A Companion to Literature and Arts*. New York: Garland, 1999. 563–690.

Gardaphé, Fred. "The Gangster as Surburbian Trickster." *A Sitdown with The Sopranos: Watching Italian American Culture on TV's Most Talked-About Series*. Ed. Regina Barreca. 1st ed. New York: Palgrave Macmillan, 2002. 89–112.

Gibson, Brian. "'Black Guys, My Ass': Uncovering the Queerness of Racism in *The Sopranos*." *Reading The Sopranos: Hit TV from HBO*. Ed. David Lavery. Reading Contemporary Television. London, New York: I.B. Tauris, Palgrave Macmillan, 2006. 194–213.

Hipsky, Martin. "Post-Cold War Paranoia in the Corrections and The Sopranos." *Postmodern Culture: An Electronic Journal of Interdisciplinary Criticism* 16.2 (2006).

Kocela, Christopher. "Unmade Men: The Sopranos after Whiteness." *Postmodern Culture: An Electronic Journal of Interdisciplinary Criticism* 15.2 (2005): 30.

McPhee, Michele. "TV Wisegay 'Sopranos' Fella Hits the Other Way." *New York Daily News* 3 May 2004, sec. I.

Nochimson, Martha P. "Waddaya Lookin' At? Rereading the Gangster Film through *The Sopranos*. Mob Culture: Hidden Histories of the American Gangster Film. Eds. Lee Grieveson, Esther Sonnet, and Peter Sanfield. New Brunswick, New Jersey: Rutgers University Press, 2005. 185–204.

Parini, Jay. "The Cultural Work of *The Sopranos*." *A Sitdown with The Sopranos: Watching Italian American Culture on TV's Most Talked-About Series*. Ed. Regina Barreca. 1st ed. New York: Palgrave Macmillan, 2002. 75–88.

Rotundo, E. Anthony. "Wonderbread and Stugots." *A Sitdown with The Sopranos*. Ed. Regina Barreca. New York: Palgrave Books, 2002. 47–75.

Sedgwick, Eve Kosofsky. *Epistemology of the Closet*. Berkeley: University of California Press, 1990.

Walker, Joseph S. "'Cunnilingus and Psychiatry Have Brought Us to This': Livia and the Logic of False Hoods in the First Season of The Sopranos." *This Thing of Ours: Investigating The Sopranos*. Ed. David Lavery, New York: Columbia University Press, Wallflower, New York, 2002. xviii, 285.

White, Rob. "Hitting the High Notes." *Sight and Sound* 11.1 (2001): 12–13.

Yacowar, Maurice. *The Sopranos on the Couch: Analyzing Television's Greatest Series*. 3rd ed. New York: Continuum, 2005.

Until the Fat Man Sings: Body Image, Masculinity, and Sexuality in *The Sopranos*

Keith B. Mitchell

"Always eating, always, always eating. It's like drugs, I guess, for them."[1]
—DREA DE MATTEO (Adriana La Cerva)

In Hollywood, body image, often even more than talent, determines an actor's net worth. Women in Hollywood have known and dealt with this cultural edict for years: the heavier one is, the less likely she will be hired. In other words, if a woman is fat in Hollywood and in society she is largely seen as sexless. Women such as Mae West and Marilyn Monroe are still seen as the epitome of eroticism. Today, however, thin is in. While it is true that some large women certainly have made a name for themselves in Hollywood, mostly on the small screen and mostly as comedic actresses, they are usually relegated to roles, in the words of T. V.'s Roseanne Barr, as "domestic goddesses."[2] Nor can one say that traditionally fat male actors in Hollywood have been treated any better. As with women, whether on the small screen or the silver screen, fat men traditionally have been relegated to the role of the dumb sidekick, the clown, or the disgusting reprobate.[3] With very few exceptions does the public or the media view fat male actors as virile, strong, sex symbols.

Case in point: Marlon Brando's meteoric rise and subsequent fall in Hollywood is illustrative of Hollywood's tendency to relegate fat male actors to specific, usually nonsexual, roles. In the prime of his film career, Brando was considered by movie viewers and the media one of the sexiest actors and most virile men in Hollywood. However, over the course of his career, Brando ballooned to over three hundred pounds, and this drastic transformation in his corporeal image affected the kinds of roles he was offered and considered for; from the late 1960 up until his death in 2004, studio moguls rarely considered Brando as a viable candidate for big screen movie roles, mainly due to his morbid obesity. More often than not, because of his large size and seemingly unorthodox life, Marlon Brando became fodder for numerous comedic acts. Even in the early 70s, with his huge success in the *Godfather* (1972), Brando's acting skills could not be denied.[4] As a sex symbol, however, he was no longer on the media's or the public's radar. Brando's weight wasn't the only issue inherent in the media's and the public's view of him: as his bisexuality became more generally known, in addition to other more tumultuous events in his life, the media's image of Brando changed so drastically that the public began to view him as both physically and psychologically aberrant. In short, his image as a virile, tough sex symbol had come undone.

We may never know the reasons for Brando's deliberate corporeal transformation, but today, almost without exception, society and the medical community have pathologized fat men especially because "America's public health establishment ... has prefigured body weight as a barometer of wellness, so that being thin is equated with being healthy" (Oliver 5). Today, unlike at different times in the past, society views fat people as having no control over themselves. The reasonable man is also the healthy man; the fat boy is neither of these. Clearly it is in the world of dietetics, Sander L. Gilman professes, "that the link between the fat and the male body, perhaps sexless, but certainly gendered, is made" (*Fat Boys* 28). One only has to observe the complicity between the diet industry and the mainstream media to see that body fat, whether female or male, has become one of the most written about and media-scrutinized social issues in recent memory. And the media's and the diet industry's obsession with weight has certainly trickled down to the general public, and it has greatly influenced how the public views overweight people in American society. Instead of focusing on Marlon Brando and the image of the fat male body — its significance in the eyes of the public and the media — I feel that Brando's corporeality is a representative site of comparison and contextualization for the discussion of other fat male bodies, masculinity, and power to increase our awareness of what Mark Graham coins *lipoliteracy*, that is, "the way we see fat or the absence of fat as conveying a message, as telling us something good or bad about food, bodies and people" (Kulick and Menely 7).

My intention is to further critical discourse about the fat body that has been theorized in texts such as Susie Orbach's *Fat Is a Feminist Issue* (1979), Naomi Wolf's *The Beauty Myth* (1990), and Susan Bordo's *Unbearable Weight: Feminism, Western Culture, and the Body* (1993). These works focus on the heterosexual female body, but I want to explore how fat male bodies have become sites of contestation about how society views masculinity, virility, and power. Whether we label a person as stout, overweight, fat, or obese, the bottom line is that fat bodies are viewed as degenerate bodies, as Orbach, Wolf and Bordo conclude. Moreover, the fat body tends to reflect a weak and degenerate mind in Western society as well:

> The fat boy or the fat man is an exception even unto the law. The normal is a cultural standard to be found in all aspects of society from the law to medicine. The fat boy is unreasonable even in the implied claim that his masculinity is the default definition in the law of the human being as male. He is not normal; he is not a reasonable man [*Fat Boys* 30].

Sander Gilman's text *Fat Boys: A Slim Book* (2004) performs groundbreaking work in the area of *lipoliteracy* and explores the signification and the significance of the fat heterosexual male body throughout Western history; however, he fails to address the fat male body, masculinity, and power in terms of queer sexuality. This essay seeks to redress this important omission and expand our understanding of these weighty issues through one of the most popular television shows in recent memory, David Chase's *The Sopranos*. Through Tony Soprano (James Gandolfini) and Vito Spatafore (Joe Gannascoli), whose characters are straight and queer, respectively, upholds the idea of the fat male body and psychology as pathological and grotesque, while at the same time investing these two characters with virility and power not normally associated with fat males. The revelation that Vito is fat, queer, and an important Captain in Tony's mob family adds another even more interesting dimension to the subject that has not been explored in other texts about *The Sopranos* such as David Lavery's edited collection of essays, *This Thing of Ours: Investigating the Sopranos* (2002) and Regina Barreca's edited collection of essays, *A Sitdown with the Sopranos: Watching Italian American Culture on T.V.'s Most Talked-About Series* (2002). I want to begin, however, by interrogating Sander L. Gilman's theories of the "fat detective" in nineteenth and twentieth century popular culture and to review his theory's applicability to the fat criminal in contemporary popular culture.

In "How Fat Detectives Think," Sander L. Gilman exposes the "unique ... depiction of portly detectives in nineteenth and twentieth century German, English and American crime fiction" ("The Belly and Beyond" 9). Gilman asserts that in overweight, male amateur sleuths, such as the German writer Wilhelm Raabe's Tubby Schaumann and Arthur Conan Doyle's Mycroft Holmes (Sherlock Holmes' corpulent, amateur detective brother) depicted in the popular literature of the 19th century, the fat detective's body, although passive, allows him to "[remember] the forgotten, [to sense] that which cannot be experienced, which shapes their ability to discover hidden or forgotten truths. It [the fat detective's corpulence] seems to be primitive (like a sloth or walrus), but it is indeed the hallmark of the most sophisticated and highly developed male body. It is the body that thinks" ("How Fat Detectives Think" 226). Moreover, Gilman lovingly describes these fat, amateur, sleuths as gentle, kind, and lovable creatures whose, "bodies provide an image of obesity that masks their sharp powers of observation and deduction" (230). Gilman ends his essay with a critique of a contemporary detective, Andy Sipowicz, played by Dennis Franz, on the popular television show *NYPD Blue*. Gilman sees Sipowicz's character as a descendent of Tubby Schaumann; Sipowicz is a "muscular man gone to fat," through which "he is able to be empathetic with his colleagues and generally to have insight into his own character" (234). In short, Sipowicz's "flawed," fat body is the medium through which he is able to understand his own flaws and to empathize with others' shortcomings and weaknesses. I wonder, however, would Gilman similarly apply his theories to more and more frequent images of overweight crime figures that have sprung up in film and television over the last thirty years? Earlier, I mentioned Marlon Brando's pivotal role as Vito Corleone, the head of an Italian-American crime family in *The Godfather*. Certainly, Brando's character is one of the primary models that David Chase used to develop the character of Anthony Soprano. One major difference, however, is where Don Corleone wears his weight well, Tony Soprano is depicted as a parody of Corleone. Corleone, despite his weight, exemplifies elegance and class; Tony Soprano, the product of a working class Italian-American family, is generally depicted as a fat slob that has great difficulty not only controlling the chaos of his immediate family, as well as his crime Family, but he also has great difficulty controlling himself in most other aspects of his life, including his weight.

Fat as an issue rears itself in the very first episode of *The Sopranos*. One of our first views of Tony Soprano's corporeality is unflattering. It is early morning and Tony, his hair slightly mussed, is in his boxers, a wife-beater t-shirt (hairy chest exposed) and an open robe; he is barefoot. But most important perhaps is that for the first time we get a good look at just how fat is. His corporeality, in fact, epitomizes a character out of nineteenth-century naturalist fiction: the brute. Yet, we also see a side of Tony that contradicts this image. The chaos evoked by his bodily image in this scene is in direct contrast to the opening scene's evocation of tranquility and peace as Tony is in the backyard happily musing about a family of ducks who decide to make a migratory pit stop in his swimming pool. The scene evokes a kind of baptism as Tony gingerly enters the pool to feed bread to the ducks. His emotions sparked by seeing and interacting with the ducks, are one of joy and awe. Moreover, the exterior shot of Tony's grandiose house reflects his corporeality and tranquility. It is a massive structure fit for a king. But his world is anything but halcyon. The scene moves from the peace and tranquility of Tony's sprawling backyard to the chaos simultaneously taking place in the kitchen between his wife Carmela (Edie Falco) and their teenage daughter Meadow (Jamie-Lynn Sigler). Carmela tries to coax Meadow and her friend to eat breakfast before going to school and offers them some left over *boula delle*. Meadow replies, "Eww, get away with that fat." And her friend then asks, "How do you stay so skinny, Mrs. Soprano?" As Susan Bordo suggests in *Unbearable Weight*, "female hunger—for public power, for independence, for sexual gratification—[must] be contained, and the public space that women be allowed to take up be circumscribed, limited..." (171). This is certainly the case in the Soprano household as the camera soon cuts to Tony (this time wrapped only in a towel) alone in the kitchen with Carmela, the ever-dutiful and long suffering stay-at-home wife and mother. Here we get an even clearer picture of Tony's corpulence and a hint of his strained, contentious relationship with Carmela due to his numerous infidelities. In many respects, Tony and Carmela's marriage is an atavistic almost parodic marriage reminiscent of the 1950s. Tony and Carmela are Ward and June Cleaver on steroids. Tony's corpulence and his role as primary provider remind us, as Tara Eastland explains, that "women who remain thin are being obedient; it is another way for patriarchy to control women" ("Eating Disorders: A Feminist Issue"). Tony's body, in contrast to Carmela's, evinces power and control as well impotence and chaos. One of the primary aggravations in Tony's life is with Carmela, other women in his family, and the plethora of women he has affairs with throughout the show's six seasons. When it comes to women, Tony's sexual libido, like his lust for money and power, is insatiable, despite the fact that Tony's corpulence would belie this. Whether or not these women are attracted to Tony because of his money or his power as a capo of a crime family is not the point. "Hypersexuality is a quality," writes Sander Gilman, "ascribed to the pre-modern fat boy, but is repressed in modernity" (*Fat Boys* 24). Tony defies the stereotype of the desexualized, impotent, fat male body. Yet, we cannot ignore the fact that Tony consumes these women. As a crime boss whose name frequently appears in the media and whose reputation is generally known to the public, Tony Soprano has celebrity status. To these women, he is a star:

The star thus becomes the food of dreams; the dream, unlike the ideal tragedy of Aristotle, does not purify us truly from our fantasies but betrays their obsessive presence; similarly, the stars only partially provoke catharsis and encourage fantasies which would like to but cannot liberate themselves in action. Here, the role of the star becomes "psychotic": it polarizes and fixes obsessions [Morin 164].

Practically all of the women Tony becomes involved with are consumed with desire for him, and he consumes them as though they were his last supper.[5] As soon as there is a hint of a problem with any of his *goomaras* (mistresses), he dumps them, which is symbolically apt given that his supposedly legitimate business is as a waste management consultant.

That Tony Soprano is figuratively and literally a heavyweight player among New Jersey crime bosses is clear in the series. Yet, unlike other mobster figures in popular culture such as Tony Montana (Al Pacino) in *Scarface* (1983) and Jimmy Conway (Robert De Niro) in *Goodfellas* (1990), Tony Soprano's physicality does not resemble Pacino or De Niro in the least. Whereas Pacino's and De Niro's sinister performances in these two seminal mob movies are based more on their psychological acumen to instill fear and respect among their enemies and their respective crime Families, Tony Soprano's weight, in addition to his sociopath psychology, significantly adds to his ability to instill fear in his enemies. Nevertheless, Tony's weight marks both a sign of his strength and his weakness. His body represents a plethora of signs that point to who he is a husband, father, and crime boss. His large body, unlike Tony Montana's and Jimmy Conway's relatively thin bodies, adds to an accumulation of signs that signify his affluence, influence, power, heterosexuality, and masculinity. Tony's "masculinity is not simply a parallel construct to femininity but has its own complex history, as do the meanings attached to the fat boy's body" (*Fat Boys* 7). These meaning are made manifest in *The Sopranos* in connection to Tony's relationship to the women in his life.

When Tony first goes to see Dr. Melfi for his ongoing panic attacks, he sits alone in the waiting room, anticipating this meeting with trepidation. The waiting room scene in this premier episode represents the primal scene from which the roots of his panic attacks derive. It is not until much later in the series that we learn that women, and in particular Tony's mother, Livia, is the greatest contributor to his neuroses. Tony's pathological relationship with women is hinted at when he is in the waiting room studying a life-size statue of a nude woman, who stares directly at him with unseeing eyes. He stares back with great intensity, agitation, and contemplation before Dr. Melfi ushers him into her office.[6]

As Tony relates to Dr. Melfi one of the more stressful events that leads up to his panic attack, "an issue of an outstanding loan," Melfi stops him and says, "I don't know where this story is going but there are a few ethical ground rules we should quickly get out of the way" (1.1). If he tells her a story where someone is going to get killed, she is supposed to let the authorities know.

Thus, from the very brief time that Dr. Melfi and Tony have been talking she figures out what Tony's real occupation is. And so, in order not to reveal to her anything that would incriminate him or place her in an awkward position, he simply tells her that he and the guy had coffee. This summation hits on a trope that is consistent throughout the show's six seasons: food and its juxtaposition with violence. As Christopher and Tony drive by an HMO, Tony spots Mahaffey, and he immediately spots them. Mahaffey quickly drops the tray of coffee he has been carrying back to his office and takes off running. Tony is in hot pursuit in Christopher's new car.[7] Tony runs Mahaffey down, breaking his leg. Rather than leaving it at that Tony and Christopher corner him and give him the beating of his life as Tony screams, "Where's our fuckin' money!" Of course, he doesn't have it, and more violence ensues as Tony and Christopher leave him bruised and bloody. To add insult to injury, as Mahaffey lies on the grass writhing in pain, Tony screams, "Shut up, what are you crying about? HMO! You're covered, ya prick! Degenerate, fuckin' gambler!" (1.1) Tony's behavior is shockingly brutal, but at the same time quite funny. Where we might generally be outraged at his display of sheer, unadulterated violence, oddly enough, we are not. What this scene accomplishes, rather, is to inure the viewer to more violence to come. Violence specifically associated with food.

That same morning, Tony has a breakfast meeting with the members of his crew at Satriale's Meat Market which advertises a life-size replica of pig on its roof. Tony and his Mafioso discuss how to fix a problem he is having with a Czechoslovakian mob family intent on moving in on his waste management scheme. Christopher volunteers to take care of the problem and secretly invites one of the Czechoslovakian mob boss' sons, Emile Kolar (Bruce Smolanoff), unbeknownst to Emile's father, to discuss the situation. The meeting is to take place that night in Satriale's, an establishment that Tony owns and operates. When Emile arrives, the conversation begins with Christopher and Emile talking about something as mundane as sausages:

> EMILE: Hey, in Czech Republic, too, we love our pork. You ever have our sausages.
>
> CHRISTOPHER: No, no, I thought the only sausages they had were Italian and *Jimmy Dean*. See what you learn when you cross cultures and shit. [...] We have issues in common [1.1].

One of those common issues is a coke habit, which he effectively uses to catch Emile off guard. As Emile, bend over to snort a line that Christopher has ironically placed on a meat clever, he puts a bullet in the back of Emile's head and blood splatters across the meat clever and the table. He then fires three more rounds into Emile's head to make sure that he dead. It is excessive violence. The scene is perfectly constructed, for as Christopher shoots Emile, directly to the side of him is a meat locker filled with pigs' heads on hooks, staring intently down upon the bloody scene like cherubs from heaven.[8] The scene ends as Christopher, with a look of fascination and satisfaction with a job well done, quickly glances in the direction of the dead pigs and then turns his attention back to the deceased Emile.

In *The Poetics and Politics of Transgression* (1986), Peter Stallybrass and Allon White, referencing Edmond Leach's essay "Anthropological Aspects of Language: Animal Categories and Verbal Abuse," about "the use of animals as social categories of thought," and the "culturally specific" categorization of animals thought of as taboo and those which are not focus their attention on the transhistorical cultural significance of the pig in western society (*Transgression* 45). Stallybrass and White assert that across time pigs have not always been thought of as low, disgusting animals willing and able to devour practically anything. This is generally how pigs are viewed it is a word often used to denigrate fat people. We associate fat people with being diseased and having no self-control. The pig is an apt metaphor for Tony, who is overweight, *and* Christopher. It is not weight which anchors Tony, Christopher, and the other members of both of Tony's families to the pig as metaphor; it is monstrous excess, whether in the form of overeating and obesity, womanizing, drug and alcohol abuse, uncaring, violence or consumerism. Metaphorically, they are animals in human form, but they are literally butchers.[9]

Stallybrass and White go on to make a transhistorical distinction between rural and urban existence and the symbolization of the pig. They claim that during the Middle Ages pigs had a ritual role within the family unit; pigs were thought of as members of the family, sometimes abused, but not wholly canvassed as disgusting creatures with very little purpose except to consume waste and eventually to be consumed. In urban dwellings, "their symbolic ambivalence was slowly lost as they became more clearly objects of hatred, fear, and abuse" (*Transgression* 48–49). Chase's symbolic use of the pig in this particular episode of *The Sopranos* is telling because the pig represents the baser qualities of human nature. Avarice and excess (porcine qualities) motivates practically all of the characters. The show's narrative is a continuous dialectic about the nature of and the thin line between law and anarchy. In this manner, *The Sopranos* embraces the carnavalesque that

Mikhail Bakhtin theorizes in *Problems of Dostoevsky's Poetics* (1984). Bakhtin surmises:

> It could be said (with reservations of course) that a person of the Middle Ages lived, as it were, *two lives*: one that was the *official life*, monolithically serious and gloomy, subjugated to a strict hierarchical order, full of terror, dogmatism, reverence, and piety; the other was the *life of the carnival square*, free and unrestricted, full of ambivalent laughter, blasphemy, the profanation of everything sacred, full of debasing and obscenities, familiar contact with everyone and everything. Both these lives were legitimate, but separated by strict temporal boundaries [129–130].

The dark, violent world of *The Sopranos* is not much different from England (or Italy) during the Middle Ages. The show is replete with paradox and irony. Allegiances quickly change and often friends become enemies. Tony is the center of this paradoxical world; he is the calm eye of the tornado *and* its destructive fury. He tries to keep his two lives separate: the seemingly orthodox, mundane world of his home life and the violent world of his professional life. What differs between Bakhtin's notion of carnival and what occurs in *The Sopranos* is there are no temporal boundaries. It is difficult for viewer and Tony to determine where one life ends and the other one begins. His home life and professional life elide. His home life, his material wealth, his power, his sense of manhood and his excessive libido are absolutely derived from his role as mob boss and "a repudiation of femininity"[10] ("Melancholy Gender" 26).

In Season Five, being the man of the house helps define Tony.[11] He is a habitual philanderer. Carmela knows this and tacitly accepts it. When one of his mistresses actually calls the house and confronts Carmela, she decides to throw him out and to seek a divorce. For a while their relationship is like the War of the Roses, but they reconcile in Season Six as Carmela realizes that when she married Tony she made a pact with the devil. She is at peace with the type of man she has married and he realizes that his world is not complete without her. He promises her never to cheat again and she allows him to move back into the house. The family unit remains intact. Tony's mantra is that no matter what family and loyalty are the most important things. This includes his mob family as well. This is why it is so difficult for Tony to seek vengeance against members of his mob family who do not conform to or who transgress his mantra. Season Six of *The Sopranos* deals headlong with the issue of transgression and loyalty when he learns that one of his top earning capos, Vito Spatafore, is a homosexual.

David Chase's *The Sopranos* deftly presents to the viewer the duality of conformity and anarchy within mob families.[12] Tony's associates consist of white males who are older, third-generation Italian Americans.[13] All of the men are presumed to be heterosexual. Vito Spatafore is a quiet, married man with two children; he is a good husband and provider, just like Tony and his other associates.[14] He is, according to Tony, the most reliable of his capos. He is level headed, yet ruthless and calculating when necessary. He possesses all of the qualities that go into making an excellent mobster. Vito's dual life though is incompatible with mob family values. The mob prides itself on the predication of heteronormative sexual behavior. His associates liberally use anti-gay slurs when angry. They refer to the objects of their verbal abuse as "cocksuckers," "faggots," "homos," "pillow-biters," "ass-munchers," and "flambé's." These are words meant to emasculate, to weaken and to dehumanize others. Judith Butler writes, "The utterances of hates speech are part of the continuous and uninterrupted process [of] ... an on-going subjection (*assujetissement*) that is the very operation of interpellation, that continually repeated action of discourse by which subjects are formed in subjugation ... [it is] "injurious language" (*Excitable Speech* 27). The mob world is one where even a hint of weakness leaves one open to destruction. Society equates homosexuality with femininity and weakness. It does not matter that Vito is neither weak nor effeminate. He is a homosexual. No matter how tough and manly he is, this makes him a liability.

Finn DeTrolio (Will Janowitz), Meadow Soprano's fiancé, is the first to discover Vito's secret when he spies Vito giving a construction worker a blowjob at his worksite ("Unidentified Black Males," 5.9). Finn wisely only confides in Meadow about Vito's indiscretion and subsequent sexual harassment by him. Vito's sexual proclivity is then discovered when two members of the New York mob arrive at a gay leather bar to pick up protection money from its owner. There, they happen to run into Vito dressed in full leather attire and dancing with another man. A surprised Vito acts as if his being at the gay club is a misunderstanding, but the other mobsters don't buy it ("Mr. and Mrs. John Sacrimoni Request," 6.5). The jig is up for Vito, and he knows it. In the middle of the night, he kisses his sleeping children goodbye and goes into hiding. He knows the price of being queer and in the mob. The parallel between Vito's situation as a closet gay man in the mob and the question of gays in the military is relevant here.[15] Before his outing, Vito existed under a self-imposed "Don't Ask, Don't Tell" policy. He was safe. Once outed, he becomes the object of verbal derision and physical harm by not only members of the Soprano mob family but also by his wife's cousin, Phil Leotardo (Frank Vincent), the acting head of the one of the more powerful New York mob families. Having a brother-in-law who is homosexual is an affront to Phil's sense of manhood and all that is associated with the term; he asks Tony's permission to whack Vito. Tony, at least initially, cannot decide what to do about Vito. His associates, on the other hand, are in agreement with Phil. They cannot have a homosexual mob member in the Family. Sal reminds Tony that not whacking Vito could lead to an all out mutiny against his leadership. Tony's fate is closely tied to Vito's fate, and they act as doubles. Both men have a great deal in common in their beliefs about family and loyalty. Their strength and ability to survive resides in their strategic acumen and in their sizable girth. They differ in that Tony does not make a concerted effort to loose weight and Vito does. But it is not only for health reason that Vito decides to loose weight. His dramatic weight loss is tied to a gradual acceptance of his homosexuality. It is linked to his coming out process as a gay man.

Vito's body moves from one that is morbidly obese to one whose weight is manageable. Vito takes pride in his new, slimmer waistline, and he begins to wear clothes that fit his new bodily image. That his new bodily image coincides with his acceptance of his homosexuality is not coincidental. Jane Ogden writes, "From the 1800s the male body as the object of idealization was replaced by the female body until the 1980s, when images of naked and semi-clothed men reemerged in the mainstream media. This re-emergence has been credited to the influence of gay culture" (Ogden 73–74). More physically fit, Vito becomes psychologically confident to explore a life that does not conform to cultural norms promulgated in a society that views homosexuality as an anathema. His weight-loss enables him to open the closet door and explore his sexuality. The cult of the beautiful male body is central to gay male culture. Vito is no Brad Pitt, but within certain quarters of the gay community he does not need to conform to this idea of male corporeal beauty. This he learns when he is on the lam.

He winds up in Dartford, New Hampshire, a quiet, idyllic little town that looks like something from a bygone era. There he encounters a short order cook and volunteer firefighter named Jim (John Costelloe); the two hit it off almost instantly, and Vito somehow senses a kindred spirit. When he witnesses Jim save a child from a burning house, Vito is smitten. Jim is very fit and masculine; he is divorced with kids and he also happens to be gay. This episode establishes a counter-discourse which disrupts most viewers' notions of how a gay man looks and behaves.[16] Neither Vito nor Jim meets most peoples' preconceived notions of gay men and homosexuality. Jim is a firefighter and Vito is a construction worker: two occupations which people normally associate with masculinity, strength, and machismo. They are men who just happen to be homosexual.[17] But what society cannot wrap its head around is the seemingly incongruity between masculinity and queerness. Nor does it understand that sexuality is not a bifurcation; sexuality exists on a continuum and that what is considered "normal" sexuality is arbitrary. Vito and Jim seem to understand this; the conundrum, the writers imply, lies within a society of non-acceptance and discursive acts that bolster, through naming, "the linguistic constitution of the subject" (*Excitable Speech* 33). Society dehumanizes Vito and Jim by naming them degenerate. Vito sees that in Dartford gay couples are more accepted and they are vital members of the neighborhood. He comes to believe that perhaps it is a place where he might settle. Tellingly, Vito also goes off of his diet once he meets Jim and tries his famous Johnny Cakes. He tells him, "I gotta warn ya, they're addictive" ("Live Free or Die," 6.6). Vito's repudiation of his diet is symbolic of his repudiation of societal norms concerning fat bodies and represents a rekindling of libidinal desire. Others may deem his fat body revolting, but by going off of his diet Vito is also revolting against corporeal restraints inherent in gay culture. In this way, "he alters the relational topography around [desire], body size, and shape" (LeBesco 75). Vito is not, as Christopher refers to him, a "fat piece of shit" ("Live Free or Die," 6.6). He rejects societies' dehumanization of him because of his weight. He is not waste. Unlike Tony Soprano, Vito's fat does not represent uncontrollable desire. Rather, his excessive body is a site of desire that transgresses the withering gaze of heterosexual male patriarchy. He accepts his same-sex desiring fat body not as disgraceful, disgusting or aberrant.[18] Phil, unfortunately, does not feel the same way, and he wants Vito dead for disgracing his family. He implores Tony to allow him to track him down and kill him:

TONY: So, what do you want me to do, put out an APB on the guy cause he takes it up the ass? It's a victimless crime.

PHIL: Marie is a victim. The children are victims. They've done nothing. And they're forced to live with the shame and humiliation. I gotta be frank, in your father's day we wouldn't be having this conversation [6.6].

Tony reluctantly agrees that Vito has become too much of a liability and gives Phil his blessing to go after Vito. Phil's homophobia is in line with Tony's and societies' defense of family values that underpin heteronormative sexual behavior.[19]

Vito is still ambivalent about his desire. He enjoys being free of the social constraints that force him to suppress his sexuality. Yet, he misses his family. He makes a clandestine phone call to Marie who begs him to come back home so they can work things out. She tells him that he can see a psychiatrist to make him straight. The look of despondency on Vito's face after he talks with Marie speaks volumes. He mourns his old life. Psychologically, Vito resides in a No Man's Land; he is caught between his old, familiar life and a new life that beacons to him. After a night out with Jim and the other members of the volunteer fire department, Jim moves in close to Vito, and they begin to kiss. Suddenly, Vito explodes with rage and pushes Jim away screaming. Jim calls Vito a "closet queen." They fight; Vito catches the worst of it and Jim angrily rides off on his motorcycle ("Johnny Cakes," 6.8). Vito's confrontation with Jim is a confrontation with the Self. He later tells Jim, "Sometimes you tell lies so long, you don't know when to stop. You don't know when it's safe" (6.8).

For a while, Vito feels safe with Jim, but he cannot fully repudiate his old life. He decides to leave Jim and return to New Jersey to ask Tony for a place back in the family. As Vito drives through the neighborhood, out of the corner of his eye, he sees Satriale's Meat Market, a prescient indicator of Vito's fate. Tony gives Phil permission to whack Vito. When he returns to his hotel, Vito is attacked, and his mouth is bound with duct tape. In a very symbolic scene, Phil emerges from the motel room's closet. He sits on edge of the bed and says to Vito, "You're a fuckin' disgrace" ("Cold Stones," 6.11). Phil's henchmen pound Vito with metal pipes until he dies and then shove a pool stick up his rectum. His face is so disfigured from the beating that he is barely recognizable. Phil physically and psychologically annihilates him. Phil saves face, and Vito's corporeality goes the way of all flesh. Phil's obsession with killing Vito goes beyond revenge and family honor. Vito's sexuality "haunts" Phil so much so that he has to completely eradicate its presence. Nikki Sullivan writes that "heterosexuality (and/or) the 'natural') includes what it excludes (homosexuality and/or the 'unnatural'); homosexuality is internal to heterosexuality (and vice-versa) and not external to it" (51). When Dr. Melfi confronts Tony about the sexual activity of associates who serve long stints in prison, Tony replies, "You get a pass for that" ("Mr. and Mrs. Sacrimoni Request," 6.5). Phil served a twenty year prison sentence during which he probably participated in homosexual activities. He displaces his self-disgust onto Vito. Perhaps this is another reason he is so intent on murdering him and "accounts for [his] extreme defensiveness," and pathological hatred (Seidman 131).

Elizabeth Grosz asserts that when it comes to the body "control is a matter of vigilance, never guaranteed" (194). We see this played out in representations of Tony Soprano's and Vito Spatafore's fat bodies. Their bodies engender multiple signs that manifest fluidity which on the one hand reinforce societies' imagined construction of fat bodies as innervated, weak, depraved, and out of control while simultaneously imbuing the very same body with notions of power, wealth, and unimpeded libidinal energy. These fat bodies express a kind of liberation from cultural norms and expectations. Vito and Tony, through their corpo/reality, provide us other ways of seeing the world in all of its complexities and largess.

Notes

1. This quotation is from Drea De Matteo's audio commentary about Season Five, Episode 12 titled "Long Term Parking."

2. With Mae West perhaps being the exception, and even she was viewed more as a comedienne, most fat female actresses found roles as sexless, comedic domestics on the small and silver screen. Hattie McDaniels, Shirley Booth, Mabel King, and Ann B. Davis are a few examples. Roseanne Barr, for all her feminist feistiness, never quite broke out of this mold.

3. W. C. Fields, Roscoe "Fatty" Arbuckle, Jackie Gleason, John Candy, Chris Farley are a few of these overweight actors.

4. It is well known that Frances Ford Coppola had a very difficult time convincing studio heads to allow him to cast Marlon Brando as Don Corleone and that Brando, because of his obesity, prevented him from getting roles he might otherwise have.

5. Tony's mistresses frequently fantasize that they are the love of Tony's life. A number of them become so obsessed with him that they frequently end up physically or psychologically scarred or killed. In Season Four, Tony's mistress, Gloria Trillo (Annabella Sciorra) hangs herself; and in Season Five, Valentina La Paz (Leslie Bega) is severely burned while trying to cook eggs for Tony.

6. The statue is interesting in its composition. It is green which generally symbolizes nature and nurturing and its arms rest crossed behind its back, with its breasts exposed, yet the statue's visage is disturbing because of its unseeing eyes and because of its cold demeanor. Strangely enough, given the prevalence of women in Tony's life and the numerous problems that arise out of these relationships, in the commentary about this particular scene, David Chase responds that he does not know why he chose to use the statue in this scene (1.1).

7. This scene is both funny and disturbing because it is the first opportunity the viewer gets to see Tony enjoying his work. And enjoy it he does. As he attempts to run down Mahaffey, we see the sheer pathological joy on Tony's face.

8. Pigs and pork are tropes that recur throughout the series.

9. In the first episode, it is symbolic that Christopher murders Emile in a butcher's shop. Emile's grisly murder establishes Christopher's psychopathology. One of the more gruesome means that the New Jersey mob employs to dispose of a dead body is by literally cutting it into pieces and then disposing of those pieces in various locations across the state. This is what happens to Janice Soprano's (Aida Turturro) intended fiancé, Richie Aprile (David Proval).

10. In the early episodes of the series, Carmela is partially in denial about how Tony makes his money. Although from time to time she feels pangs of guilt, she does not question him. She believes that her religious piety and Madonna-like role as wife and mother absolves her from any guilt by association. Meadow suspects about her father's business dealings but she does not immediately confront her father, and A. J. is completely oblivious about his father's mob connections.

11. Carmela is actually the one who deals with family issues more than Tony does. He always seems to step in only when things at home have reached a crisis point.

12. The teachings of the Catholic Church, the idea of the American Dream, and the importance of family solidarity and loyalty all play a part in *The Sopranos* in constructing a social body that does not tolerate radical difference.

13. Two of the exceptions are Herman "Hesh" Rabkin, who is Jewish, and Furio Giunta (Federico Castelluccio), who is Italian.

14. The character, Vito Spatafore, appeared in the First Season of *The Sopranos*. He, however, was originally named Joe. The character next appeared in Season Five as Vito Spatafore.

15. The mob is run very much like the military and the members are referred to as an army with various captains. Tony is extremely interested in military history and often watches the historical programs and movies about World War II. Tony also read and enjoyed Sun Tzu's *The Art of War*.

16. This episode titled "Johnny Cakes" undermines as well as reinforces gay stereotypes. Jim's masculinity is not in question. How he dresses, however, is a site of 70s gay iconography. His mustache and his biker gear may remind the viewer of The Village People. On the other hand, numerous straight men with similar interests look like Jim. Vito works construction that also points to gay iconography. It is ironic that Tony Soprano is frustrated by his son A. J.'s lack of toughness and that to remedy this he gets him a job working construction. A. J.'s thinness symbolizes weakness.

17. I do not want to suggest here that effeminate (gay) men are not men, just that society, by and large, equates effeminate men with femininity and weakness. These categories are simply abstractions that, by and large, have been sanctioned by society; the faces of sexuality are indeed social constructions.

18. Vito's love affair with Jim suggests that alternative views of the fat body as desirous are possible.

19. Ironically, those who decry homosexual sex acts usually do have a problem when similar sex acts are performed between a heterosexual man and woman. As the activity in Tony's strip club, The Bada, Bing!, demonstrates, lesbian sexual acts are not only tolerated but encouraged, as long a straight man is part of the equation, either gazing at the sex act or participating in it with the two women.

Works Cited

Bahktin, Mikhail. *Problems of Dostoevsky's Poetics*. Trans. Caryl Emerson. Minneapolis: University of Minnesota Press, 1984.

Barreca, Regina, ed. *A Sitdown with the Sopranos: Watching Italian American Culture on T.V.'s Most Talked-About Series*. New York: Palgrave, 2002.

Butler, Judith. *Excitable Speech: A Politics of the Performative*. New York: Rutledge, 1997.

_____. "Melancholy Gender/ Refused Identification." *Constructing Masculinity*. Maurice Berger, Brian Wallis and Simon Watson, eds. New York: Routledge, 1995. 21–36.

Dyer, Richard. *Stars*. London: British Film Institute, 1998.

Eastland, Tara. "Eating Disorders: A Feminist Issue." 4 Mar. 2007 http://www.vanderbilt.edu/AnS/psychology/health_psychology/feminist.htm.

Forth, Christopher E., and Ana Carden-Coyne. ed. *Cultures of the Abdomen: Diet, Digestion and Fat in the Modern World*. New York: Palgrave, 2005.

Gilman, Sander L. *Fat Boys: A Slim Book*. Lincoln and London: University Nebraska Press, 2004.

Grosz, Elizabeth. *Volatile Bodies: Toward a Corporeal Feminism*. Bloomington: Indiana University Press, 1994.

Kulick, Don, and Anne Meneley, ed. *Fat: The Anthropology of an Obsession*. New York: Jeremy P. Tarcher/Penguin, 2005.

Lavery, David, ed. *This Thing of Ours: Investigating the Sopranos*. New York: Columbia University Press, 2002.

LeBesco, Kathleen. "Queering Fat Bodies/Politics." *Bodies Out of Bounds: Fatness and Transgression*. Ed. Jana Evans Braziel and Kathleen LeBesco. Los Angeles: University of California Press, 2001.

Morin, Edward. *The Stars*. Trans. Richard Howard. New York: Grove Press, 1960.

Ogden, Jane. *The Psychology of Eating: From Healthy to Disordered Behavior*. Malden: Blackwell Publishing, 2003.

Oliver, J. Eric. *Fat Politics: The Real Story Behind America's Obesity Obsession.* Oxford University Press, 2006.

Seidman, Steven. "Deconstructing Queer Theory or the Undertheorization of the Social and the Ethical." *Social Postmodernism: Beyond Identity Politics.* Eds. Steven Seidman and Linda J. Nicholson. Cambridge: Cambridge University Press, 1995. 116–41.

Stallybrass, Peter, and Allon White. *The Politics and Poetics of Transgression.* New York: Cornell University Press, 1986.

Sullivan, Nikki. *A Critical Introduction to Queer Theory.* New York: New York University Press, 2003.

From Troy to 95 Lincoln Place, Irvington, N.J.: A Virgilian Reading of *The Sopranos* Underworld

Michael Calabrese

The Sopranos tells stories of loss and of past(s), historical, personal, familial, imperial, mythic, and filmic that are no more. Every viewer/reader engages the text though his own personal vision of loss and of pathos, but Italian Americans in particular find themselves exposed and revealed in its camera's eye. The show therefore appeals to the universal, the specific, and the personal, fulfilling all the classical requirements of great art and then some. As you watch it, you think it's about you, and you're right, no matter who you are. Its specific literary allegiances are to Western Classical literature, despite what David Chase says about having studied in college mainly "The Rolling Stones"[1]: its tragic movements are indebted to Aeschylus (the fall of a great house), to Sophocles (a good man polluted and polluting), and to Euripides (frenzy, immorality, and injustice), and in every sense it fulfills the Aristotelian paradigms for tragedy, as Lippman has revealed well.[2] In the terms of the late-classical discourse "On the Sublime," attributed to Longinus, the show appeals to "all and always" across cultures and time.[3] The psychic paradigms of love, desire, and the complex family relationships (themselves often rooted in the Classics) provide a universal appeal as well; everyone, we now notice in the experiential world, has a brother like Tony, a son like AJ, a sister like Janice, a girlfriend like Gloria, and so on.[4] I am amazed at how many non–Italians proudly quote the show to me and boast that they have spent the summer renting and re-watching the entire published saga. *The Sopranos* now belongs to the world.[5] It strikes a universal chord that all can hear: love, death, sin, sex, friendship, brotherhood, food, family, work. We could be reading Homer or Shakespeare, watching Kurosawa, Zhang Yimou, or John Ford.

But to leave aside for the moment what the eighteenth-century humanist, philologist, and critic Dr. Samuel Johnson would call the show's "just representations of general humanity,"[6] we see, as we zoom in, like on one of those internet maps where you can see satellite images of your childhood home, that our intensified attention to specific detail creates unique points of entry for each viewer. The show may not be designed only for the narrowest demographic, which is specifically Italian Americans from Essex county, but as a member of that exact group, I have to exploit and explore the specific points of regional contact that the show provides. My personal resonances are many: Like Meadow, I went to Columbia, riding the 45 minute bus much as she does, shacking up in the hot, City summer with my freshman girlfriend (circa 1980, when Columbia and New York were a lot grittier than now), feeling like hip adults on the urban edge, with a full fridge less than an hour away, neglected, in Jersey. The goal of the artist, as Johnson writes, is not to "paint the streaks on the tulip" (See Johnson's *Rasselas* in Richter, 224). That is, the poet need not render specifics in anatomical, mimetic detail; the poet's truth lies in capturing a universal truth. But for the botanist, the streaks that other observers ignore could prove critically convincing. Chase is secure in the universality, in the just depiction of general nature. Johnson says of Shakespeare that he writes of kings but "thinks always on men" (Richter, 227), that is, on a humanity beyond social or historically contingent position or status. One can say the same about Chase, substituting for "kings" a host of terms— WOPS, cooks, drug addicts, capos, cons, massage therapists. Chase depicts mimetically the exact world of Essex county. He can therefore paint the tulip in the Garden State as it has never quite been painted before, while still tapping into mythic and psychic narratives that compel the emotional sympathy of readers across cultures, nations, and ethnicities.

The streaks on the tulip are the smoke stacks, the Parkway "exits," the CBS FM Oldies Radio, the "coke and a slice." Most viewers have never really had the "coke and a slice" of *The Sopranos*; it's even now hard to find in Jersey; it's not the same as when we were kids. But all viewers have their own versions of that lost, mythic "coke and a slice," "red lead," the "pepper and egg sangwitches"— the meat and drink of "home."[7] In short, one can smell the chemical plants and the dumpsters in *The Sopranos* and also hear, at once, the strain of the ancient bard guiding Odysseus home to the rocky shores of Ithaca, where he can sit in peace with mellowed wine and roasted sides of beef and give his thanks to the gods.

I find myself, therefore, the target audience of any host of particulars that mark the distinct landscape of my old home. But also, as a Literature of Humanities student at Columbia and now as a professor who teaches Homer, Virgil, and Dante (a WOP with my ambition gets called "Professor Cucumber" derisively in Italian), I am also the audience of the universal and the mythic. This essay explores *The Sopranos* as part of the continuing "Italian" saga that was begun specifically in the Roman continuation of Homer, Virgil's *Aeneid*. This is the original story of how our people (then Trojans) escaped a land of decay and woe to venture westward to found a new life and a new home. Placing *The Sopranos* in this context opens up readings of the show that embrace the particular and the universal, the local and the epic, the Jersian and Virgilian, as they permeate *The Sopranos* and as I myself have witnessed it as a child and as a man. I begin where it all began, in Irvington.

Irvington

As a kid, I lived from birth to eighteen (before "growing up" and hitting the City) at 95 Lincoln Place, Irvington, NJ 07111. Jerry Lewis comes from Irvington, and the town is now in state-receivership, a Pottersville version of Beaver Falls from *It's a Wonderful Life*: a nightmare of drugs, poverty and horror, such that my dreams are haunted by images of my father's cabinet work in our old kitchen, likely now decaying, unpolished, unloved, and unknown as the art of the greatest man in my own mythic vision of paternity and heroism. When my dad did the kitchen, we ate from trays of eggplant parmesan that my mother double battered and egged to give it a heavier consistency — best with a slice of salami and with bread that, of course, you just can't get any more. I remember putting on plays in the garage with my cousin Susan and the neighborhood kids, games of Twister and Green Ghost, and the very first time some kids came around to scan the backyards to steal our bikes, which we had never had to lock up. Tony, showing AJ his old neighborhood in Newark, encounters a less than nostalgic welcome: "It's our neighborhood now, Ginny mother-fucker," says a drug-dealer, who does not appreciate the ironical brotherhood implied by that racial epithet ("Watching Too Much Television," 4.7).[8] After college, my family sold the home for almost nothing in 83; the value then tripled the next year before plummeting; I saw it last in 2000 in a quick drive by with Ralphie D, religion teacher at Seton Hall Prep and old friend (Tony you recall, did a semester and a half at Seton Hall and in those days, the U and the Prep shared a campus—I saw him once, I think). My house looked small, and I had to count from the corner to remember which one it was.

Irvington itself functions in the *Soprano* universe as an infernal zone of despair, violence, and horror.[9] When Tony B needs an explanation for his hurt foot, wounded when Joey Peeps's car, carrying the dead bodies of him and his whore, rolled over it, he confidently tells Tony, "Fucking Irvington," which, metonymically, would have been enough but to which he adds that "Two black guys jumped me outside a bar," in the episode whose title refers to that very scene, "Unidentified Black Males" (5.9). When Chris needs men outside the family to whack Carmine, he summons black hit men from Irvington, and when the assassination is called off they are massacred ("Whitecaps," 4. 13). When the wife of Paulie's school chum, Chucky Cirillo grows impatient with her mother-in-law Cookie's snubbing of Paulie's mother Nucci (as then was thought she was), a situation that already has earned Chucky a broken arm, she threatens to move her from the lush confines of Green Grove to an Salvation Army home in "Irvington." The very word concludes the scene and the debate, and the viewer knows that there won't be any more trouble from the old gal. Her son's punishment meant nothing, but "Irvington" is a name that would strike fear in the residents of Purgatory and even of Hell.

These instances underline for me, of course, the loss of my Irvington, and much of *The Sopranos*, like all good epic, is indeed about loss. "What is left," in Old English "*lāf,*" permeates, for example, the epic poem *Beowulf:* the sword of giants, the rusted useless treasure, the unpolished helmet, the burning body of the dead leader, peoples, and civilizations decaying, and the laments of the last survivors. Homer's *Odyssey,* too, is about what was left behind, a wife, a father, and a son, but Homer's poem is a romance, essentially comic in genre and moves toward restoration and re-union.[10] Virgil's *Aeneid,* however, is closest in heritage and tone to the *Sopranos,* as are the epics of John Ford. It tells the story of a home and a nation, Troy, lost in violence and destruction. If great things can be compared to small, this makes Irvington (not Naples; not Calabria) my Troy. To trace all of the Homeric, Virgilian, Dantesque, to say nothing of the other "literary" references in the *Sopranos,* would be the subject of a longer, "catalogue" analysis that is beyond my scope here, but a review of even simply the first few episodes reveals that Chase lays literary, and those often distinctly Italian, foundations right from the show's inception.[11]

Tony's mother is named "Livia," the mother of the future emperors Tiberius and Nero and the wife, in her second marriage, of Caesar Augustus, Virgil's (and the young Jesus's) emperor. In Robert Graves's book and the popular mini-series, *I Claudius*, Livia is a poisoning murderess, and Chase himself explicitly acknowledges *I Claudius*, and a maternal aunt, as the source of the name, while the character herself is also "somewhat" based on his own mother, "an acerbic and fearful woman" (Chase, viii).[12] The name could not be more dominant and imperial, casting Tony, the subject of Livia's attempted "hit," as both Augustus, whom Livia was said to have poisoned, and as the son Tiberius, his heir. Tony's own father, a "saint" in Livia's assessment, continues to be, in his ghostly "recurring role" in Tony's imaginary, "a formidable paternal presence," as Melfi puts it in very first episode (1.1). Tony's report that Livia wore his father down to a nub and that he died a "squeaking gerbil" might refer to Livia's treatment of the enfeebled Augustus in *I Claudius*, and one could write an essay simply on the connections of these, perhaps the two greatest television events about Italians. But unraveling exactly this web of potential allusions to the Roman royal "family" is irrelevant. What's most important is that the name Livia bespeaks, in Roman lore and in "TV land," a character as far as possible removed from Aeneas's own mother, the goddess Venus herself. Venus saves her son's life in battle with Achilles, controls—in a good way—his love life, ensures that he eats, and guides him to find a home in Italy. Livia is the antitype of this epic maternal guidance.

Another significant name is that of Silvio Dante; the Dante is obvious, but Silvio is likely drawn from the mythic *Silvius*, son of Aeneas and Lavinia. The tie between van Zant's character and Virgil is powerfully wrought in a nearly inaudible, seeming throwaway line in the pilot episode; as the boys discuss Junior's resentment of Tony's position, Silvio notes that "sadness accrues." A Google of the phrase indicates that is has become an emblematic favorite among fans and journalists, but does not suggest, as I am now, that it echoes Aeneas's own emblematic phrase, *sunt lacrimae rerum*, once romantically translated as "the world is a veil of tears." Such sadness is the constant underscore of both Virgil's and Chase's epics, and giving the line to the namesake of the son of Aeneas, the very father of tears in Italian history, anchors the show from its very inception in the specific imagery of epic pathos, a sadness that has moved us imperceptibly from Irvington to Troy.

"One"

Central to this restless pathos in the *Sopranos* is the theme of "loss," but what exactly is lost in the *Sopranos*? And, what, also, is artistically *gained* by Chase through the show's rich pattern of Classical and literary allusion? Among the losses are pride in identity. The Italians are supplanted over and over by other, newer and better minorities, by American Indians, by the wizards of Starbucks who corner the market in espresso, by Jamba juice, by Russians, by Arabs, by Puerto Rican priests, Mexican cooks, and also by "real" Italians themselves, as seen in *Vesuvio*'s being supplanted by an *Italian* restaurant and also in Furio's manly, old world-love for Carmela, which trumps philandering Tony's infantile dependency.[13] But perhaps the most pathetic episode is the tragic failure of the crew, during their Italian visit, to assert themselves meaningfully in the realms of love, sex, speech and food; one wonders how failure could be more comprehensive for Italians ("Commendatori," 2.4).

Chris can't even be a good tourist during the visit to the "Old Country," failing to see Vesuvius in favor of heroin; old men on the street and in cafes either ignore Paulie or accuse him of the NATO severing of a ski gondola. "Do you know me?" one old man says. Paulie thought he did, but the *commendatore* saw no brotherhood in him. There is no greater horror for a proud Italian American than to be seen as a "medighan" who puts butter on bread and mayonnaise on sandwiches—ketchup on egg noodles in Henry's Hill's formulation in *Goodfellas*.[14] However, the most grim of all scenes in Italy is Paulie's encounter with the whore. He uses his few cherished phrases in dialect to little avail while she condescendingly corrects his pronunciation to the proper Tuscan she aspires to. The scene is based on Dante's encounter with the "foul disheveled" whore Thaïs in *Inferno* 18, in the circle of the flatterers. "Now she squats and now she's standing up," Dante says of her, in words that aptly describe Paulie's escort when we first see her, leaning over a sink, knees slightly bent, cleaning her private parts; a moment later, Paulie carefully sprays breath freshener into her open mouth. As he prattles on about heritage, she smokes, indifferently, then begins aggressively scratching her foot, enacting more lines from Dante's scene, where Thaïs "scratches herself with her filthy nails" [si graffa con l'unghie merdose] (see *Inferno* 18, 130–32).[15] At this absurdly grotesque moment, the sentimental marriage of old and new worlds and the celebrated homecoming of the native son come to an end.

But the only victory for the crew in Italy, such as it is, is significant, as Tony, like his forefather Aeneas before him, visits the cave of the Cumean Sybil, who tells the lost Trojan of his fate and his need to descend to the underworld to consult his father: the "way down from lake Avernus is easy" [*facilis descendus Averno*], she famously says—the doors are open 24/7 [*noctes atque dies patet atri*], but getting back up, that's the task: *hic opus, hic labor est* [*Aeneid* 6. 126, 29]. Tony becomes Aeneas. Aeneas, called *pater* throughout Virgil's poem, hopes to lead the lost Trojans to a peaceful, prosperous homeland, with his father now gone but his young adolescent son carrying the future promise of the family and of the race. Tony leads a wandering band of second generation Italians, founders of new national identities, with their household gods safely conveyed from the "old country" and enshrined in the houses and temples of the New World—the stone churches wrought by Italian masons. The Roman foundation myth traces the wanderings of the ragged Trojan exiles, leaving a home as sterile and useless as the poor villages of southern Italy were to the peasants in the late-19th and the early 20th-century. Our mythic ancestors finally do set up their "thing" in Italian soil. They pick up the local language, "kick ass" in the neighborhood, and steal women away from the locals. In this migration, this quest, this new founding, Chase explores the failed historical systems of identity that his Italians have inherited, from Virgil on down. Finally, however, the art of the show, its self-awareness as a continuation of Classical drama and epic, its universal emotional textures, and its ongoing significance to the sons and daughters of *pater* Aeneas, all finally redeem the cascading failures of Italian identity. Virgil was a poet not simply of nationalistic self-congratulation but of ambiguity and oblique hope. When I was at Columbia, I heard Professor Matthew Santirocco, while lecturing on Virgil, quote Steele Commager's observation that the entire *Aeneid* is qualified with a big *forsan*, a big "maybe"; *maybe* one day it will delight us to look back on all this pain.[16] Chase's own Virgilian accomplishment lies in his appeal to a viewership attuned to the twin forces of loss and redemption that have marked Classical and Medieval Italian literature and perpetually mark the creative lives of Italian Americans.

Central to this problem of identity is the show's relations to a more proximate epic, the *Godfather*. Like everybody in New Jersey, the characters love and know the Trilogy, though, as noted by Massive Genius, "Three" is unworthy of citation—a conclusion somehow lost on Silvio.[17] The *Sopranos* characters readily associate their behavior with the epic paradigms in Coppola's films. Big Pussy refers to Chris's henchman Brendan being shot through the eye as a "Moe Green," "like in One." He here establishes that the simple term, "One" refers to *Godfather* I, the first volume of near sacred scripture and a guide for Italian living.[18] Chris's own failed attempt to "allude" to One comes as he plans to plant the body of his Czech rival as a visible "Sicilian message" to his crew. Chris can't pronounce "Lucca Brazzi," and the plan itself is vetoed by Pussy, who functions as an expert scriptural scholar in such matters. But while the crew may fail at the *Godfather*, they are simultaneously and ironically succeeding, as Chase is, at the *Aeneid*. They do not consciously try to do so—the poem is never mentioned by name in the show, but as the disposed and the dislocated, they are natural inheritors of the loss and pathos of their epic ancestors, whose story they are playing out in bathetic parody. Chase has crafted a telescopic literary universe, expanding out from the streets of Newark (properly pronounced "Nork") to the *Godfather* universe, to Italy, to Dante's infernal landscape, and finally to the smoldering timbers and crumbled stone of fallen Troy. They all perpetually bear witness that there *are*, indeed, tears for the way the world goes.

Tony at Cumae

Each action and desire in the *Sopranos* resonates along this continuum. That the show is immersed so deeply in the classics, in spirit, if not always in explicitly crafted or self-conscious allusion, is seen poignantly in the episode where Burt Young, old Hollywood warrior of *Chinatown* and *Rocky* fame, appears as Bobby Baccalieri's father ("Another Toothpick," 3.5). The scene recalls the end of Homer's *Odyssey*, where Odysseus's father Laertes is infused with strength by the goddess Athena and hurls a spear that fells the leader of the "suitors'" family, who come to seek revenge on Odysseus's house after the Ithacan king has butchered that worthless lot. Whether the writer, in this case Terrance Winter, had Homer in mind or not is irrelevant, because the paradigms of dignity, strength, heroism, and perhaps above all, fatherhood, themselves link the episode and the entire show to the classical literary past. Chase crafts such moments of epic "connectedness" to shape the *Sopranos* as part of the continuing Mediterranean, Classical, and specifically Italian saga. That the band "America" is playing on the car radio as Bobby, Sr., his inhaler unreachable, meets his end in a crash, confirms that emotionally and mythically, only the locale has changed since Homer first wrote such an episode about old fathers.

We could compound these Homeric moments, but, among the classics, I want to focus now on the *Aeneid* — the definitive foundational myth of Italy and the highest literary achievement of Imperial Rome — as a model that illuminates the *Sopranos*.[19] Like the *Sopranos*, Virgil's poem is all about betrayal and loss. Troy fell through infiltration, treachery, and the ungrateful heart of Achilles's son Pyrrhus, who slaughters the helpless king Priam despite his father's separate peace with the old king. The history of New Troy's survivors is filled as well with treachery, betrayal, and sacrificial death: Jimmy, Big Pussy, Adrianna, Vito, Gloria. In Virgil, the losses of the wandering Trojan exiles and associates, Palinaurus, Anchises, Nisus, Euryalus, and Dido among them, are not meaningless, for they slowly rebuild fallen Troy, restoring hope, home, and the legitimate integrity of Rome — to be *re*-restored, finally, as Dante hopes, in a new reign of earthy monarchy and justice (*Inferno* 1, 106–08). However, the *Sopranos* crew has no redemptive political or civic *telos*, no divinely-guided quest to find a home, no universal paternity to maintain, and no final redemption to build toward.[20] Tony tells Melfi, there are two possible outcomes for a man like him, death or prison. As the Sybil remarked long ago to Aeneas, the way *down* to the underworld is easy, and our new–Trojans, with nowhere to go but down, labor in consistent, parodic disjunction from the epic destiny of their mythic forebears.

In the *Aeneid*, the ghost of Aeneas's father, old Anchises, visits him in dreams to provide wisdom and guidance. In the underworld, he announces the future of Roman glory in politics, culture, and law, with the obligation to "spare the conquered and battle down the proud" (Fitzgerald, 190); these personal, public and imperial virtues will devolve in Jersey into merciless bust-outs, garbage routes, cocaine deals, cell-phone scams, and stolen airbags. Later in Virgil's poem, with his mother Venus's loving intervention, Aeneas receives a shield with his people's future hammered upon it; "knowing nothing of the events themselves, / He felt joy in their pictures" (Fitzgerald 256), which display men, wars, and histories yet unborn but spawned by him. He heaves this history up upon his shoulders, a symbol of the great weight he must bear for his family, his troops, and his people. Chase, whether intentionally Virgilian or simply employing the powerful Classical and psychological metaphor of weight, offers his own version of Aeneas's burdens in Tony's frighteningly increasing weight gain, un-ameliorated by stripping off his belt or by his hospital stay in which, tellingly, he lost "mostly muscle mass" ("Members Only," 6.1).[21]

A somewhat obscure but grimly extended Virgilian conceit is achieved when the hapless duo, Matt Bevelaqua and Sean Gismonte, enact a mock version of the doomed Trojan lovers Nisus and Euryalus. Virgil's pair contemplate the inner god of ambition and zeal inside them and leap to accomplish a daring military feat during the Trojans' war with the native Latins. Overeager for glory and spoils, they push themselves hubristically unto their deaths, with Nisus himself dying while avenging his younger lover's death. The pathos is driven by the magnificent image of Euryalus's death:

> his neck
> Collapsing let his head fall on his shoulders—
> As a bright flower cut by a passing plow
> Will droop and wither slowly, or a poppy
> Bow its head upon its tired stalk
> When overborne by a passing rain [Fitzgerald 275].

The scene inspires the plaintive promise of the poet that these two will live forever in memory *as long as Rome lives*. Rome still stands today and some of it is in New Jersey however debased into this pseudo–Virgilian duo. The two may not be homosexual lovers in Chase's story, but, in order to forge the parodic link, they are explicitly accused of such when the Neapolitan Furio, observing their casual, near-naked intimacy, examines with disgust their bikini briefs and says to his *paesano* that "these two suck each other off" ("Full Leather Jacket," 2.8).[22] In their attempt to rise to glory and get noticed by killing Christopher, we witness a profanation of Virgilian love, grandeur, loyalty, and pathos. But Virgil's promise of immortality for his lovers is nonetheless fulfilled in Chase's dark and twisted homage. Chase even preserves the pathos and the tears of Virgil's story in Bevelaqua's last moments, weeping and crying for his mother, in a final tragic allusion to Vergil's aftermath in which Euryalus's mother receives the sad news of her son's death (see Fitzgerald, 277). Virgil is transported westward, miserably but emotionally whole, from aqueduct to turnpike.

The centerpiece of the Virgilian analogy is, of course, Gloria Trillo as Aeneas's lover *infelix* (unhappy) Dido, who lives forever in the formulation of both St. Augustine and Dante as "Dido, who killed herself for love" [colei che s'ancise amorosa] (*Inferno* 5, 61).[23] Aeneas makes love to Dido in a cave, fleeing a storm but igniting a frenzy of love in the Tryian queen — *amor fou* as Dr. Melfi depicts it, garbled to "mo fo" by Tony. (We recall that Gloria goes to North Africa, not far from Dido's ancient kingdom, for the Holidays). Dido, Virgil tells us, called her adventure with the captain of the Trojans "marriage," and "in this name hid her fault" (see Fitzgerald's rendering 101). Once in love, she neglects her administrative life as queen, and her kingdom begins to fall apart. When Aeneas leaves to tend his epic duties, Dido, humiliated and disgraced, kills herself with his sword. The smoke from her pyre rises to the sight of the Trojans sailing away, for they knew, Virgil tells us, what would result from the events that unfolded. Mad, violent, wishing she had minced Aeneas's child Ascanius to a paste and served him to his "perfidious" father, unhappy Dido still inspires our tears as she did Augustine's — a perpetual reminder of what must be sacrificed, what is lost, left behind and burned away in the westward march of empire, law, civilization, and order.

The personal will of Aeneas is irrelevant, for what we could easily call "this thing of his" this "Rome" must dictate his every action, and he has no choice but to abandon Dido to her fate. Tony, for his part, as Gloria herself tells him, "deprives himself of nothing." Yet, as Dido in the underworld continues to haunt Aeneas with her punishing silence, so does the shade of the dead Gloria haunt Tony. But the *Sopranos* versions of all these Virgilian elements, Gloria, Bevelaqua, the Cumean Sybil, never contribute to any glorious, divinely-fated march toward *paternitas*, *clementia*, and *justitcia*; they are parodically "Virgilian," rather, in their twisted, sterile, and unending pathos. Chase gives us the blood, the tears, and the cascading sacrifices of the *Aeneid* but not the guarantee of a mythic destiny fulfilled.

The *Aeneid*, by contrast, is replete with moments of redemptive hope. When Aeneas the unhappy wanderer (to borrow and adjust one of Tony's phrases) first comes to Carthage in North Africa, he sees the sad story of the Trojan war depicted in murals adorning the walls of Dido's Carthage. These images were painted as part of the construction of a new kingdom she is founding after fleeing her evil brother Pygmalion, who has killed her noble husband Sychaeus. Though it will not last for long for her, she has found a new home. Amazed that their story is so widely known and more importantly *felt*, Aeneas examines the art in detail and famously exclaims:

> "What spot on earth...
> What region of the earth...
> Is not full of the story of our sorrow?"
> "They weep here
> For how the world goes, and our life that passes
> Touches their hearts. [*sunt lacrimae rerum et mentem mortalia tangunt*]
> Throw off your fear. This fame insures some kind of refuge."[24]

Recognizing themselves in art, in the expression of a culture so far away, and thus seeing their story inspire tears, is the only comfort for the wandering exiles, their home gone, their gods in a sac aboard ship, en route to an unknown shore. Fitzgerald translates as "comfort" Virgil's word *salutem* [L. *salus*, gen. *salutis*, health], a sound heard every day at dinner in Italian American households, as we raise a glass and give thanks for each other, for the food and for the memories that we are forever making together at the table.

The immigrant Italians, in the *Sopranos* and in real life, ever searching for *salutem*, carry into the future the emotional hopes of the Trojan exiles, who crossed the sea, as they would later cross one, "without papers" but with a glorious mythic history behind them. If Aeneas could see the *Sopranos* as he saw the story of Troy on Dido's "big screen," he would recognize his own story and would know yet again that they "weep here" as well. Chase re-writes, relocates, re-imagines Virgil at a gritty, lower register, but he continues the epic pathos in a modern manifestation of *translatio imperii*, not to the Lavinian shore and the great gates of Rome but to the "Jersey Shore" and the high arches of the Pulaski Skyway. Here the Roman virtues of law and paternity plod on in fractured chaos, but the *lacrimae rerum* still fall in basements, boardwalks, bars, and brothels. For the Italian-American fan who, like Aeneas, sees his own life-story depicted here, these tears (*lacrimae*) are the final redemptive reward, the "comfort" for the things (*res*) lost and left behind in fallen ancient kingdoms, boarded-up two family homes, and empty toy-closets.

In "Commendatori" (2.4), Chase invites these detailed parallels by boldly placing Tony in the cave at Cumae, tracing Aeneas's very steps. The cave also recall the cave of love the Trojan enters with Dido, and there is sex in the air between Tony and Annalisa, the sexy Neapolitan boss and surrogate voice of the Sybil. Tony, not "shitting where he eats," declines the offer, but in one brilliant flash into Tony's dreamscape, we see him in Roman military dress, stroking her ably from behind, in a triumph of Classical *eros* and grandeur possible only in mythological flicker. The price of the stolen cars is settled in the cave; in the mystic light of ancient myth at least a small profit is guaranteed to Tony to enjoy in his New Troy, his New Jersey to which the alienated band of New-Trojans returns. The comfort they feel is tangible as the camera pans across the vista of Turnpike, swamp, industry, shack — the last fruits of the *translatio imperii* begun with Aeneas, now erecting its final kingdom in the Meadowlands and environs. Back on friendly soil, far from Italy, the boys can now voice their g's in *manicotti* freely and can be "Italian" again in peace.

However, the peace is temporary. The Sybil had warned Aeneas of "Wars, vicious wars ... and Tiber foaming blood" (Fitzgerald 162). And for Tony too, war and blood are to come. Aeneas carried his father on his back, calling him "no great burden," but the history of myth and of paternity weigh down the new–Trojans at every turn. Christopher is haunted by the death of his father whom he believes he has finally avenged; Tony won't get a vasectomy because he fears his heir is weak, and he himself carries his father Johnny on his back constantly. In turn, AJ's own loafing father weighs so heavily on his back that he can neither succeed nor effectively fail, floundering in a silly hit attempt on his uncle and lost in a media sea of "growing up Soprano." The heroic, mythic task, the "labor" the "opus," is left to Meadow, the Columbia student. My own father never finished high school because of the depression and the War, but when he visited his son's lecture on the *Aeneid*, he read aloud for my students, with grace, clarity and power, the episode in which the *pius* one lifts his father and carries him safely from burning Troy. "This is the task, this the labor," to find a way to bring the past safely to a new home, to honor the father and the household gods. The weight of the past and the demands of the future rest with Meadow.

Thus when Tony visits the Sybil, learning from the graffiti-covered tourist sign that ancient visitors would ask the prophetess within to "deliver unto them their fates," he picks up the entire mythic weight of Virgil's poem and also the detailed history of violence and blood it depicts. The scene compels us to search into the future, to ponder Tony's unknown fate as we ponder that of Aeneas, knowing all along for both men that the way down to hell, in both Classical and Catholic moral geography, is easy. And the number of dead there seems as countless, Aeneas observes, "as leaves that yield their hold on boughs and fall / Through forests in the early frost of autumn, or as migrating birds from the open sea" (Fitzgerald 170). "It was something special them commin' here, eh," says Tony with innocent emotion, about his own migrating birds, whose loss will leave him empty and in near despair.

As I write, the end of the *Sopranos* story, the final 8 episodes, remain untold. How will it end? How does the *Aeneid* end? That great poem is not only, as its famous first line announces, about a *man [virum]*, but also about *war [arma]*, misleadingly translated by the great Fitzgerald as "man of arms." That the world of the *Sopranos*, in its murder and mayhem, can only be a parody of the epic elegance of the *Aeneid* is belied once we realize that the poem about piety and paternity itself ends with murder. In the climatic scene, Aeneas, "burning with fury and anger" [*furiis accensus et ira*] (12. 946), slaughters the beaten, begging Turnus, who submits, offering his land and his woman, and beseeching the Trojan to "go no further out of hatred." The final line depicts the indignant spirit of Turnus hurrying down to the underworld, "with a groan" (see Fitzgerald, 402) in a less than glorious moment of personal vengeance that Aeneas takes for the death of his young, beloved charge, Pallas— his "Christopher" we could say — whom Turnus has killed.[25]

I end my essay with a non–Italian moment from the very first episode of *The Sopranos*. It powerfully sets the show's epic tone and prepares the viewer for how the entire literary tradition, "from Homer on down" as T. S. Eliot had put it, will inform the saga's many tragic movements to come. In the pilot episode, Hesh and Big Pussy take a degenerate and increasingly frightened gambler to the bridge over the falls at Paterson, home of Lou Costello (who is actually entombed here in LA a mile or so from my office in East LA) and locus of the great modern, *neo–Vergilian* epic poem *Paterson*, the greatest achievement of New Jersey's greatest poet, William Carlos Williams. "Sing me a song," writes Williams, echoing the *Aeneid*, "to make death tolerable, a song of a man and a woman: the riddle of a man and a woman" (Williams 107). In Jersey's first epic before the *Sopranos*, the falls at Paterson are the literal and metaphorical center of that story of empire, emotion, work, nature, and pollution, complete with the personal letters of an emotionally unraveling Dido, as the Dr. bears his own sad history of fury and loss.[26] The mind of the poet and of modern man moves like the gathering waters of the falls in lines that echo the ease of infernal descent and the tireless wanderings we witness in the Roman epic. The thoughts are "Jostled as are the waters approaching the brink," and, finally,

they leap to the conclusion and
fall, fall in air! as if
floating, relieved of their weight,
split apart, ribbons; dazed, drunk
with the catastrophe of the descent
floating unsupported
to hit the rocks; to a thunder,
as if lightning had struck
                              [Williams 8].

Williams brought Virgil to Jersey, just as Chase does here at the inception of his epic and will continue to do for the next seven seasons, as the dry leaves, with the catastrophe of their own descent, "yield their hold on boughs and fall" on the Garden State, on the surging waters of Paterson, and on the well-wrought steps my father built at 95 Lincoln Place, Irvington, NJ.

Notes

1. See the interview printed in Rucker. Chase notes as well that he read much Shakespeare, whom we can certainly isolate as a source of Classical literary transmission. For not a Classical but a Renaissance Italian reading of the show, see DeFino's assessment of Tony's debt to the political doctrines of leadership and control in Nicolo Macchiavelli's *The Prince* (*Il Principe*).

2. Lippman thoughtfully aligns Tony and the show itself with the prominent features of Aristotelian tragedy, including the notions of the "flawed tragic hero," fear, and pity. Lippman also convincing interprets the complex concept of *catharsis*, not, as some have, as a purging that leads to "beatific detachment" but as a healthy" bringing [of] our emotions forward" (Green and Vernezze, 156) as we witness the tragedy unfold.

3. See David Richter's anthology, 38ff. for the text of Aristotle's poetics, esp. 50–51 on the nature of the tragic character: "[he must be] a person who is neither perfect in virtue and justice, nor one who falls into misfortune through vice and depravity; but rather one who succumbs through miscalculation. He must also be a person who enjoys greet reputation and good fortune." The goal of tragedy, for Aristotle, is to provoke "fear and pity." Readers may want to debate whether Tony Soprano fulfills these definitions, and the very theme of "tragedy" as the genre of the program would have to be the subject of a separate inquiry. For Longinus, see the text of "On the Sublime" in the same anthology, pp. 79ff. Se esp. the definition of the sublime as transcending time and culture: "In general consider those examples of sublimity to be fine and genuine which please all and always. For when men of different pursuits, lives, ambitions, ages, languages, hold identical views on one and the same subject, then the verdict which results, so to speak, from a concert of discordant elements makes our faith in the object of admiration strong and unassailable" (Richter, 84).

4. These themes and the shows "unprecedented" "degree of psychiatric realism" prompted Dr. Glen O Gabbard to explore the show's portrayal of the psyche, of emotion, and of therapy. For him, the show "brilliantly illuminates what it means to be human" (xi–xii).

5. For example, see Lacey on its appeal to a broad sector of men (from 16 to 55) in non–Italian British society.

6. See a selection of Johnson's writings in Richter, 218 ff; here, 225 from the "Preface to Shakespeare."

7. Dunne, 216, notes how food at times bespeaks "us-ness," creating a familial connection between the viewers and the characters, while at other points it participates as well in the scenarios of violence and power. She offers a comprehensive survey of the role of food in the *Sopranos*.

8. The subject of race in the *Sopranos* has not been adequately studied or understood. Gibson, for example, summons the history of lynching and innuendo about the war on terror in order to frame a series of what turn out to be no more than simple indictments and condemnations of the characters' attitudes toward race. But see Kocela's insightful discussion of the distinctions between "white" and "Italian" identities, particularly in reference to Tony's allegiance to "symbolic fathers" (120).

9. An appreciation of the unique geography, both physical and cultural, of what he calls "Sopranoland," is offered by Lance Strate, who also explores the odd "pleasures of recognition" that I myself am practicing here.

10. Johansson, exploring the show's opening sequence as Tony heads home to Jersey from the City, effectively relates the *Sopranos* to saga and epic in the tradition of "that other epic hero, the Greek Odyseus" who braves monsters on all sides in his quest to get home.

11. Though it does not focus on Classical allusions, per se, Lavery's "Intertextual Moments and Allusions in the Sopranos" (Lavery 235–53, Appendix C) offers an excellent catalogue the reveals the richness of both literary and cultural reference in the show. Peter J. Vernezze effectively addresses the Danteque qualities of sin in the show, employing Dante's major divisions of incontinence, violence and fraud. Playfully entering into the spiritual fray, Vernezze anticipates Tony's final fate and hopes he can avoid "eternal damnation" (194).

12. On the origins of some other characters' names, unrelated to Roman history, see Chase, viii. On Livia, see also Gabbard, 106; and See Stoehr, 36–454 passim, on Tony's relationship with his mother in the context of the show's comprehensive philosophical nihilism.

13. Kocela, passim, addresses the Columbus question (and the episode "Christopher")as it pertains, in part, to "the struggle for ethnic identity in the age of victimhood" (115).

14. See Dunne, 217, on Paulie's displeasure with squid-ink pasta and also on the idea of the "Wonder-bread WOP."

15. References to the *Inferno*, both text and translation, are to Robert's and Jean Hollander's translation.

16. I refer to Aeneas's hope that "some day even remembering this / Will be a pleasure" [forsan et haec olim meminisse iuvabit] (Fitzgerald, 10). Santirocco was quoting Steele Commager, 13. who wrote that "A perpetual forsan, 'perhaps,' hovers over the *Aeneid*." I express my thanks to Professor Santirocco for this reference and for the insight, shared some 23 years ago.

17. It is worth noting that Chase was originally approached about creating "a TV version of the Godfather," an idea in which he "wasn't interested" (Chase, vii).

18. Gabbard mentions this scene in the context of the show's cinematic debts and allusions, 11ff.; he notes, as well, that Chase explicitly refers to that other influential film, *Goodfellas* as "The Koran." Auster, 11, notices as well that the *Sopranos* characters treat the Godfather as "holy writ." And see Pattie, who offers the fullest assessment of Coppola's and Scorsese's films as influences and frames of reference for the *Sopranos* characters, arguing, essentially, that *Goodfellas* is muted in the show because it is "too close to Tony's grubby, meaningless, and contingent reality" while the Godfather presents an "idealized version of their lives" (145).

19. In this vein see Gabbard's chapter "Medea, Oedipus and other Family Myths" (Gabbard 99–123), exploring the literary, mythic, and psychological paradigms, with particular application to Livia and also Janice.

20. This lack of redemption no doubt relates to the nihilism Stoehr locates in the show; see 36–54 in the chapter, "The Nihilistic Vision of Film Noir and *The Sopranos*": "[n]ihilism ... signals the loss of unity and wholeness on both personal and collective levels of existence" (40). An earlier, shorter version of his essay appears in Greene and Vernazze, 37–47.

21. For a study of Tony's weight as a capitalist metaphor for material "consumption," and also in the dynamics of middle class masculinity, see Santo. Since Santo's essay, Tony has grown ever heavier, partially supporting that author's conclusions: "Self-made manhood is ... doomed to destroy itself. Its very reliance on success in the capitalism marketplace in order to define its identity requires that it constantly exploit new areas of consumption" (94). Santo offers convincing close readings of the imagery of food and of the dramatic relations of characters with different body types.

22. On the pair as fastidious dandies, see Santo, 86–90.

23. See Gabbard, 139ff. for a psychological profile of Gloria.

24. Citations of the *Aeneid* are to the edition of R. D. Williams; here Book 1, 462; translations are Fitzgerald's with lineation occasionally adjusted, here p. 20. Where not cited, the translation is mine.

25. On the role of "bloodlust" in the *Sopranos*, particularly as it is incited in the viewers in "Employee of the Month," and "Another Toothpick," see Baldanzi.

26. See the personal letters directed at Williams by a woman, "C" in *Patterson*, Book 2, iii, pp. 82, 87–91; see the editor's notes, 275ff., identifying her as Marcia Nardi.

Works Cited

Auster, Albert. "*The Sopranos:* The Gangster Dedux." Lavery (2002), 10–15.

Baldanzi, Jessica. "Bloodlust for the Common Man: *The Sopranos* confronts its Volatile American Audience." Lavery (2006), 81–92.

Chase, David. *The Sopranos: Selected Scripts from Three Seasons.* New York: HBO, 2002.

Commager, Steele. *Virgil: A Collection of Critical Essays.* Englewood Cliffs, NJ: Prentice-Hall, 1966.

Dante, *The Inferno.* Trans. Robert and Jean Hollander. New York: Anchor Books, 2002.

DeFino, Dean. "The Price of North Jersey." Lavery (2006), 181–95.

Dunne, Sarah Lewis. "'The Brutality of Meat and the Abruptness of Seafood': Food, Violence, and Family in *The Sopranos.* Lavery (2002), 215–226.

Gibson, Brian. "'Black Guys, My Ass': Uncovering the Queerness of Racism in the *Sopranos.*" Lavery (2006), 197–216.

Greene, Richard and Peter Vernezze, eds. *The Sopranos and Philosophy.* Chicago: Open Court, 2004.

Kocela, Christopher. "From Columbus to Garry Cooper: Mourning the Lost White Father in *The Sopranos.*" Lavery (2006), 107–120.

Lacey, Joanne. "One for the Boys? *The Sopranos* and its Male, British Audience." Lavery (2002), 95–108.

Lavery, David. *This Thing of Ours: Investigating The Sopranos.* New York: Columbia University Press, 2002.

_____. *Reading The Sopranos.* New York: McMillan, 2006.

Lippman, Mike. "Know Thyself, Asshole: Tony Soprano as an Aristotelian Tragic Hero." Greene and Vernezze, 147–56.

Noyes, Russell. *English Romantic Poetry and Verse*. New York: Oxford, 1956.

Pattie, David. "Mobbed Up: *The Sopranos* and the Modern Gangster Film." Lavery (2002), 135–45.

Richter, David. *The Critical Tradition: Classic Texts and Contemporary Trends*. 2d ed. Boston and New York: Bedford/St. Martins, 1998.

Rucker, Allen. *The Sopranos: A Family History*. New York: New American Library, 2001.

Santo, Avi. "'Fat Fuck! Why Don't You Take a Look in the Mirror': Weight, Body Image, and Masculinity in *The Sopranos*." Lavery (2002), 72–94.

Strate, Lance. "No(rth Jersey) Sense of Place: The Cultural Geography (and Media Ecology) of *The Sopranos*." Lavery, 178–94.

Stoehr, Kevin L. *Nihilism in Film and Television: A Critical Overview from Citizen Kane to The Sopranos*. Jefferson, North Carolina: McFarland, 2006.

Vernezze, Peter J. "Tony Soprano in Hell: Chase's Mob in Dante's Inferno." Greene and Vernezze, 185–94.

Virgil. *The Aeneid*. Trans. Robert Fitzgerald. New York: Vintage, 1992.

_____. *The Aeneid of Virgil*. Ed. R.D. Williams. London: McMillan, 1972.

Williams, William Carlos. *Paterson*. Ed. Christopher MacGowan. New York: New Directions, 1995.

Episode Listing for
The Rockford Files
(1974–1980)

Season 1 (1974-75)

Episode 1 (1:1) "The Rockford Files: Backlash of the Hunter." Teleplay: John Thomas James. Dir.: Richard T. Heffron. NBC. 27 March 1974.

Episode 2 (1:2) "The Kirkoff Case." Teleplay: Stephen J. Cannell. Dir.: Lou Antonio. NBC. 13 September 1974.

Episode 3 (1:3) "The Dark and Bloody Ground." Teleplay: Juanita Bartlett. Dir.: Michael Schultz. NBC. 20 September 1974.

Episode 4 (1:4) "The Countess." Teleplay: Stephen J. Cannell. Dir.: Russ Mayberry. NBC. 27 September 1974.

Episode 5 (1:5) "Exit Prentiss Carr." Teleplay: Juanita Bartlett. Dir.: Alexander Grasshoff. NBC. 4 October 1974.

Episode 6 (1:6) "Tall Woman in Red Wagon." Teleplay: Stephen J. Cannell. Dir.: Jerry London. NBC. 11 October 1974.

Episode 7 (1:7) "This Case Is Closed." Teleplay: Stephen J. Cannell. Dir.: Bernard L. Kowalski. NBC. 18 October 1974.

Episode 8 (1:8) "The Big Ripoff." Teleplay: Robert Hamner and Jo Swerling Jr. Dir.: Vincent McEveety. NBC. 25 October 1974.

Episode 9 (1:9) "Find Me If You Can." Teleplay: Juanita Bartlett. Dir.: Lawrence Doheny. NBC. 1 November 1974.

Episode 10 (1:10) "In Pursuit of Carol Thorne." Teleplay: Stephen J. Cannell. Dir.: Charles S. Dubin. NBC. 8 November 1974.

Episode 11 (1:11) "The Dexter Crisis." Teleplay: Gloryette Clark. Dir.: Alexander Grasshoff. NBC. 15 November 1974.

Episode 12 (1:12) "Caledonia—It's Worth a Fortune." Teleplay: Juanita Bartlett. Dir.: Stuart Margolin. NBC. 6 December 1974.

Episode 13 (1:13) "Profit and Loss: Part I." Teleplay: Stephen J. Cannell. Dir.: Lawrence Doheny. NBC. 20 December 1974.

Episode 14 (1:14) "Profit and Loss: Part II." Teleplay: Stephen J. Cannell. Dir.: Lawrence Doheny. NBC. 27 December 1974.

Episode 15 (1:15) "Aura Lee, Farwell." Teleplay: Edward J. Lakso. Dir.: Jackie Cooper. NBC. 3 January 1975.

Episode 16 (1:16) "Sleight of Hand." Teleplay: Stephen J. Cannell and Jo Swerling. Dir.: William Wiard. NBC. 17 January 1975.

Episode 17 (1:17) "Counter Gambit." Teleplay: Juanita Bartlett and Howard Berk. Dir.: Jackie Cooper. NBC. 24 January 1975.

Episode 18 (1:18) "Claire." Teleplay: Stephen J. Cannell and Edward J. Lakso. Dir.: William Wiard. NBC. 31 January 1975.

Episode 19 (1:19) "Say Goodbye to Jennifer." Teleplay: Juanita Bartlett and Rudolph Borchert. Dir.: Jackie Cooper. NBC. 7 February 1975.

Episode 20 (1:20) "Charlie Harris at Large." Teleplay: Zekial Marko. Dir.: Russ Mayberry. NBC. 14 February 1975.

Episode 21 (1:21) "The Four Pound Brick." Teleplay: Juanita Bartlett. Dir.: Lawrence Doheny. NBC. 21 February 1975.

Episode 22 (1:22) "Just by Accident." Teleplay: Charles Sailor and Eric Kalder. Dir.: Jerry London. NBC. 28 February 1975.

Episode 23 (1:23) "Roundabout." Teleplay: Edward J. Lakso. Dir.: Lou Antonio. NBC. 7 March 1975.

Season 2 (1975-76)

Episode 24 (2:1) "The Aaron Ironwood School of Success." Teleplay: Stephen J. Cannell. Dir.: Lou Antonio. 12 September 1975.

Episode 25 (2:2) "The Farnsworth Stratagem." Teleplay: Juanita Bartlett. Dir.: Lawrence Doheny. NBC. 19 September 1975.

Episode 26 (2:3) "Gearjammers: Part I." Teleplay: Don Carlos Dunaway. Dir.: William Wiard. NBC. 26 September 1975.

Episode 27 (2:4) "Gearjammers: Part II." Teleplay: Don Carlos Dunaway. Dir.: William Wiard. NBC. 3 October 1975.

Episode 28 (2:5) "The Deep Blue Sleep." Teleplay: Juanita Bartlett. Dir.: William Wiard. NBC. 10 October 1975.

Episode 29 (2:6) "The Great Blue Lake Land and Development Company." Teleplay: Juanita Bartlett. Dir.: Lawrence Doheny. NBC. 17 October 1975.

Episode 30 (2:7) "The Real Easy Red Dog." Teleplay: Stephen J. Cannell. Dir.: Ivan Dixon. NBC. 31 October 1975.

Episode 31 (2:8) "Resurrection in Black and White." Teleplay: Juanita Bartlett and Stephen J. Cannell. Dir.: Russ Mayberry. NBC. 7 November 1975.

Episode 32 (2:9) "Chicken Little is a Little Chicken." Teleplay: Stephen J. Cannell. Dir.: Lawrence Doheny. NBC. 14 November 1975.

Episode 33 (2:10) "2 Into 5.56 Won't Go." Teleplay: Stephen J. Cannell. Dir.: Jeannot Szwarc. NBC. 21 November 1975.

Episode 34 (2:11) "Pastoria Prime Pick." Teleplay: Gordon Dawson. Dir.: Lawrence Doheny. NBC. 29 November 1975.

Episode 35 (2:12) "The Reincarnation of Angie." Teleplay: Stephen J. Cannell. Dir.: Jerry London. NBC. 5 December 1975.

Episode 36 (2:13) "The Girl in the Bay City Boys Club." Teleplay: Juanita Bartlett. Dir.: James Garner. NBC. 19 December 1975.

Episode 37 (2:14) "The Hammer of C Block." Teleplay: Gordon Dawson. Dir.: Jerry London. NBC. 9 January 1976.

Episode 38 (2:15) "The No-Cut Contract." Teleplay: Stephen J. Cannell. Dir.: Lou Antonio. NBC. 16 January 1976.

Episode 39 (2:16) "A Portrait of Elizabeth." Teleplay: Stephen J. Cannell. Dir.: Meta Rosenberg. NBC. 23 January 1976.

Episode 40 (2:17) "Joey Blue Eyes." Teleplay: Walter Dallenbach. Dir.: Lawrence Doheny. NBC. 30 January 1976.

Episode 41 (2:18) "In Hazard." Teleplay: Juanita Bartlett. Dir.: Jackie Cooper. NBC. 6 February 1976.

Episode 42 (2:19) "The Italian Bird Fiasco." Teleplay: Edward J. Lakso. Dir.: Jackie Cooper. NBC. 13 February 1976.

Episode 43 (2:20) "Where's Houston?" Teleplay: Don Carlos Dunaway. Dir.: Lawrence Doheny. NBC. 20 February 1976.

Episode 44 (2:21) "Foul on the First Play." Teleplay: Stephen J. Cannell. Dir.: Lou Antonio. NBC. 12 March 1976.

Episode 45 (2:22) "A Bad Deal in the Valley." Teleplay: Donald L. Gold and Lester William Berke. Dir.: Jerry London. NBC. 19 March 1976.

Season 3 (1976-77)

Episode 46 (3:1) "The Fourth Man." Teleplay: Juanita Bartlett. Dir.: William Wiard. NBC. 24 September 1976.

Episode 47 (3:2) "The Oracle Wore a Cashmere Suit." Teleplay: David Chase. Dir.: Russ Mayberry. NBC. 1 October 1976.

Episode 48 (3:3) "The Family Hour." Teleplay: Gordon Dawson. Dir.: William Wiard. NBC. 8 October 1976.

Episode 49 (3:4) "Feeding Frenzy." Teleplay: Stephen J. Cannell. Dir.: Russ Mayberry. NBC. 15 October 1976.

Episode 50 (3:5) "Drought at Indianhead River." Teleplay: Stephen J. Cannell. Dir.: Lawrence Doheny. NBC. 5 November 1976.

Episode 51 (3:6) "Coulter City Wildcat." Teleplay: Don Carlos Dunaway. Dir.: Russ Mayberry. NBC. 12 November 1976.

Episode 52 (3:7) "So Help Me God." Teleplay: Juanita Bartlett. Dir.: Jeannot Szwarc. NBC. 19 November 1976.

Episode 53 (3:8) "Rattlers' Class of '63." Teleplay: David Chase. Dir.: Meta Rosenberg. NBC. 26 November 1976.

Episode 54 (3:9) "Return to the Thirty-Eight Parallel." Teleplay: Walter Dallenbach. Dir.: Bruce Kessler. NBC. 10 December 1976.

Episode 55 (3:10) "Piece Work." Teleplay: Juanita Bartlett. Dir.: Lawrence Doheny. NBC. 17 December 1976.

Episode 56 (3:11) "The Trouble with Warren." Teleplay: Juanita Bartlett. Dir.: Christian I. Nyby II. NBC. 24 December 1976.

Episode 57 (3:12) "There's One in Every Port." Teleplay: Stephen J. Cannell. Dir.: Meta Rosenberg. NBC. 7 January 1977.

Episode 58 (3:13) "Sticks and Stones May Break Your Bones, but Waterbury Will Bury You." Teleplay: David Chase. Dir.: Jerry London. NBC. 14 January 1977.

Episode 59 (3:14) "The Trees, the Bees, and T. T. Flowers: Part I." Teleplay: Gordon Dawson. Dir.: Jerry London. NBC. 21 January 1977.

Episode 60 (3:15) "The Trees, the Bees, and T. T. Flowers: Part II." Teleplay: Gordon Dawson. Dir.: Jerry London. NBC. 28 January 1977.

Episode 61 (3:16) "The Becker Connection." Teleplay: Juanita Bartlett. Dir.: Reza Badiyi. NBC. 11 February 1977.

Episode 62 (3:17) "Just Another Polish Wedding." Teleplay: Stephen J. Cannell. Dir.: William Wiard. NBC. 18 February 1977.

Episode 63 (3:18) "New Life, Old Dragons." Teleplay: David C. Taylor. Dir.: Jeannot Szwarc. NBC. 25 February 1977.

Episode 64 (3:19) "To Protect and Serve: Part I." Teleplay: David Chase. Dir.: William Wiard. NBC. 11 March 1977.

Episode 65 (3:20) "To Protect and Serve: Part II." Teleplay: David Chase. Dir.: William Wiard. NBC. 18 March 1977.

Episode 66 (3:21) "Crack Back." Teleplay: Juanita Bartlett. Dir.: Reza Badiyi. NBC. 25 March. 1977.

Episode 67 (3:22) "Dirty Money, Black Light." Teleplay: David C. Taylor. Dir.: Stuart Margolin. NBC. 1 April 1977.

Season 4 (1977–78)

Episode 68 (4:1) "Beamer's Last Case." Teleplay: Stephen J. Cannell. Dir.: Stephen J. Cannell. NBC. 16 September 1977.

Episode 69 (4:2) "Trouble in Chapter 17." Teleplay: Juanita Bartlett. Dir.: William Ward. NBC. 23 September 1977.

Episode 70 (4:3) "The Battle of Canoga Park." Teleplay: Juanita Bartlett. Dir.: Ivan Dixon. NBC. 30 September 1977.

Episode 71 (4:4) "Second Chance." Teleplay: Gordon Dawson. Dir.: Reza Badiyi. NBC. 14 October 1977.

Episode 72 (4:5) "The Dog and Pony Show." Teleplay: David Chase. Dir.: Reza Badiyi. NBC. 21 October 1977.

Episode 73 (4:6) "Requiem for a Funny Box." Teleplay: James Crocker. Dir.: William Wiard. NBC. 4 November 1977.

Episode 74 (4:7) "Quickie Nirvana." Teleplay: David Chase. Dir.: Meta Rosenberg. NBC. 11 November 1977.

Episode 75 (4:8) "Irving the Explainer." Teleplay: David Chase. Dir.: James Coburn. NBC. 18 November 1977.

Episode 76 (4:9) "The Mayor's Committee From Deer Lick Falls." Teleplay: William R. Stratton. Dir.: Ivan Dixon. NBC. 25 November 1977.

Episode 77 (4:10) "Hotel of Fear." Teleplay: Juanita Bartlett. Dir.: Russ Mayberry. NBC. 2 December 1977.

Episode 78 (4:11) "Forced Retirement." Teleplay: William R. Stratton. Dir.: Alexander Singer. NBC. 9 December 1977.

Episode 79 (4:12) "The Queen of Peru." Teleplay: David Chase. Dir.: Meta Rosenberg. NBC. 16 December 1977.

Episode 80 (4:13) "A Deadly Maze." Teleplay: Juanita Bartlett. Dir.: William Wiard. NBC. 23 December 1977.

Episode 81 (4:14) "The Attractive Nuisance." Teleplay: Stephen J. Cannell. Dir.: Dana Elcar. NBC. 6 January 1978.

Episode 82 (4:15) "The Gang at Don's Drive-In." Teleplay: James Crocker. Dir.: Harry Falk. NBC. 13 January 1978.

Episode 83 (4:16) "The Paper Palace." Teleplay: Juanita Bartlett. Dir.: Richard Crenna. NBC. 20 January 1978.

Episode 84 (4:17) "Dwarf in a Helium Hat." Teleplay: Stephen J. Cannell and David Chase. Dir.: Reza Badiyi. NBC. 27 January 1978.

Episode 85 (4:18) "South by Southeast." Teleplay: Juanita Bartlett. Dir.: William Wiard. NBC. 3 February 1978.

Episode 86 (4:19) "The Competitive Edge." Teleplay: Gordon Dawson. Dir.: Harry Falk. NBC. 10 February 1978.

Episode 87 (4:20) "The Prisoner of Rosemont Hall." Teleplay: Stephen J. Cannell and David Chase. Dir.: Ivan Dixon. NBC. 17 February 1978.

Episode 88 (4:21) "The House on Willis Avenue: Part I." Teleplay: Stephen J. Cannell. Dir.: Hy Averback. NBC. 24 February 1978.

Episode 89 (4:22) "The House on Willis Avenue: Part II." Teleplay: Stephen J. Cannell. Dir.: Hy Averback. NBC. 24 February 1978.

Season 5 (1978-79)

Episode 90 (5:1) "Heartaches of a Fool." Teleplay: Stephen J. Cannell. Dir.: William Wiard. NBC. 22 September 1978.

Episode 91 (5:2) "Rosendahl and Gilda Stern Are Dead." Teleplay: Juanita Bartlett. Dir.: William Wiard. NBC. 29 September 1978.

Episode 92 (5:3) "The Jersey Bounce." Teleplay: David Chase. Dir.: William Wiard. NBC. 6 October 1978.

Episode 93 (5:4) "White on White and Nearly Perfect." Teleplay: Stephen J. Cannell. Dir.: Stephen J. Cannell. NBC. 20 October 1978.

Episode 94 (5:5) "Kill the Messenger." Teleplay: Juanita Bartlett. Dir.: Ivan Dixon. NBC. 27 October 1978.

Episode 95 (5:6) "The Empty Frame." Teleplay: Stephen J. Cannell. Dir.: Corey Allen. NBC. 3 November 1978.

Episode 96 (5:7) "A Three-Day Affair With a Thirty-Day Escrow." Teleplay: David Chase. Dir.: Ivan Dixon. NBC. 10 November 1978.

Episode 97 (5:8) "A Good Clean Bust With Sequel Rights." Teleplay: Rudolph Borchert. Dir.: William Wiard. NBC. 17 November 1978.

Episode 98 (5:9) "Black Mirror: Part I." Teleplay: David Chase. Dir.: Arnold Laven. NBC. 24 November 1978.

Episode 99 (5:10) "Black Mirror: Part II." Teleplay: David Chase. Dir.: Arnold Laven. NBC. 24 November 1978.

Episode 100 (5:11) "A Fast Count." Teleplay: Gordon Dawson. Dir.: Reza Badiyi. NBC. 1 December 1978.

Episode 101 (5:12) "Local Man Eaten by Newspaper." Teleplay: Juanita Bartlett. Dir.: Meta Rosenberg. NBC. 8 December 1978.

Episode 102 (5:13) "With the French Heel Back, Can the Nehru Jacket Be Far Behind?" Teleplay: Rudolph Borchert. Dir.: Ivan Dixon. NBC. 5 January 1979.

Episode 103 (5:14) "The Battle-Ax and the Exploding Cigar." Teleplay: Rogers Turrentine. Dir.: Ivan Dixon. NBC. 12 January 1979.

Episode 104 (5:15) "Guilt." Teleplay: Juanita Bartlett. Dir.: William Wiard. NBC. 19 January 1979.

Episode 105 (5:16) "The Deuce." Teleplay: Gordon Dawson. Dir.: Bernard McEveety. NBC. 26 January 1979.

Episode 106 (5:17) "The Man Who Saw the Alligators." Teleplay: David Chase. Dir.: Corey Allen. NBC. 10 February 1979.

Episode 107 (5:18) "The Return of the Black Shadow." Teleplay: Stephen J. Cannell. Dir.: William Wiard. NBC. 17 February 1979.

Episode 108 (5:19) "A Material Difference." Teleplay: Rogers Turrentine. Dir.: William Wiard. NBC. 24 February 1979.

Episode 109 (5:20) "Never Send a Boy King to Do a Man's Job: Part I." Teleplay: Juanita Bartlett. Dir.: William Wiard. NBC. 3 March 1979.

Episode 110 (5:21) "Never Send a Boy King to Do a Man's Job: Part II." Teleplay: Juanita Bartlett. Dir.: William Wiard. NBC. 3 March 1979.

Episode 111 (5:22) "A Different Drummer." Teleplay: Rudolph Borchert. Dir.: Reza Badiyi. NBC. 13 April 1979.

Season 6 (1979-80)

Episode 112 (6:1) "Paradise Cove." Teleplay: Stephen J. Cannell. Dir.: Stephen J. Cannell. NBC. 28 September 1979.

Episode 113 (6:2) "Lions, Tigers, Monkeys and Dogs: Part I." Teleplay: Juanita Bartlett. Dir.: William Wiard. NBC. 12 October 1979.

Episode 114 (6:3) "Lions, Tigers, Monkeys and Dogs: Part II." Teleplay: Juanita Bartlett. Dir.: William Wiard. NBC. 12 October 1979.

Episode 115 (6:4) "Only Rock 'n' Roll Will Never Die: Part I." Teleplay: David Chase. Dir.: William Wiard. NBC. 19 October 1979.

Episode 116 (6:5) "Only Rock 'n' Roll Will Never Die: Part II." Teleplay: David Chase. Dir.: William Wiard. NBC. 26 October 1979.

Episode 117 (6:6) "Love Is the Word." Teleplay: David Chase. Dir.: John Patterson. NBC. 9 November 1979.

Episode 118 (6:7) "Nice Guys Finish Dead." Teleplay: Stephen J. Cannell. Dir.: John Patterson. NBC. 16 November 1979.

Episode 119 (6:8) "The Hawaiian Headache." Teleplay: Stephen J. Cannell. Dir.: William Wiard. NBC. 23 November 1979.

Episode 120 (6:9) "No Fault Affair." Teleplay: Juanita Bartlett. Dir.: Corey Allen. NBC. 30 November 1979.

Episode 121 (6:10) "The Big Cheese." Teleplay: Shel Willens. Dir.: Joseph Pevney. NBC. 7 December 1979.

Episode 122 (6:11) "Just a Coupla Guys." Teleplay: David Chase. Dir.: Ivan Dixon. NBC. 14 December 1979.

Episode 123 (6:12) "Deadlock in Parma." Teleplay: Lester William Berke, Don L. Gold, and Rudolph Borchert. Dir.: Winrich Kolbe. NBC. 10 January 1980.

Season 7 (1994–99)

Episode 124 (7:1) "I Still Love L. A." Teleplay: Juanita Bartlett. Dir.: James Whitmore Jr. CBS. November 27, 1994.

Episode 125 (7:2) "A Blessing in Disguise." Teleplay: Stephen J. Cannell. Dir.: Jeannot Szwarc. CBS. May 14, 1995.

Episode 126 (7:3) "If the Frame Fits...." Teleplay: Juanita Bartlett. Dir.: Jeannot Szwarc. CBS. January 14, 1996.

Episode 127 (7:4) "Godfather Knows Best." Teleplay: David Chase. Dir.: Tony Wharmby. CBS. February 18, 1996.

Episode 128 (7:5) "Friends and Foul Play." Teleplay: Stephen J. Cannell. Dir.: Stuart Margolin. CBS. April 25, 1996.

Episode 129 (7:6) "Punishment and Crime." Teleplay: David Chase. Dir.: David Chase. CBS. September 18, 1996.

Episode 130 (7:7) "Murder and Misdemeanors." Teleplay: Juanita Bartlett. Dir.: Tony Wharmby. CBS. November 21, 1997.

Episode 131 (7:8) "If It Bleeds, It Leads." Teleplay: Reuben Leder. Dir.: Stuart Margolin. CBS. April 20, 1999.

Episode Listing for *Northern Exposure* (1990–1995)

Season 1 (1990)

Episode 1 (1:1) "Pilot." Teleplay: John Falsey and Joshua Brand. Dir.: Joshua Brand. CBS. 12 July 1990.

Episode 2 (1:2) "Brains, Know How, and Native Intelligence." Teleplay: Stuart Stevens. Dir.: Peter O'Fallon. CBS. 19 July 1990.

Episode 3 (1:3) "Soapy Sanderson." Teleplay: Jerry Stahl and Karen Hall. Dir.: Stephen Cragg. CBS. 26 July 1990.

Episode 4 (1:4) "Dreams, Schemes, and Putting Greens." Teleplay: Sean Clark. Dir.: Dan Lerner. CBS. 2 August 1990.

Episode 5 (1:5) "Russian Flu." Teleplay: David Assael. Dir.: David Carson. CBS. 9 August 1990.

Episode 6 (1:6) "Sex, Lies, and Ed's Tapes." Teleplay: John Falsey and Joshua Brand. Dir.: Sandy Smolan. CBS. 16 August 1990.

Episode 7 (1:7) "A Kodiak Moment." Teleplay: Jessica Klein and Steve Wasserman. Dir.: Max Tash. CBS. 23 August 1990.

Episode 8 (1:8) "Aurora Borealis—A Fairy Tale for Big People." Teleplay: Charles Rosin. Dir.: Peter O'Fallon. CBS. 30 August 1990.

Season 2 (1991)

Episode 9 (2:1) "Goodbye to All That." Teleplay: Robin Green. Dir.: Stuart Margolin. CBS. 8 April 1991.

Episode 10 (2:2) "The Big Kiss." Teleplay: Henry Bromell. Dir.: Sandy Smolan. CBS. 15 April 1991.

Episode 11 (2:3) "All is Vanity." Teleplay: Andrew Schneider and Diane Frolov. Dir.: Nick Marck. CBS. 22 April 1991.

Episode 12 (2:4) "What I Did for Love." Teleplay: Ellen Herman. Dir.: Steve Robman. CBS. 29 April 1991.

Episode 13 (2:5) "Spring Break." Teleplay: David Assael. Dir.: Rob Thompson. CBS. 6 May 1991.

Episode 14 (2:6) "War and Peace." Teleplay: Robin Green and Henry Bromell. Dir.: Bill D'Elia. CBS. 13 May 1991.

Episode 15 (2:7) "Slow Dance." Teleplay: Andrew Schneider and Diane Frolov. Dir.: David Carson. CBS. 20 May 1991.

Season 3 (1991-92)

Episode 16 (3:1) "The Bumpy Road to Love." Teleplay: Sybil Adelman and Marin Sage. Dir.: Nick Marck. CBS. 23 September 1991.

Episode 17 (3:2) "Only You." Teleplay: Ellen Herman. Dir.: Dill D'Elia. CBS. 30 September 1991.

Episode 18 (3:3) "Oy, Wilderness." Teleplay: Robin Green. Dir.: Miles Watkins. CBS. 7 October 1991.

Episode 19 (3:4) "Animals 'R' Us." Teleplay: Robin Green. Dir.: Nick Marck. CBS. 14 October 1991.

Episode 20 (3:5) "Jules et Joel." Teleplay: Stuart Stevens. Dir.: James Hayman. CBS. 28 October 1991.

Episode 21 (3:6) "The Body in Question." Teleplay: Henry Bromell. Dir.: David Carson. CBS. 4 November 1991.

Episode 22 (3:7) "Roots." Teleplay: Dennis Koenig. Dir.: Sandy Smolan. CBS. 11 November 1991.

Episode 23 (3:8) "A-Hunting We Will Go." Teleplay: Craig Volk. Dir.: Dill D'Elia. CBS. 18 November 1991.

Episode 24 (3:9) "Get Real." Teleplay: Andrew Schneider and Diane Frolov. Dir.: Michael Katleman. CBS. 9 December 1991.

Episode 25 (3:10) "Seoul Mates." Teleplay: Andrew Schneider and Diane Frolov. Dir.: Jack Bender. CBS. 16 December 1991.

Episode 26 (3:11) "Dateline: Cicely." Teleplay: Jeff Melvoin. Dir.: Michael Fresco. CBS. 6 January 1992.

Episode 27 (3:12) "Our Tribe." Teleplay: David Assael. Dir.: Lee Shallat-Chemel. CBS. 13 January 1992.

Episode 28 (3:13) "Things Become Extinct." Teleplay: Robin Green. Dir.: Dean Parisot. CBS. 20 January 1992.

Episode 29 (3:14) "Burning Down the House." Teleplay: Robin Green. Dir.: Rob Thompson. CBS. 3 February 1992.

Episode 30 (3:15) "Democracy in America." Teleplay: Jeff Melvoin. Dir.: Michael Katleman. CBS. 24 February 1992.

Episode 31 (3:16) "Three Amigos." Teleplay: Robin Green and Mitchell Burgess. Dir.: Matthew Nodella. CBS. 2 March 1992.

Episode 32 (3:17) "Lost and Found." Teleplay: Andrew Schneider and Diane Frolov. Dir.: Steve Robman. CBS. 9 March 1992.

Episode 33 (3:18) "My Mother, My Sister." Teleplay: Mitchell Burgess and Kate Boutillier. Dir.: Rob Thompson. CBS. 16 March 1992.

Episode 34 (3:19) "Wake Up Call." Teleplay: Andrew Schneider and Diane Frolov. Dir.: Nick Marck. CBS. 23 March 1992.

Episode 35 (3:20) "The Final Frontier." Teleplay: Jeff Vlaming. Dir.: Tom Moore. CBS. 27 April 1992.

Episode 36 (3:21) "It Happened in Juneau." Teleplay: Robert Rabinowitz and David Assael. Dir.: Michael Katleman. CBS. 4 May 1992.

Episode 37 (3:22) "Our Wedding." Teleplay: Andrew Schneider and Diane Frolov. Dir.: Nick Marck. CBS. 11 May 1992.

Episode 38 (3:23) "Cicely." Teleplay: Andrew Schneider and Diane Frolov. Dir.: Rob Thompson. CBS. 18 May 1992.

Season 4 (1992-93)

Episode 39 (4:1) "Northwest Passages." Teleplay: Robin Green. Dir.: Dean Parisot. CBS. 28 September 1992.

Episode 40 (4:2) "Midnight Sun." Teleplay: Geoffrey Neigher. Dir.: Michael Katleman. CBS. 5 October 1992.

Episode 41 (4:3) "Nothing's Perfect." Teleplay: Andrew Schneider and Diane Frolov. Dir.: Nick Marck. CBS. 12 October 1992.

Episode 42 (4:4) "Heroes." Teleplay: Jeff Vlaming. Dir.: Chuck Braverman. CBS. 19 October 1992.

Episode 43 (4:5) "Blowing Bubbles." Teleplay: Mark B. Perry. Dir.: Rob Thompson. CBS. 2 November 1992.

Episode 44 (4:6) "On Your Own." Teleplay: Christian Williams and Sy Rosen. Dir.: Joan Tewkesbury. CBS. 9 November 1992.

Episode 45 (4:7) "The Bad Seed." Teleplay: Mitchell Burgess. Dir.: Randall Miller. CBS. 16 November 1992.

Episode 46 (4:8) "Thanksgiving." Teleplay: David Assael. Dir.: Michael Fresco. CBS. 23 November 1992.

Episode 47 (4:9) "Do the Right Thing." Teleplay: Andrew Schneider and Diane Frolov. Dir.: Nick Marck. CBS. 30 November 1992.

Episode 48 (4:10) "Crime and Punishment." Teleplay: Jeff Melvoin. Dir.: Rob Thompson. CBS. 14 December 1992.

Episode 49 (4:11) "Survival of the Species." Teleplay: Denise Dobbs. Dir.: Dean Parisot. CBS. 4 January 1993.

Episode 50 (4:12) "Revelations." Teleplay: Andrew Schneider and Diane Frolov. Dir.: Daniel Attias. CBS. 11 January 1993.

Episode 51 (4:13) "Duets." Teleplay: Geoffrey Neigher. Dir.: Win Phelps. CBS. 18 January 1993.

Episode 52 (4:14) "Grosse Point, 48230." Teleplay: Mitchell Burgess and Robin Green. Dir.: Michael Katleman. CBS. 1 February 1993.

Episode 53 (4:15) "Learning Curve." Teleplay: Jeff Vlaming. Dir.: Michael Vittes. CBS. 8 February 1993.

Episode 54 (4:16) "Ill Wind." Teleplay: Jeff Melvoin. Dir.: Rob Thompson. CBS. 15 February 1993.

Episode 55 (4:17) "Love's Labour Mislaid." Teleplay: Jeff Melvoin. Dir.: Joe Napolitano. CBS. 21 February 1993.

Episode 56 (4:18) "Northern Lights." Teleplay: Andrew Schneider and Diane Frolov. Dir.: Bill D'Elia. CBS. 1 March 1993.

Episode 57 (4:19) "Family Feud." Teleplay: David Assael. Dir.: Adam Arkin. CBS. 8 March 1993.

Episode 58 (4:20) "Homesick." Teleplay: Jeff Vlaming. Dir.: Nick Marck. CBS. 15 March 1993.

Episode 59 (4:21) "The Big Feast." Teleplay: Robin Green and Mitchell Burgess. Dir.: Rob Thompson. CBS. 22 March 1993.

Episode 60 (4:22) "Kaddish, For Uncle Manny." Teleplay: Jeff Melvoin. Dir.: Michael Lange. CBS. 3 May 1993.

Episode 61 (4:23) "Mud and Blood." Teleplay: Andrew Schneider and Diane Frolov. Dir.: Jim Charleston. CBS. 10 May 1993.

Episode 62 (4:24) "Sleeping with the Enemy." Teleplay: Mitchell Burgess and Robin Green. Dir.: Frank Prinzi. CBS. 17 May 1993.

Episode 63 (4:25) "Old Tree." Teleplay: Robin Green and Diane Frolov. Dir.: Michael Fresco. CBS. 24 May 1993.

Season 5 (1993-94)

Episode 64 (5:1) "Three Doctors." Teleplay: Andrew Schneider and Diane Frolov. Dir.: Daniel Attias. CBS. 20 September 1993.

Episode 65 (5:2) "The Mystery of the Old Curio Shop." Teleplay: Rogers Turrentine. Dir.: Michael Fresco. CBS. 27 September 1993.

Episode 66 (5:3) "Jaws of Life." Teleplay: Mitchell Burgess and Robin Green. Dir.: Jim Charleston. CBS. 4 October 1993.

Episode 67 (5:4) "Altered Egos." Teleplay: Jeff Melvoin. Dir.: John David Coles. CBS. 11 October 1993.

Episode 68 (5:5) "A River Doesn't Run Through It." Teleplay: Jeff Melvoin. Dir.: Nick Marck. CBS. 25 October 1993.

Episode 69 (5:6) "Birds of a Feather." Teleplay: Mitchell Burgess and Robin Green. Dir.: Mark Horowitz. CBS. 1 November 1993.

Episode 70 (5:7) "Rosebud." Teleplay: Barbara Hall. Dir.: Michael Fresco. CBS. 8 November 1993.

Episode 71 (5:8) "Heal Thyself." Teleplay: Diane Frolov and Andrew Schneider. Dir.: Michael Katleman. CBS. 15 November 1993.

Episode 72 (5:9) "A Cup of Joe." Teleplay: Mitchell Burgess and Robin Green. Dir.: Michael Lange. CBS. 22 November 1993.

Episode 73 (5:10) "First Snow." Teleplay: Andrew Schneider and Diane Frolov. Dir.: Daniel Attias. CBS. 13 December 1993.

Episode 74 (5:11) "Baby Blues." Teleplay: Barbara Hall. Dir.: Jim Charleston. CBS. 3 January 1994.

Episode 75 (5:12) "Mr. Sandman." Teleplay: Diane Frolov and Andrew Schneider. Dir.: Michael Fresco. CBS. 10 January 1994.

Episode 76 (5:13) "Mite Makes Right." Teleplay: Andrew Schneider and Diane Frolov. Dir.: Michael Vittes. CBS. 17 January 1994.

Episode 77 (5:14) "A Bolt from the Blue." Teleplay: Jeff Melvoin. Dir.: Michael Lange. CBS. 24 January 1994.

Episode 78 (5:15) "Hello, I Love You." Teleplay: Mitchell Burgess and Robin Green. Dir.: Michael Fresco. CBS. 31 January 1994.

Episode 79 (5:16) "Northern Hospitality." Teleplay: Barbara Hall. Dir.: Oz Scott. CBS. 28 February 1994.

Episode 80 (5:17) "Una Volta in L'Inverno." Teleplay: Jeff Melvoin. Dir.: Michael Vittes. CBS. 7 March 1994.

Episode 81 (5:18) "Fish Story." Teleplay: Jeff Melvoin. Dir.: Bill D'Elia. CBS. 14 March 1994.

Episode 82 (5:19) "The Gift of the Maggie." Teleplay: Robin Green and Mitchell Burgess. Dir.: Patrick McKee. CBS. 28 March 1994.

Episode 83 (5:20) "A Wing and a Prayer." Teleplay: Mitchell Burgess and Robin Green. Dir.: Lorraine Senna Ferrara. CBS. 11 April 1994.

Episode 84 (5:21) "I Feel the Earth Move." Teleplay: Jed Seidel. Dir.: Michael Fresco. CBS. 2 May 1994.

Episode 85 (5:22) "Grand Prix." Teleplay: Barbara Hall. Dir.: Michael Lange. CBS. 9 May 1994.

Episode 86 (5:23) "Blood Ties." Teleplay: Robin Green and Mitchell Burgess. Dir.: Thomas R. Moore. CBS. 16 May 1994.

Episode 87 (5:24) "Lovers and Madmen." Teleplay: Jeff Melvoin. Dir.: James Hayman. CBS. 23 May 1994.

Episode 6 (1994-95)

Episode 88 (6:1) "Dinner at Seven-Thirty." Teleplay: Andrew Schneider and Diane Frolov. Dir.: Michael Fresco. CBS. 19 September 1994.

Episode 89 (6:2) "Eye of the Beholder." Teleplay: Mitchell Burgess and Robin Green. Dir.: Jim Charleston. CBS. 26 September 1994.

Episode 90 (6:3) "Shofar, So Good." Teleplay: Jeff Melvoin. Dir.: James Hayman. CBS. 3 October 1994.

Episode 91 (6:4) "The Letter." Teleplay: Meredith Stiehm. Dir.: Jim Charleston. CBS. 10 October 1994.

Episode 92 (6:5) "The Robe." Teleplay: Sam Egan. Dir.: Lorraine Senna Ferrara. CBS. 17 October 1994.

Episode 93 (6:6) "Zarya." Teleplay: Andrew Schneider and Diane Frolov. Dir.: Jim Charleston. CBS. 31 October 1994.

Episode 94 (6:7) "Full Upright Position." Teleplay: Mitchell Burgess and Robin Green. Dir.: Oz Scott. CBS. 7 November 1994.

Episode 95 (6:8) "Up River." Teleplay: Andrew Schneider and Diane Frolov. Dir.: Michael Fresco. CBS. 14 November 1994.

Episode 96 (6:9) "Sons of the Tundra." Teleplay: Jeff Melvoin. Dir.: Michael Vittes. CBS. 28 November 1994.

Episode 97 (6:10) "Realpolitik." Teleplay: Sam Egan. Dir.: Victor Lobl. CBS. 12 December 1994.

Episode 98 (6:11) "The Great Mushroom." Teleplay: Diane Frolov and Andrew Schneider. Dir.: James Hayman. CBS. 4 January 1995.

Episode 99 (6:12) "Mi Casa, Su Casa." Teleplay: Robin Green and Mitchell Burgess. Dir.: Daniel Attias. CBS. 11 January 1995.

Episode 100 (6:13) "Horns." Teleplay: Jeff Melvoin. Dir.: Michael Fresco. CBS. 18 January 1995.

Episode 101 (6:14) "The Mommy's Curse." Teleplay: Robin Green and Mitchell Burgess. Dir.: Michael Lange. CBS. 1 February 1995.

Episode 102 (6:15) "The Quest." Teleplay: Diane Frolov and Andrew Schneider. Dir.: Michael Vittes. CBS. 8 February 1995.

Episode 103 (6:16) "Lucky People." Teleplay: Diane Frolov and Andrew Schneider. Dir.: Janet Greek. CBS. 15 February 1995.

Episode 104 (6:17) "The Graduate." Teleplay: Sam Egan. Dir.: James Hayman. CBS. 8 March 1995.

Episode 105 (6:18) "Little Italy." Teleplay: Jeff Melvoin. Dir.: Stephen Cragg. CBS. 15 March 1995.

Episode 106 (6:19) "Balls." Teleplay: Jeff Melvoin. Dir.: Scott Paulin. CBS. 6 April 1995.

Episode 107 (6:20) "Buss Stop." Teleplay: Robin Green and Mitchell Burgess. Dir.: Daniel Attias. CBS. 24 April 1995.

Episode 108 (6:21) "Ursa Minor." Teleplay: Sam Egan. Dir.: Patrick McKee. CBS. 12 July 1995

Episode 109 (6:22) "Let's Dance." Teleplay: Sam Egan. Dir.: Michael Vittes. CBS. 19 July 1995.

Episode 110 (6:23) "Tranquility Base." Teleplay: Robin Green, Mitchell Burgess, and Jeff Melvoin. Dir.: Michael Fresco. CBS. 26 July 1995.

Episode Listing for
The Sopranos
(1999–2007)

Season 1 (1999)

Episode 1 (1:1) "Pilot: The Sopranos." Teleplay: David Chase. Dir.: David Chase. HBO. 10 January 1999.

Episode 2 (1:2) "46 Long." Teleplay: David Chase. Dir.: David Chase. HBO. 17 January 1999.

Episode 3 (1:3) "Denial, Anger, Acceptance." Teleplay: Mark Saraceni. Dir.: Nick Gomez. HBO. 24 January 1999.

Episode 4 (1:4) "Meadowlands." Teleplay: Jason Cahill. Dir.: John Patterson. HBO. 31 January 1999.

Episode 5 (1:5) "College." Teleplay: Jim Manos, Jr. and David Chase. Dir.: Allen Coulter. HBO. 7 February 1999.

Episode 6 (1:6) "Pax Soprana." Teleplay: Frank Renzulli. Dir.: Alan Taylor. HBO. 14 February 1999.

Episode 7 (1:7) "Down Neck." Teleplay: Robin Green and Mitchell Burgess. Dir.: Lorraine Senna. HBO. 21 February 1999.

Episode 8 (1:8) "The Legend of Tennessee Moltisanti." Teleplay: Frank Renzulli and David Chase. Dir.: Tim Van Patten. HBO. 28 February 1999.

Episode 9 (1:9) "Boca." Teleplay: Jason Cahill, Robin Green, and Mitchell Burgess. Dir.: Andy Wolk. HBO. 7 March 1999.

Episode 10 (1:10) "A Hit is a Hit." Teleplay: Joe Bosso and Frank Renzulli. Dir.: Matthew Penn. HBO. 14 March 1999.

Episode 11 (1:11) "Nobody Knows Anything." Teleplay: Frank Renzulli. Dir.: Henry J. Bronchtein. HBO. 21 March 1999.

Episode 12 (1:12) "Isabella." Teleplay: Robin Green and Mitchell Burgess. Dir.: Allen Coulter. HBO. 28 March 1999.

Episode 13 (1:13) "I Dream of Jeannie Cusamano." Teleplay: David Chase. Dir.: John Patterson. HBO. 4 April 1999.

Season 2 (2000)

Episode 14 (2:1) "Guy Walks into a Psychiatrist's Office." Teleplay: Jason Cahill. Dir.: Allen Coulter. HBO. 16 January 2000.

Episode 15 (2:2) "Do Not Resuscitate." Teleplay: Robin Green, Mitchell Burgess, and Frank Renzulli. Dir.: Martin Bruestle. HBO. 23 January 2000.

Episode 16 (2:3) "Toodle-Fucking-Oo." Teleplay: Frank Renzulli. Dir.: Lee Tamahori. HBO. 30 January 2000.

Episode 17 (2:4) "Commendatori." Teleplay: David Chase. Dir.: Tim Van Patten. HBO. 6 February 2000.

Episode 18 (2:5) "Big Girls Don't Cry." Teleplay: Terence Winter. Dir.: Tim Van Patten. HBO. 13 February 2000.

Episode 19 (2:6) "The Happy Wanderer." Teleplay: Frank Renzulli. Dir.: John Patterson. HBO. 20 February 2000.

Episode 20 (2:7) "D-Girl." Teleplay: Todd A. Kessler. Dir.: Allen Coulter. HBO. 27 February 2000.

Episode 21 (2:8) "Full Leather Jacket." Teleplay: Robin Green and Mitchell Burgess. Dir.: Allen Coulter. HBO. 5 March 2000.

Episode 22 (2:9) "From Where to Eternity." Teleplay: Michael Imperioli. Dir.: Henry J. Bronchtein. HBO. 12 March 2000.

Episode 23 (2:10) "Bust Out." Teleplay: Frank Renzulli, Robin Green, Mitchell Burgess, and David Chase. Dir.: John Patterson. HBO. 19 March 2000.

Episode 24 (2:11) "House Arrest." Teleplay: Terence Winter. Dir.: Tim Van Patten. HBO. 26 March 2000.

Episode 25 (2:12) "The Knight in White Satin Armor." Teleplay: Robin Green and Mitchell Burgess. Dir.: Allen Coulter. HBO. 2 April 2000.

Episode 26 (2:13) "Funhouse." Teleplay: David Chase and Todd A. Kessler. Dir.: John Patterson. HBO. 9 April 2000.

Season 3 (2001)

Episode 27 (3:1) "Mr. Ruggerio's Neighborhood." Teleplay: David Chase. Dir.: Allen Coulter. HBO. 4 March 2001.

Episode 28 (3:2) "Proshai, Livushka." Teleplay: David Chase. Dir.: Tim Van Patten. HBO. 4 March 2001.

Episode 29 (3:3) "Fortunate Son." Teleplay: Todd A. Kessler. Dir.: Henry J. Bronchtein. HBO. 11 March 2001.

Episode 30 (3:4) "Employee of the Month." Teleplay: Robin Green and Mitchell Burgess. Dir.: John Patterson. HBO. 18 March 2001.

Episode 31 (3:5) "Another Toothpick." Teleplay: Terence Winter. Dir.: Jack Bender. HBO. 25 March 2001.

Episode 32 (3:6) "University." Teleplay: Terence Winter and Salvatore Stabile. Dir.: Allen Coulter. HBO. 1 April 2001.

Episode 33 (3:7) "Second Opinion." Teleplay: Lawrence Konner. Dir.: Tim Van Patten. HBO. 8 April 2001.

Episode 34 (3:8) "He is Risen." Teleplay: Todd A. Kessler. Dir.: Allen Coulter. HBO. 15 April 2001.

Episode 35 (3:9) "The Telltale Moozadell." Teleplay: Michael Imperioli. Dir.: Daniel Attias. HBO. 22 April 2001.

Episode 36 (3:10) "To Save Us All from Satan's Power." Teleplay: Robin Green and Mitchell Burgess. Dir.: Jack Bender. HBO. 29 April 2001.

Episode 37 (3:11) "Pine Barrens." Teleplay: Terrence Winter. Dir.: Steve Buscemi. HBO. 6 May 2001.

Episode 38 (3:12) "Amour Fou." Teleplay: Frank Renzulli. Dir.: Tim Van Patten. HBO. 13 May 2001.

Episode 39 (3:13) "The Army of One." Teleplay: David Chase and Lawrence Konner. Dir.: John Patterson. HBO. 20 May 2001.

Season 4 (2002)

Episode 40 (4:1) "For All Debts Public and Private." Teleplay: David Chase. Dir.: Allen Coulter. HBO. 15 September 2002.

Episode 41 (4:2) "No Show." Teleplay: David Chase and Terence Winter. Dir.: John Patterson. HBO. 22 September 2002.

Episode 42 (4:3) "Christopher." Teleplay: Michael Imperioli and Maria Laurino. Dir.: Tim Van Patten. HBO. 29 September 2002.

Episode 43 (4:4) "The Weight." Teleplay: Terence Winter. Dir.: Jack Bender. HBO. 6 October 2002.

Episode 44 (4:5) "Pie-O-My." Teleplay: Robin Green and Mitchell Burgess. Dir.: Henry J. Bronchtein. HBO. 13 October 2002.

Episode 45 (4:6) "Everybody Hurts." Teleplay: Michael Imperioli. Dir.: Steve Buscemi. HBO. 20 October 2002.

Episode 46 (4:7) "Watching Too Much Television." Teleplay: David Chase, Robin Green, Mitchell Burgess, and Terence Winter. Dir.: John Patterson. HBO. 27 October 2002.

Episode 47 (4:8) "Mergers and Acquisitions." Teleplay: David Chase, Robin Green, Mitchell Burgess, and Terence Winter. Dir.: Daniel Attias. HBO. 3 November 2002.

Episode 48 (4:9) "Whoever Did This." Teleplay: Robin Green and Mitchell Burgess. Dir.: Tim Van Patten. HBO. 10 November 2002.

Episode 49 (4:10) "The Strong, Silent Type." Teleplay: Terence Winter, Robin Green, and Mitchell Burgess. Dir.: Allen Taylor. HBO. 17 November 2002.

Episode 50 (4:11) "Calling All Cars." Teleplay: Robin Green, Mitchell Burgess, David Chase, and David Flebotte. Dir.: Tim Van Patten. HBO. 24 November 2002.

Episode 51 (4:12) "Eloise." Teleplay: Terence Winter. Dir.: James Hayman. HBO. 1 December 2002.

Episode 52 (4:13) "Whitecaps." Teleplay: Robin Green, Mitchell Burgess, and David Chase. Dir.: John Patterson. HBO. 8 December 2002.

Season 5 (2004)

Episode 53 (5:1) "Two Tonys." Teleplay: David Chase and Terence Winter. Dir.: Tim Van Patten. HBO. 7 March 2004

Episode 54 (5:2) "Rat Pack." Teleplay: Matthew Weiner. Dir.: Alan Taylor. HBO. 14 March 2004.

Episode 55 (5:3) "Where's Johnny?" Teleplay: Michael Caleo. Dir.: John Patterson. HBO. 21 March 2004.

Episode 56 (5:4) "All Happy Families." Teleplay: Toni Kalem. Dir.: Rodrigo García. HBO. 28 March 2004.

Episode 57 (5:5) "Irregular Around the Margins." Teleplay: Robin Green and Mitchell Burgess. Dir.: Allen Coulter. HBO. 4 April 2004.

Episode 58 (5:6) "Sentimental Education." Teleplay: Matthew Weiner. Dir.: Peter Bogdanovich. HBO. 11 April 2004.

Episode 59 (5:7) "In Camelot." Teleplay: Terence Winter. Dir.: Steven Buscemi. HBO. 18 April 2004.

Episode 60 (5:8) "Marco Polo." Teleplay: Michael Imperioli. Dir.: John Patterson. HBO. 25 April 2004.

Episode 61 (5:9) "Unidentified Black Males." Teleplay: Matthew Weiner and Terence Winter. Dir.: Tim Van Patten. HBO. 2 May 2004.

Episode 62 (5:10) "Cold Cuts." Teleplay: Robin Green and Mitchell Burgess. Dir.: Mike Figgis. HBO. 9 May 2004.

Episode 63 (5:11) "The Test Dream." Teleplay: Matthew Weiner and David Chase. Dir.: Allen Coulter. HBO. 16 May 2004.

Episode 64 (5:12) "Long Term Parking." Teleplay: Terence Winter. Dir.: Tim Van Patten. HBO. 23 May 2004.

Episode 65 (5:13) "All Due Respect." Teleplay: David Chase, Robin Green, and Mitchell Burgess. Dir.: Tim Van Patten. HBO. 6 June 2004.

Season 6 (2006–2007)

Episode 66 (6:1) "Members Only." Teleplay: Terence Winter. Dir.: Timothy Van Patten. HBO. 12 March 2006.

Episode 67 (6:2) "Join the Club." Teleplay: David Chase. Dir.: David Nutter. HBO. 19 March 2006.

Episode 68 (6:3) "Mayham." Teleplay: Matthew Weiner. Dir.: Jack Bender. HBO. 26 March 2006.

Episode 69 (6:4) "The Fleshy Part of the Thigh." Teleplay: Diane Frolov and Andrew Schneider. Dir.: Alan Taylor. HBO. 2 April 2006.

Episode 70 (6:5) "Mr. and Mrs. John Sacrimoni Request." Teleplay: Terence Winter. Dir.: Steve Buscemi. HBO. 9 April 2006.

Episode 71 (6:6) "Live Free or Die." Teleplay: Terence Winter, David Chase, Robin Green, and Mitchell Burgess. Dir.: Tim Van Patten. HBO. 16 April 2006.

Episode 72 (6:7) "Luxury Lounge." Teleplay: Matthew Weiner. Dir.: Danny Leiner. HBO. 23 April 2006.

Episode 73 (6:8) "Johnny Cakes." Teleplay: Andrew Schneider and Diane Frolov. Dir.: Tim Van Patten. HBO. 30 April 2006.

Episode 74 (6:9) "The Ride." Teleplay: Terence Winter. Dir.: Alan Taylor. HBO. 7 May 2006.

Episode 75 (6:10) "Moe and Joe." Teleplay: Matthew Weiner. Dir.: Steve Shill. HBO. 14 May 2006.

Episode 76 (6:11) "Cold Stones." Teleplay: Andrew Schneider and Diane Frolov. Dir.: Tim Van Patten. HBO. 21 May 2006.

Episode 77 (6:12) "Kaisha." Teleplay: Terence Winter, Matthew Weiner, and David Chase. Dir.: Alan Taylor. HBO. 4 June 2006.

Episode 78 (6:13) "Soprano Home Movies." Teleplay: Diane Frolov, Andrew Schneider, David Chase, and Matthew Weiner. Dir.: Tim Van Patten. HBO. 8 April 2007.

Episode 79 (6:14) "Stage 5." Teleplay: Terence Winter. Dir.: Alan Taylor. HBO. 15 April 2007.

Episode 80 (6:15) "Remember When." Teleplay: Terence Winter. Dir.: Phil Abraham. HBO. 22 April 2007.

Episode 81 (6:16) "Chasing It." Teleplay: Matthew Weiner. Dir.: Tim Van Patten. HBO. 29 April 2007.

Episode 82 (6:17) "Walk Like a Man." Teleplay: Terence Winter. Dir.: Terence Winter. HBO. 6 May 2007.

Episode 83 (6.18) "Kennedy and Heidi." Teleplay: Matthew Weiner and David Chase. Dir.: Alan Taylor. HBO. 13 May 2007.

Episode 84 (6.19) "The Second Coming." Teleplay: Terence Winter. Dir.: Tim Van Patten. HBO. 20 May 2007.

Episode 85 (6.20) "The Blue Comet." Teleplay: Matthew Weiner and David Chase. Dir.: Alan Taylor. HBO. 3 June 2007.

Episode 86 (6.21) "Made in America." Teleplay: David Chase. Dir.: David Chase. HBO. 20 June 2007.

About the Contributors

Thomas Fahy is the director of the American Studies Program and an assistant professor of English at the C. W. Post campus of Long Island University. He has published nine books, including *Freak Shows and the Modern American Imagination* (2006), *Gabriel García Márquez's Love in the Time of Cholera: A Reader's Guide* (2003), two novels, *The Unspoken* (2008) and *Night Visions* (2004), and several edited collections, *Considering Alan Ball* (McFarland, 2006), *Considering Aaron Sorkin* (McFarland, 2005), *Captive Audience: Prison and Captivity in Contemporary Theater* (2003), and *Peering Behind the Curtain: Disability, Illness, and the Extraordinary Body in Contemporary Theater* (2002).

Victoria E. Johnson is an assistant professor in the Department of Film and Media Studies, the Program in Visual Studies, and the Program in African American Studies at the University of California–Irvine. Her *Heartland TV: Prime Time Television and the Struggle for U.S. Identity* (2007) examines the imagination of the American Midwest as "Heartland" in critical moments in prime time and social history. Her prior publications examine the politics of place, race, and popular music in television and film, and have appeared in journals including *Film Quarterly*, *The Velvet Light Trap* and *Continuum* as well as in anthologies such as *The Television Studies Reader* (2004) and *The Revolution Wasn't Televised: Sixties Television and Social Conflict* (1997).

Robert F. Gross teaches theatre at Hobart and William Smith colleges. He is the author of *Words Heard and Overheard* and *S. N. Behrman: A Research and Production Sourcebook* and the editor of volumes on Christopher Hampton and Tennessee Williams in the Garland/Routledge Casebook Series on Modern Drama. His recent work includes essays on the plays of A. R. Gurney, Sidney Howard's *Lucky Sam McCarver*, and the television series *Six Feet Under*.

Heather E. Epes is an assistant professor of English and assistant director of the Writing Center at Francis Marion University. She uses radical and writing center pedagogies to question the role of relationship in classroom settings. She also has an interest in the history of pulp fiction in America and its continuing cultural influence, especially as seen in comics and graphic novels, the ever present influence of film noir, and science fiction film and television. Much of the rest of her time is spent gardening, in meditation and indulging her cat, Luna Nyx. A recent publication was an article for the anthology *After the Pain: Critical Essays on Gayl Jones*.

Kirstin Ringelberg is an associate professor of art history at Elon University. She has an article in the forthcoming anthology *Representing Pain*, edited by James Elkins, and has published in *Prospects: An Annual of American Cultural Studies*. As a scholar, she is interested in gender and class in nineteenth-century American art, the dialogic relationship between Japanese and American art from the nineteenth century to the present, and television and film studies.

Susann Cokal is an assistant professor of English at Virginia Commonwealth University and author of the novels *Mirabilis* and *Breath and Bones*. She has published articles on authors such as Jeanette Winterson, Marianne Wiggins, and Georges Bataille, and on pop culture subjects such as supermodels and Mary Poppins.

Ann C. Hall is a professor of English at Ohio Dominican University. She has published widely on drama, women's studies, and contemporary literature. She is currently at work on a book on the *Phantom of the Opera*, editing a collection of essays, *PopPorn: Pornography in American Culture*, and completing a collection of short stories on Old Spice cologne.

Mardia J. Bishop has presented and published on contemporary theatre, popular culture, the fabrication of the female body, and body image. She teaches theatre and communication courses at Shorter College and directs performance events in the Atlanta area. She holds a Ph.D. in theatre from Ohio State University.

Lorena Russell is an associate professor at the University of North Carolina–Asheville, where she teaches in the Department of Literature and Language. Her articles have appeared in *Considering Alan Ball*, *Straight Writ Queer*, *Horror Film: Creating and Marketing Film*, and *Gothic Studies*. Current projects include an article on queer intimacies and family violence in *The Deep End* and *In the Bedroom*, and a book project on Angela Carter, Jeanette Winterson and Fay Weldon.

Keith B. Mitchell is currently an assistant professor of English and ethnic literature at the University of Massachusetts–Lowell. His areas of research are francophone and anglophone Caribbean literature and African American literature. His writing has appeared in *Rhetoric of the Other*, *The Oxford Companion to African American Literature*, *Changing Currents: Anglophone, Francophone, and Hispaniophone Literary and Cultural Criticism*, and *James Baldwin and Toni Morrison: Comparative Critical and Theoretical Essays*. He is currently co-editing a special issue of the *Xavier Review* titled "Sex and Spirit: Reading the Intersections of Sexuality and Spirituality in the Creative Arts."

Michael Calabrese, a graduate of Columbia University with a Ph.D. from the University of Virginia, is a professor of English at California State University, Los Angeles, where he teaches Medieval English literature. He is the author of *Chaucer's Ovidian Arts of Love* (1994) and numerous essays on medieval literature. He lived for many years at 95 Lincoln Place, Irvington, New Jersey.

Index